P9-CQL-810

A REMARKABLE STORY OF COURAGE
AND HOPE.
AN EXTRAORDINARY WOMAN
WITH THE STRENGTH TO ENDURE
A DEVASTATING FAMILY TRAGEDY
—AND FIGHT FOR WHAT SHE
BELIEVES IN.

YOU WILL NEVER FORGET
HER INSPIRING STORY . . .

Elizabeth Glaser

IN THE ABSENCE
OF ANGELS

"Elizabeth Glaser's courage and determination are
truly inspirational."
—Meryl Streep

"A story about courage, love, and hope. Faced with
a parent's most terrifying nightmare, Elizabeth Glaser chose to fight for her family and all of us. She
took on Congress and aroused an unsuspecting nation."
—Senator Orrin Hatch

"A powerful story . . . an extraordinary book."
—*Kirkus*

(continued . . .)

IN THE ABSENCE OF ANGELS

ELIZABETH GLASER
AND LAURA PALMER

BERKLEY BOOKS, NEW YORK

All photographs not otherwise credited are from Elizabeth Glaser's personal collection.

This Berkley book contains the complete text of the original hardcover edition. It has been completely reset in a typeface designed for easy reading and was printed from new film.

IN THE ABSENCE OF ANGELS

A Berkley Book/published by arrangement with the author

PRINTING HISTORY
G.P. Putnam's Sons edition/February 1991
Berkley edition/November 1991

All rights reserved.
Copyright © 1991, 1992 by Elizabeth Glaser.
Cover photograph Reuters-Bettmann.
This book may not be reproduced in whole or in part, by mimeograph or any other means, without permission.
For information address: The Berkley Publishing Group,
200 Madison Avenue, New York, New York 10016.

ISBN: 0-425-13023-1

A BERKLEY BOOK ® TM 757,375
Berkley Books are published by The Berkley Publishing Group,
200 Madison Avenue, New York, New York 10016.
The name "BERKLEY" and the "B" logo
are trademarks belonging to Berkley Publishing Corporation.

PRINTED IN THE UNITED STATES OF AMERICA

10 9 8 7 6 5 4 3

To Ariel, Jake, and Paul,
who will be my family for ever and ever

ELIZABETH GLASER'S SPEECH —

DEMOCRATIC NATIONAL CONVENTION

JULY 14, 1992, 8:05 P.M.

I'm Elizabeth Glaser.

Eleven years ago, while giving birth to my first child, I hemorrhaged and was transfused with seven pints of blood. Four years later, I found out that I had been infected with the AIDS virus and had unknowingly passed it on to my daughter, Ariel, through my breast milk, and my son, Jake, in utero.

Twenty years ago I wanted to be at the Democratic Convention because it was a way to participate in our country.

Today I am here because it's a matter of life and death.

Exactly four years ago my daughter died of AIDS — she did not survive the Reagan administration. I am here because my son and I may not survive four more years of leaders who say they care, but do nothing. I am in a race with the clock. This is *not* about being a Republican or an Independent or a Democrat — it's about the future . . . for each and every one of us.

I started out just a mom — fighting for the life of her child. But along the way I learned how unfair America can be. Not just for people who have HIV, but for many, many people — gay people, people of color, children. A strange spokesperson for such a group — a well-to-do white woman — but I have learned my lessons the *hard way,* and I *know* that America has lost her path and is at *risk* of losing her soul. America wake up — we are all in a struggle between life and death.

I understand the sense of frustration and despair in our country, because I know firsthand about screaming for help and getting no answer. I went to Washington to tell Presidents Reagan and Bush we needed to do much, much more for AIDS research and care, and that children couldn't be forgotten. The first time, when nothing happened, I thought, Oh, they just didn't hear. The second time, when nothing happened, I thought, Maybe I didn't shout loud enough. But now I realize that they don't hear because they don't *want* to listen. When you cry for help and no one listens you start to lose hope.

I began to lose *faith* in America. I felt my country was letting me down — and it was.

This is not the America I was raised to be proud of. I was raised to believe that others' problems were my problems as well. But when I tell most people about HIV, hoping they will care and try to help, I see the look in their eyes — it's *not my* problem they're thinking — well, it's *everyone's problem* and we need a leader who will tell us that.

We need a visionary to guide us — to say it *wasn't* all right for Ryan White to be banned from school because he had HIV or a man or woman denied a job because they were infected with this virus. We need a leader who is truly committed to educating us.

I *believe* in America — but *not* with a leadership of selfishness and greed where the wealthy get health care and insurance and the poor don't. Do you know how much my AIDS care costs? More than $40,000 a year. Someone without insurance can't afford this. Even the drugs that I hope will keep me alive are out of reach for others. Is their life any less valuable? Of course not. *This* is not the America I was raised to be proud of — where the rich people get care and drugs that poor people can't. We need health care for all. We need a leader to say this, and do something about it.

I *believe* in America — but *not* with a leadership that talks about problems but is incapable of solving them. Two HIV commission reports with recommendations about what to do to solve this crisis are sitting on shelves, gathering dust. We need a leader who will not only listen to these recommendations, but will implement them.

I *believe* in America — but *not* with a leadership that doesn't hold government accountable. I go to Washington to the National Institutes of Health and say, "Show me what you're doing on HIV." They hate it when I come because I try to tell them how to do it better. But that's why I *love* being a taxpayer — because it's *my* money and they *must* become accountable.

I *believe* in an America where our leaders talk straight. When anyone tells President Bush that the battle against AIDS is seriously underfunded, he juggles the numbers to mislead the public into thinking we're spending twice as much as we really are. While they play games with numbers, people are dying.

I *believe* in America — but an America where there is a light *in every* home. One thousand points of light just wasn't enough — my house has been dark for too long.

Once every generation, history brings us to an important crossroads. Sometimes in life there is that moment when it's possible to make a change for the better. *This* is one of those moments.

For me, this is not politics. It's a crisis of caring.

In this hall is the future: women, men of all colors saying, Take America back. We are just real people wanting a more hopeful life. But words and ideas are not enough. Good thoughts won't save my family. What's the point of caring if we don't do something about it? We *must* have ACTION: a President *and* a Congress who can work together so we can get out of this gridlock and move ahead. Because I don't win my war if the Congress cares and the President doesn't — or if the President cares and the Congress doesn't support the ideas.

The people in this hall — this week, the Democratic party — all of us can begin to deliver that partnership, and in November *we can all* bring it home.

My daughter lived seven years, and in her last year, when she couldn't walk or talk, her wisdom shone through. She taught me to love when all I wanted to do was hate. She taught me to help others, when all I wanted to do was help myself. She taught me to be brave, when all I felt was fear.

My daughter and I loved each other with simplicity. America, we can do the same.

This was the country that offered hope. This was the place where dreams could come true. Not just economic dreams, but dreams of freedom, justice and equality. We *all* need to hope that our dreams can come true. I challenge you to make it happen, because *all our lives,* not just mine, depend on it.

PROLOGUE

There were no words, no sounds. Everything was lost in a single focus, getting to the hospital. I was concentrating totally on the shapes of the buildings moving past. Western, La Brea, La Cienega, the avenues slipped by. Everything familiar seemed suddenly strange. It was as though I were motionless and the scenery was being pulled past me.

When I arrived at Cedars-Sinai Hospital, my husband, Paul, rushed over to me, and I could see the fear in his face. "It will be all right," I assured him. An orderly helped me into a wheelchair and we were immediately taken to labor and delivery. I wasn't in labor and I wasn't supposed to be delivering. I breathed deeply, trying to stay calm. I was six months pregnant and had started bleeding. This wasn't supposed to be happening. My baby wasn't due for eleven more weeks. I had lost control of my body and was riveted with fear.

Paul stayed in my room with me. He was brave, and for his sake I tried to be, too. IVs were running into my veins, and a fetal monitor tracked my baby's heartbeat in beeps and blips across a screen. Doctors, residents, and nurses crisscrossed our room throughout a night that never seemed to end.

I was diagnosed as having placenta previa, which meant the placenta was growing across my cervix. All we could do was pray that I would stop bleeding because my child was probably too small to live outside my body. I was given a shot to stimulate the baby's lung development so it would have a better chance of surviving in case I delivered prematurely. I still had seventy-seven days to go. It was all too hard to believe. I felt like my life was no longer in my hands, that there was nothing I could do to save myself or to save my baby. I didn't even want to move for fear of causing more problems. I lay there, day after day, with Paul by my side, waiting, counting the hours. All I wanted to do was fall asleep and wake up when my baby was ready to be born.

On the sixth day, my doctor felt I was stronger and stable enough to go. I was sent home and told to stay in bed for the rest of my pregnancy. I was so afraid that I did less than whatever the doctor said I could. I showered once a day, walked to the living room, walked briefly outside, and then went back to bed. As in the hospital, I was going to do everything I could for my baby.

Paul was rehearsing during the days for a play called *The Lady Cries Murder*. My mother came and took care of me. She brought me my breakfast on a tray and we sat in bed all morning doing crossword puzzles. I didn't want to see many people, but it was wonderful to have her there. I needed to relax and have someone take care of me. I was always her good luck girl and she kept saying, "Betsy, you're going to make it. Everything will be fine. It will all work out."

I wanted to believe her, but whenever I was by myself, I would feel cold from the constant fears. There was the fear of bleeding, and the fear of dying. There was the fear of having a dead baby and the fear of having a baby that was not normal. If something really went wrong, there was the fear of a hysterectomy and then, the fear of never having any children of my own at all.

I would talk to the baby and say, "Hang in there. You and I can make it. We can do it. I know we can." Each day was a victory; the next, a challenge.

Paul and I were holding our breath. We didn't speak much during those weeks about what might happen. I didn't tell him of my many fears. The less we said, the easier it was to keep our balance.

Finally, on August 4, 1981, after I started to bleed again, Paul drove me to the hospital and Ariel Glaser was delivered by caesarean section. She was three and a half weeks early and weighed five pounds, two ounces, but I didn't care. When Paul placed her on my chest he said, "We have a beautiful baby daughter. She's perfect." We were so relieved.

When I looked into her eyes for the first time I was amazed that this miracle was mine. Our two hearts had beaten together for months inside my body. Now here she was, alive and magnificent. I kissed her. I stared at her exquisite hands, which were curling and uncurling in little fists. I looked at her lips and wondered about all she would say. I kissed her and watched her breathe and blink. Then I gave her to her dad. Our fears were gone. Paul took Ariel to bathe her, and the doctor began to stitch me up.

I was trying to talk to the doctors, to tell them how glad I was that it was over, when I heard the anesthesiologist saying that something was wrong.

More doctors came in. I couldn't breathe. I was hemorrhaging. It felt like . . . I was gasping for air, like I was suffocating. Paul was back in the room. Someone put an oxygen mask over me. My doctor pushed on my stomach and I could feel the warm blood gushing out. I was too horrified to even scream. What was happening to me? Paul stepped outside with the doctors. He had watched three unsuccessful attempts to stop the bleeding. He demanded to know what was going on but no one really knew.

I was losing too much blood too fast. I heard someone asking if they should prepare for a hysterectomy. I heard the words "life threatening" and, suddenly realizing that I might die in that room, I began fighting back for my life. I would not feel helpless again. I didn't want to die! If it would save me, I prayed, let them take my uterus.

The blood transfusions began. I watched the dark red blood drip out of the squat plastic bag, flow through an IV tube and into a vein in my arm. I was transfused with seven pints. It was not until the doctors packed me with cotton, an old and rarely used procedure, that I finally stopped bleeding.

When I was wheeled into the recovery room, I looked at Paul and said, "Am I okay?" In his most reassuring voice he said, "You're fine—everything is fine." But I was still too scared to feel any relief. A nurse asked me if I wanted to see my daughter. "Not if I am going to die," I said.

Hours passed and I remained stable. It wasn't until I saw my baby daughter again that the weariness and terror began to drift away, replaced with an instinctive love. She *was* beautiful and we had both survived. It was over. Nothing more could happen to us. I'll never forget the moment I realized for the first time I was a mother and the three of us were a family. Ariel was by my bed in a plastic Isolette, snug in a pastel cotton blanket, and Paul and I just looked at her. She was breathing quietly—the only sound in the room. I finally fell asleep listening to her breathe, thinking about the wonderful life the three of us had to look forward to.

The next day I nursed my baby for the first time. It was a lovely feeling, full of tender intimacy. Ariel and I would be such pals. I pictured her taking her first steps and chasing sea gulls on the beach. I saw her in pigtails and riding a bicycle, in party dresses and patent leather shoes. Her daddy would teach her to paint and I would teach her to ski. She had Paul's blue eyes and my brown hair. Ariel was the most beautiful baby we had ever seen and Paul and I fell in love with her. She was our daughter.

There were moments when I felt a cold sense of foreboding. I had been so scared for so long, it didn't just stop the next minute and go away. I desperately wanted my good feelings to last, but I was worried. I wondered whether I would start bleeding again.

Once we got home, I gradually began to calm down as the terror of the hospital ebbed into memory. My tiny daughter snuggled beside me, perfect and safe. We were beginning our lives together. I still smile when I think of those moments and how happy we all were.

Three weeks later I was reading the newspaper in bed one morning when I saw an article about a new virus called AIDS. I called my obstetrician immediately.

"I just read an article in the paper about AIDS, a virus that may be transmitted by blood transfusions. I just got seven pints!"

"Oh, Elizabeth," he said, "you've been through a difficult ordeal, but it's behind you. Relax and enjoy your baby. Your nightmare is over. AIDS isn't ever going to have anything to do with you."

CHAPTER

❧ 1 ❧

I had pork chops, not passion, on my mind when I first met Paul. I was coming home from a session with my therapist and determined to defrost two chops and have supper by myself.

I had, in fact, just spent fifty minutes explaining why I didn't need a man. I must have sounded like a string of self-help book titles as I explained to my therapist that I would take charge of my own happiness and that my life could be complete by myself. Its meaning was up to me and, thank you very much, I'd be finding my own fulfillment. It sounds a bit foolish now, but I know I meant it wholeheartedly at the time.

Then, while waiting for the light to change at the intersection of Santa Monica and Beverly boulevards I looked at the car next to me.

Oh, my God, that is the cutest guy I have ever seen, I thought. I smiled. He smiled. The light changed.

His dark blue Mazda stayed beside mine. I decided to look one more time to see if he was really as cute as I thought he was. Feeling as though I was doing something silly, I subtly glanced sideways. He saw me. I smiled again. He waved. I turned right. He turned right.

My heart started to pound. Now the only thing I could think of was serial killers. A stranger was following me with my encouragement. What was I doing? They'd find my body parts in a canyon.

I glanced into the rearview mirror, and he signaled me over with his arm. I was near my apartment and decided to stop before I showed him where I lived. I dismissed the idea of trying to lose him in a high-speed chase—that was television.

My friend Donna Arost lived in the neighborhood so I pulled over in front of her apartment. I thought, *If he kills me here, she'll be able to identify the body.* As ridiculous as it sounds, it's what I thought.

I was anxious and jittery as I pulled over. He stepped out of his car and walked toward me. I rolled down my window and he said, "Okay, let me see your driver's license and registration."

I looked at him and laughed. He was droll and disarming. I said, "What are you talking about?"

"My God," he said, "your car is as filthy as mine." My little BMW always seemed to look like a tag sale at the end of the day with odd bits of clutter and trash. It's become a trademark of mine.

"What are you doing for dinner?" he asked.

Thinking of therapy, I told him I was going home and making pork chops.

"Wouldn't you rather go out for Chinese food?"

"Yes," I said without missing a beat. One therapy session thrown out the window. I told him to follow me to my apartment. When we got there, I parked my car and walked over to his.

"My name is Betsy. I'm Betsy Meyer."

"I'm Paul. Paul Glaser. Nice to meet you. I'll see you at eight."

I went inside and called my friend Maryly Benzian. Since we were teaching together every day, Maryly and I were very close. "I have just done the stupidest thing in the whole world. I have no idea who this guy is. You *must* call my apartment at eleven o'clock tonight. If I am not home by then, call the police. He tells me his name is Paul Glaser. He drives a blue Mazda. Damn, I should have gotten the license number. Promise me you'll call. I can't go on this date unless you do."

She said "fine" and we both laughed.

I washed my hair and tried to look pretty. The bottom line

for me was that this was still the most handsome man I had ever seen.

Paul knocked on the door at eight and when he walked in, he said quietly, "I'm in trouble."

I thought that was an unusual remark since all I had done was open the door. I lived in a small apartment with rattan furniture which was covered in a white fabric. There were a few wall hangings and potted palms. It was classic in its simplicity. It was my first apartment and I had taken great care with it. But Paul, who has always had a refined aesthetic sense, said later that, from the moment he saw my apartment, he knew I was going to be different from other women he had dated in L.A. I don't know what he expected—candles in Chianti bottles? But it wasn't what he found.

We went to Al Fong's in Beverly Hills. It was dark and the food was dreadful. Midway through the moo shu pork and cashew chicken, I asked Paul what he did. I had fantasized that here was the sensible Jewish doctor or lawyer that I had been seeking, at least until that morning in therapy.

Paul said, "I'm an actor."

Goddamnit. I was so disappointed. I had lived in Los Angeles long enough to know that being an actor meant absolutely nothing.

"Are you working?" I asked politely.

"Actually, I am. I'm in a show that's just been picked up by the network. We start filming in a month. It'll be on ABC in the fall."

"What's it called?"

" 'Starsky and Hutch.' It's a cop show about two detectives. I play Starsky."

I knew that a series could be canceled after ten weeks so this did not seem like a very big deal to me. I was looking for the long-term security that paid mortgages and college tuition. Ten weeks was not what I had in mind.

The food was unexciting, but there was a great deal of electricity between us. I told him I was a schoolteacher. We discovered we both liked to travel and play tennis and were originally from back East. Paul's father was an architect in Boston and I had lived across the street from his office when I was in graduate school at Boston University. Paul and I could have met in front of my apartment when he came to visit his dad.

He came back to my apartment and at eleven o'clock, the phone rang, as planned. I told Maryly that everything was fine. Actually, it was better than fine; it was splendid.

I knew that night that, even though he was an actor, this was the man for me. I was hooked from the moment I saw him. June 9, 1975. That was it. I never went out with anyone else.

As we got to know each other, Paul told me he'd played Perchik in the movie *Fiddler on the Roof,* which I had seen several years before. Dumb crushes were not my style (especially on someone in a film), but when I saw *Fiddler* in the movie theater I had been drawn to this man who seemed to be both classy and sexy. It was uncanny, but it seemed as though our paths were destined to cross all along.

On our third date, I was writing a check and Paul glanced over my shoulder and asked, "Why does it say Elizabeth?"

"Because that's my name."

"Then why do you call yourself Betsy?"

"That's my nickname. It's what my parents call me."

"But Elizabeth is such a beautiful name. Why don't you just call yourself Elizabeth?"

"Will you call me Elizabeth?" I asked.

"Absolutely." I've been called Elizabeth ever since.

In my journal I wrote about all the things that seem to be too silly to say out loud when you are so exuberantly in love.

> My body tingles, my mind races. All I want to do is shout and tell the whole world how ecstatic I am! But I am also scared. I tell myself not to be this happy. I try to rein myself in because I am not at all grounded, I'm floating high above in the atmosphere through billowy clouds and blue skies. It's a fantasy land. Passion seizes my body and makes me shake from the inside out. It's wonderful and frightening. Can he possibly be feeling the way I am? Things like this don't really happen.

So much for the single woman's manifesto. I wrote that twelve days after I met Paul. I was twenty-seven and in love.

I had moved to the city after my first marriage ended because Lynn Arost, my best friend from college, had settled there. Lynn and I had met during our sophomore year at the University of Wisconsin. We became roommates our junior year and have been as close as sisters ever since. Lynn's sweetness is untrammeled. The years that make some people cynical have made her kinder and more compassionate. She is the kind of friend that people yearn for.

After college, Lynn and I went to Europe together. Instinctively, we knew that being young was something to spend, not save. After Europe we lived in Boston for a year while she worked and I got a master's degree in early childhood education.

After graduate school I took a year off to ski and the following summer I married a man I had met in college, Hank Koransky. We were married on Long Island in my parents' friends' back yard that overlooked Macy Channel, and instead of coming down an aisle, I walked down the plank from Mom and Dad's houseboat.

Everyone loved Hank, who was charismatic and very gentle. He wanted to become a college professor, and we moved to Boulder, Colorado, where he would get a graduate degree in history. It was very easy to envision our life on a university campus—both of us teaching and helping to mold young minds. I looked for teaching jobs, which were scarce because men wanted them for draft deferments to avoid going to Vietnam. The Kennedy years had given teaching prestige. When you asked what you could do for your country, teaching was one of the answers. I worked nights as a waitress at the International House of Pancakes until I got a full-time job with Head Start, a program to teach disadvantaged preschoolers, in Denver.

But after two years of marriage and Hank's decision to drop out of graduate school, it was clear that we had different goals and were simply not right for each other. Sadly, we decided to separate. I had never lived alone and didn't know where to go. I could have moved back to New York where my parents were living, but they were planning to move to Puerto Rico. They encouraged me to move to the West and join Lynn, and offered to help support me until I found a teaching job.

It took me almost nine months to find the right job, but by September of 1973 I was teaching reading and social studies at a private school called the Center for Early Childhood Education in West Hollywood. I taught six- to nine-year-olds in an ungraded curriculum. I never imagined that teaching could be so much fun.

I had some of my most creative teaching experiences at the Center. In social studies we acted out Greek myths and created a complete history of Los Angeles—from dinosaurs to freeways—on cardboard. It was very stimulating for me to be able to develop an imaginative curriculum. The students were lively and creative.

At that time, my life was so thoroughly normal that it could have been plunked down in Portland or Indianapolis and continued on uninterrupted. I taught school every day and was a volunteer at a community counseling center three afternoons a week in Beverly Hills. I had little connection with the Hollywood scene. Teaching was my passion and my profession. I hardly ever went to the movies. September was my idea of an opening night. I was still new to Los Angeles and still getting used to the life-style which was so different from New York where I'd grown up. It always feels like Saturday morning in L.A.; maybe you'll work, maybe you'll play tennis, maybe you'll do both.

Because I was still getting over the emotional shoals of my divorce, I had started seeing a therapist. I wanted to be sure I was making the right choices as I began living alone for the first time in my life. I couldn't afford a private psychiatrist on my teacher's salary so I saw the chief resident at the UCLA mental health clinic for $5.00 an hour. I had just seen him when I met Paul. It was 1975. Having just decided to give up looking for the love of my life, I found it.

Paul's attraction to me was also instantaneous. He told me later he thought I was pretty, sexy, and smart. My not being "in the business" appealed to him. He knew right away this could be a significant relationship, but he was afraid of marriage and commitment. Not me. When I looked at Paul I saw happily-ever-after.

Paul and I met in June and were living together by September. I moved into the one-room bungalow on Appian Way in the Hollywood Hills he shared with a dog named Max. Like most bachelors, Paul lived in a sparsely furnished apartment with jeans on the floor and a jar of mayonnaise in the refrigerator.

He didn't even have a television. We watched the debut of "Starsky and Hutch" with David Soul, the actor who played Hutch, at the home of David's agent. The verdict was unanimous. Everyone, including the stars, felt the show would be canceled in eight weeks. Nevertheless, Paul bought a television set so we could watch the show on Wednesday nights. By Thanksgiving, it was the hottest show on TV, and Paul and David were as famous as rock stars.

This was not part of my plan. As I envisioned my life, Paul would have been a professor or possibly a lawyer or physician. I never intended to fall in love with an actor, nor was I sure I wanted to be a part of a network blockbuster. On the other hand, I was never one to shy away from challenges.

Paul worked ferociously hard. He would get up at six every morning and work until nine o'clock each night, except on Fridays, when the cast worked until midnight. We were family on the set, I would come by and we'd all go out for Italian food when the crew finally wrapped for the week.

Paul and I were both stunned by his instant celebrity status. For years, Paul had worked steadily as a serious actor, doing everything from Shakespeare to "soaps." Aside from *Fiddler on the Roof,* he had been on Broadway in *Butterflies Are Free* and *Man in the Glass Booth,* along with other off-Broadway productions. Paul took great pride in his work and was a perfectionist about his craft.

"Starsky" was not how he imagined becoming famous and he had a hard time allowing himself to enjoy his success. Because it came so easily, part of him thought he didn't deserve it. Playing Starsky was easy for Paul. He had assumed that if he ever became successful it would be for mastering something challenging.

During that first year of "Starsky and Hutch," there was a lot of adjusting to do. The fifteen hours a day Paul spent on the set were difficult but what was hardest was giving up our privacy. The simple joy of taking a weekend walk on the beach in our jeans and sweatshirts came to a halt. We would be walking barefoot beside the ocean, and amid the squawks of the gulls and the crash of the surf, we would hear the call of the "Starsky Bird." It was faint at first.

"Starsky, Starsky, Starsky."

Then it would become more noticeable.

"Starsky, Starsky, Starsky."

We would turn around and tagging behind us would be a small crowd, whispering and pointing at Paul. If they couldn't get his autograph, take his picture, or touch him, they would simply follow him. Home was the only place to relax.

We stopped going to the beach. We stopped riding our bikes along the bike path. Simple things like stopping at a supermarket for bread and juice turned into maddening events. We avoided restaurants that drew people from out of town.

One night we went to the movies with our friends Lucy Fisher and Peter Ivers. I'd met Lucy at a dinner party about a month before I met Paul. We had started talking and ignored our dates for the rest of the night. Lucy is one of the strongest women I know and one of the friends who make up the emotional bedrock of my life. Because Paul was working so much in those early years, Lucy and I would play tennis or hang out at her little house, cooking and talking. We balanced each other perfectly because Lucy is introspective and helped me keep my perspective on Paul, which wasn't always easy.

The movie we all wanted to see happened to be at Grauman's Chinese Theater in Hollywood, which is a stop on every tourist's trek through town. Paul warned us that he didn't think he should go. He was reluctant to walk into a throng of tourists. The rest of us thought "he's making too big a deal out of this." But as we walked up to the ticket window, people began clamoring at us as if we were the Beatles. Some girl came up and tried to rip Paul's shirt off and another wanted a piece of his hair. When we finally got into the lobby we just looked at Paul and said, "My God, you are really, really famous."

It was a total shock to all of us how famous Paul had become in such a short time. Most of his friends, as with Lucy and Peter, hadn't even seen the show. They gave him no congratulations and little feedback. They didn't even realize what was happening. Until you went out in public with Paul you had no sense of how overwhelming, demanding, and ridiculous being a celebrity was.

One time Paul and I were in a restaurant booth having a very difficult conversation. I was crying, although I don't remember why. While we were obviously completely involved in an intense discussion, two people came up to Paul and asked for his autograph. I was astonished that people could be so insensitive.

Paul was furious. He never signed autographs and said so, which often exacerbated the situation. Some people got angry while others would hang around and plead with him to change his mind. But he felt if he signed one he'd be opening the door for more.

When people see you on television in their living rooms and bedrooms, they think you are part of their family and have no qualms about lunging into your life to snap your picture or shake your hand. Paul hated the attention he got off the set and detested feeling like a tourist attraction. He refused to participate in the celebrity feeding frenzy. But even so, his stardom made it almost impossible to relax and enjoy the limited amount of free time that he had.

During the years that "Starsky" was on the air, we never got involved in the social side of Hollywood that people think is so exciting, nor did we have an extravagant life-style. We saved our money, knowing that actors usually have lean times, no matter how successful they are, and wanted to be prepared for that. We did our own cleaning and shopping. I loved to cook and Paul always did the dishes. (Paul's one indulgence when "Starsky" took off was to buy himself a blue BMW.) Our idea of a good time was to come home and eat dinner in front of the television. We would have a simple supper like brown rice and stir-fried chicken and vegetables, which we'd eat on the bed while watching TV. We'd be asleep by ten so Paul could get up at dawn the next day. It wasn't exactly exciting, but when you're in love none of that matters.

The price I paid for Paul's celebrity was invisibility. I learned not to rely on the show business world for any reinforcement. Wherever Paul and I would go, all of the attention would be focused on him. I had to find ways to accept that; one solution was to make a life of my own that was independent and strong.

I continued teaching and volunteering as a counselor at the Maple Center, a community counseling center, and grew even more self-reliant than I already was. I began spending more time with my women friends. I had long, endless talks about Paul and the roller-coaster ride we were on. Lucy and Lynn must have been bored many times. Lynn was now

teaching in the same school as I, so we were together again
every day.

Hollywood people would nod and smile when I would say
I was a teacher or, later, the exhibits director at the Children's Museum. I knew that many people thought what I did
was ordinary, and while Paul got extraordinary attention and
praise for his work, I got almost none. No one was ever interested in talking about my work. Los Angeles is an industry
town and most people talk business.

It was a complicated time, but it was also exciting. We
were both learning a great deal about ourselves and about
each other. By the end of 1976 Paul was a sex symbol to thousands of women. They would write to him about their fanta-
sies and say things like "I think you are the cutest and most
wonderful man in the world, and I wish you would just get
rid of that Elizabeth!" or "I'm waiting for you! When you
dump Elizabeth, just give me a call!"

When we would go out socially, women would flirt with
him relentlessly. They'd practically be unbuttoning their
blouses right in front of me. There are a lot of glamorous
young women in Los Angeles who come here to break into
the film industry or work as models until they do. I certainly
did not try to look or act like a starlet and I'm sure many
of these women thought, "She isn't pretty enough to keep
him so I'll come right in here and take my shot."

What man wouldn't get a kick out of having beautiful
women fawning over him? When someone would start coming on to him at a party I would wink and then walk away.
When I came back later I'd say with a smile, "Okay, now
what did she want?" I had to learn to laugh about it and not
be threatened.

There were times when I told Paul that if he wanted to
go out and sow his wild oats it would be fine with me. I would
have been crushed, but I knew it wasn't going to help if he
felt trapped or resentful. I did tell him that if he decided to
roam, I *would not* sit and wait for him to come back.

Paul and I had a passionate relationship. He was intense,
sensitive, and combustible, all at the same time. He could be
volatile, but I found that compelling and fascinating. He
could be spiritual, and I found that challenging. He was fun,
and I loved being with him. We could flirt endlessly.

I definitely knew I wanted to be married and have children.

I had had a wonderful childhood and was looking forward to starting a family of my own. But Paul's childhood was more complicated than mine, and marriage and family were scary to him. I explained how nurturing family life could be and how much fun I had with my parents and my brother. But we had no commitments to each other then. We were enjoying living in the moment, although I felt confident the future would work out.

Paul used to say that I enjoyed the "Starsky" years more than he did and that's probably true. I love meeting new people and going to new places. Because the show was seen in sixty-seven countries, Paul had to make publicity appearances and we flew all over the world. I never expected to see New Zealand, Argentina, or Venezuela. It was one adventure after another. I had traveled after college, but now we were flying first class and staying in five-star hotels. I was sipping aperitifs with Roger Moore and James Clavell in the south of France and having the time of my life.

Paul spent most of his time working. It was more of the celebrity treadmill he loathed. But we always found a few hours to roam through the streets of Madrid or wander along the canals of Venice, and then it was magical.

One of the most important trips we made together was to Israel, where "Starsky" was extremely popular. Paul had been to Israel before but I hadn't. His parents had never been, and he was very excited about bringing them as well. We went for the celebration of Israel's thirtieth anniversary.

While I had always known I was Jewish, we hadn't practiced much religion in my family. In fact, Christmas was a great ritual in our house. Every year, my brother and I would go with Dad to pick out a tree. Mom would say to be sure and choose a small and fat one, and each year, without fail, we would choose the tallest one we could find.

The moment I walked off the plane in Israel, I felt like I was home. It was unexpected. I felt a deep spiritual connection in Jerusalem and a quiet sense of belonging that's never left me.

Those years were filled with positives and negatives. I saw the world outside and strengthened my world inside. I was a teacher but I was on the cover of tabloids and my picture was in *US* magazine. It was a balancing act for both me and Paul right from the start.

After two years of "Starsky," Paul decided he wanted to break his contract and leave the show. He was fed up with the demands of the series and the stress of being a television star. No one thought he could be serious and when they realized he was, they thought he was crazy. His business manager and agent tried to talk him out of it.

I wasn't Paul's wife, but I knew my thoughts on what he should do would have a great impact. I told Paul he had my complete support. I knew how unhappy he was. We weren't married and didn't have children, so he could take risks. It sounds like a cliché, but I truly wanted Paul to do what would make him happiest. That's the gift my parents had given me. They had taught me to believe in myself, to be willing to take risks. I said if he was miserable in the show he should get out. I became his sounding board and staunchest supporter. Ultimately, I think this strengthened our relationship because he knew I would stand behind him. This was one of the first times we confronted a challenge together as a couple.

But in the end, there was no way out of his contract. Paul made the best of it and stayed with the show for two more years until it went off the air. Paul and I were relieved when "Starsky" was finally over. Paul vowed he'd never do another television series—and once again his agent thought he was nuts. But Paul turned down every television offer that came his way. He wanted to act in feature films and also pursue a career as a director.

He had directed several "Starsky" episodes and found out that he loved it. Creatively and intellectually, directing was very stimulating for Paul. It was a turning point for him professionally. He used to say, "When I was an actor, I was a child, but as a director, I had to become an adult." Once again, he was bucking the tide. In many ways that was part of what I liked and what scared me the most about Paul. He wasn't afraid of walking on more dangerous paths. People could not understand why someone who had been so successful as an actor would want to do something so risky as becoming a director.

But Paul was convinced this was what he wanted to do, and I supported him. It was a gamble but Paul had great talent and I knew it. I never questioned that he'd be able to do anything he wanted. Paul had stuck it out with "Starsky." We had saved money, and I wanted him to be able to have the freedom he needed to explore and experiment with his own creativity. Those transition years of 1979 to 1980 were complicated in their own ways. Paul starred in a John Huston film called *Phobia* which was never a big box office success. He was working to develop projects and have people take him seriously as a director. With so much more time on his hands, he delved into practicing yoga and playing his guitar. It was a quieting and reflective time. I had stopped teaching and was helping to start the Los Angeles Children's Museum.

About a year after "Starsky" went off the air, Paul asked me to marry him. Making the commitment was much harder than living together. Paul knew I wasn't going to push him, and finally he had decided to make the jump. I was jubilant and told everyone. Dad was working in Puerto Rico now, and we planned to stop off there en route to a Caribbean vacation.

But on the flight to San Juan, three months after he proposed, Paul told me he just couldn't go through with the marriage.

"Honey, I'm sorry, I just can't do it now." My eyes grew large in disbelief. Panic began to overtake me.

"But why? We're happy and you know we love each other."

"I don't know. It isn't anything I can put into words. My feelings haven't changed, but it's just that somehow I still don't feel ready."

I was so disappointed and angry. We had been living together for four years. I was almost thirty-one and knew I wanted to have children. I couldn't postpone my life indefinitely while he had a tug-of-war with commitment.

I thought seriously about ending our relationship. Paul and I talked it through and he finally agreed that we'd get married when we were ready to have children. I had been married once already so I had no interest in marriage for the sake of marriage. I really wanted to start a family and decided it was still worth waiting for Paul. It wasn't an easy decision and many days I was scared that I was hoping for something I would never get.

Then, about a year later we were window shopping in Beverly Hills when Paul said, "Maybe we should get married." A little smile came over my face. I asked him if he *really* wanted to do it this time and he said yes. I said, "Good—let's do it today." I guess as the bloom of first romance was wearing off and our love deepened, Paul decided he would risk starting a family even though he was scared.

That was late on a Friday afternoon and we called the rabbi but found that it was too late to get married before sunset. Saturday was the Sabbath so we made arrangements to be married on Sunday morning in the rabbi's study.

We were married in a simple ceremony on Sunday, August 24, 1980. We told no one except our four witnesses until it was over.

Afterward we both called our parents and said, "We're married!" and then we went sailing with eight friends. We told them that we had rented a sailboat for the afternoon, but not the reason why. When we all arrived it was a celebration. The day was delightful. After so much worrying about getting married, once it was done we never questioned it. Our lives actually became better as the stress of making the commitment was no longer there.

Three months later, I was pregnant. Paul was enthusiastic about fatherhood. All the goodness in the world seemed to be ours. In nine months I would have what I had always wanted most in the world, a child of my own with a man that I loved.

We were visiting Paul's sister, Connie, in Boston and talking about what to name the baby. She suggested the name Ariel, the spirit who guides the ships through the storms in Shakespeare's *The Tempest.* I thought the name was magical the moment I heard it, but dismissed it because it wasn't a Hebrew name. My trip to Israel had made me feel it was important to continue a heritage. Paul brought me a what-to-name-the-baby book a few months later and there on the first page was the name Ariel. When I saw that it was Hebrew in origin I never turned another page. The name means "Lion of God."

During my pregnancy I was working at the Los Angeles Children's Museum. I had been there three years, working without salary for the first year, and then was hired to be the first educational and program director for the museum. It was very creative and stimulating to be able to take ideas that

I'd had from the classroom and expand them for all the children of the city. One of the first projects I worked on was an exhibit called "Grandma's Attic," designed to teach children about life in the pioneer days by letting them rummage through old trunks, play with antique toys, churn butter, and experience other memorabilia in a hands-on environment.

I had developed the exhibit with a woman named Susie Zeegen. We had worked together for at least several months when we started talking one day about our past. She asked me where I grew up and I said it was a small town on Long Island that I was sure she'd never heard of.

"You're kidding! I grew up in a place like that, too."

"Well," I said, "I grew up in Hewlett Harbor."

"So did I!" she exclaimed in disbelief. As we pieced together our pasts, we realized we'd been in the same Brownie troop in second grade. Because of our different names, we hadn't recognized each other at the museum. But from the moment we reconnected, Susie and I became devoted friends. She called me every day after the trauma in my pregnancy began.

In fact, I had been working at the Children's Museum when the bleeding started. I called my obstetrician right away who told me to go to the hospital immediately. I spent the next three months at home in bed, and then on August 4, 1981, I became a mother.

After the hemorrhaging and transfusions following Ariel's birth, the doctors felt that the crisis had passed. But we were unable to let ourselves relax until a few days went by and there was no more bleeding.

We went home to our small Spanish house on Woodrow Wilson Drive in the Hollywood Hills. Protected by a giant olive tree and lush with oleander and bougainvillea, it felt like an oasis. We felt calmer and even a little bit lucky that we had made it through such a terrible ordeal. Those first few days were a time of immense love and learning. Paul was holding a baby for the first time. He changed her diaper and helped me bathe her. I was learning to breastfeed. She would sleep and we would just stare at her, talking in whispers as though a jolting noise would break her.

Ariel became colicky and cried a great deal for the first three months we were at home. This was stressful on all of us, but especially for Paul who was acting in *The Lady Cries*

Murder and needed to sleep during the daytime. We took turns getting up in the night to feed her. When it was Paul's turn, I would express breast milk and leave the bottle in the freezer for him to heat up. But when Ariel would wake up howling at five in the morning, I would get up and put her in the buggy and walk for two hours so Paul could sleep. We strolled until dawn through the Hollywood Hills where the air was fragrant with eucalyptus.

Early motherhood is an exhausting time—but I was fortunate to have wonderful help. When Ariel was two weeks old, Graciela Salazar came to work as a housekeeper. From the day she shyly walked into our home, she brought love and loyalty with her that expanded as the years went by. Graciela doted on Ariel as much as Paul and I did. One of the first words Ari learned to say was "Ga Ga," and she kept calling her that even after she learned to talk. Graciela and I were co-conspirators who were always trying to find new ways to keep the baby quiet on days when Paul was working at home. We laughed a lot together as I tried to grapple with being a new mother.

At first you expect your baby to be a miniature version of yourself. You think your moods and temperament will be in sync and that as soon as the baby starts sleeping through the night, motherhood will be a breeze. But of course life with a newborn is far more gloriously chaotic than that. Ariel was not only a delightful, bright, and strong-willed baby, but a demanding one as well. It was a challenge that I threw myself into wholeheartedly.

Paul was enchanted with Ariel. With "Starsky" finished, we could move in the world again as ordinary people. We could take her for walks together without attracting crowds. Ariel adored her father and he was an attentive dad. He loved to carry her and show her things around the house.

Many times people only see Paul's serious side but he can be quite silly as well, and Ariel seemed to bring that out in him. He loved to clown for her, and she would laugh and coax him into more antics. She used to squeeze his nose, and he would make a goofy honking noise that they both thought was a riot.

My friend Rena Kramer, who had been a volunteer counselor with me at the Maple Center, had a daughter, Sara, who was about the same age as Ariel. They lived nearby and we formed a playgroup of mothers and babies. We were all well-educated professional women who had started families in our early thirties and were suddenly overjoyed and overwhelmed with our new lives. Nothing prepares you for the exuberance and stress of being a new mother—and nothing is quite as much fun as talking about it incessantly. Women talk about their babies the way men talk about sports.

We talked about teething and husbands and the changes our marriages were going through. Every detail of our babies' development was fascinating to us. We counted new teeth, played patty-cake and "Baby is sooooo big." We clicked our babies into car seats and knew all the verses to "The People on the Bus Go Up and Down."

Ari grew quickly, developed normally, and was very alert. At six months she and Graciela were reading *Pat the Bunny* together, which became one of their favorite rituals.

Paul and I will never forget the day she first walked. We were in her room and Paul was by the door. I was across the room, and he said, "Go ahead. Walk to Mommy." And she did. We were all beaming from ear to ear. It was one of those landmark moments.

Paul and Ari had their own rituals as well. Every Sunday morning, they would drive down the canyon to Art's Deli for breakfast. They would get up at six and leave so quietly that I never woke up. It was Mommy's morning to sleep in and Daddy's morning to take out "his girl." They were regulars and it was very special. Paul had developed a very wonderful relationship with Ari. Even at such an early age they saw things with similar sensitivities.

They started painting together as soon as Ari could hold a brush and had hours of time when they created worlds on paper that no one else knew.

I think when Paul looked at Ari he saw much of the artist in himself. And when his blue eyes met her blue eyes they were one.

Ari went to sleep every night with her pink quilted blanket, which her Aunt Connie and Cousin Alisa had made, and her floppy gray bunny, which Paul and I had bought at F.A.O. Schwarz in New York when I was five months pregnant. It had been such a special moment for us. It was the first thing we had gotten for this child of ours who was yet to be born. Gray bunny was warm and soft and represented all our hopes for the future. It never left her side. She felt safe and secure with gray bunny, and Paul and I felt safe and secure in our new life.

When Ari was about a year and a half, we began looking for a larger house. Paul and I knew we wanted more children and I was trying to get pregnant. We also wanted to move into a regular neighborhood with sidewalks and back yards. The Hollywood Hills are great for panoramic views, but lousy for lemonade stands and trick-or-treating.

After some time, I found what I was looking for. From the moment I walked into the sprawling Mediterranean house in Santa Monica, I knew this was the home for my family. I was thrilled with every aspect of it. What was magical was the way the light poured into it. It was built around an atrium that is flooded with natural light. The first time I walked through the house, the living room was drenched with morning sun and I felt like I was outdoors.

I also fell in love with the gigantic kitchen. I could see Lynn and Lucy talking to me and drinking wine while we cooked lasagna and made a huge salad for dinner. Kitchens are the heartbeat of a house and this one was perfect.

I knew Paul would be comfortable in the spacious rooms of the Santa Monica house. Paul is a big man who needs a lot of space, and "quaint" doesn't work for him. Putting him in a cozy New England cottage with low ceilings is like putting a Great Dane in a Volkswagen.

All the house lacked was children. This was a house that was meant for kids. When I was standing in it, I could fast forward to my future. I could see children running up and down the stairs and slamming doors and chasing through the atrium. I could see five-year-olds with bikes and ten-year-olds with best friends and teenagers with their dates lounging around the pool in the back yard. This was a house Paul and I would never have to leave. Our children would grow up and go to college and then Glaser children would come home with Glaser grandchildren.

Paul loved the house as much as I did. We bought it and moved in six weeks before the remodeling was finished. The three of us had to sleep in the den downstairs.

This was when I started strolling with Ari in Santa Monica. When she awakened at dawn, I put her in the stroller and we slipped out the front door so Paul could sleep. We put out milk for stray cats and made friends with some of the homeless men who were sleeping in the park, or the elderly people up early on the porches of the retirement homes.

One morning we were strolling and Ariel saw her first rainbow out over the Pacific. It took her breath away. It was an immense pleasure watching Ariel grow up and experience the world. I think one of the great joys of being a teacher, and most especially being a parent, is the opportunity to rediscover life through a child's eyes. Watching Ari and her friends playing dress-up, I probably had as much fun as they did. With old crinoline slips and fluffy feather boas, they would pretend for hours.

In the car, we would sing every song she knew from nursery school and every one I knew from teaching or from my childhood days at Camp Fernwood. Then we would sing and dance like ballerinas for Paul while he played his guitar. We always knew we could get him to laugh if we sang the Fernwood songs because he hated them, and Ari loved teasing him that way.

We found a wonderful little preschool in our new neighborhood and Ari started going when she was two. The very first day I walked in I noticed another mother pushing her daughter on the swingset in the courtyard. She introduced herself as Susan De Laurentis. Her adorable daughter, Francesca, soon became Ariel's best friend and Susan became one of my closest friends. Susan and I both grew up in the East and had husbands who were part of the entertainment industry. It was like having a sister and if we didn't see each other every day, we always talked on the phone. We both shared a sense of humor and were thoroughly enjoying raising our children.

Ari made two other important and lasting friendships that year. Both Amy and Taylor became integral parts of her life and Hilary, Amy's mom, became another dear friend of mine. Looking back I would say it was truly a glorious time.

Everything seemed to be going well. I had gotten pregnant and had miscarried, but was pregnant again and this time, because I was older, I had the amniocentesis test to make sure the baby was normal. We were elated when we found out that the baby was a healthy boy.

Paul and I had known all along that we wanted more than

one child. The doctors had said that the complications in my pregnancy with Ari would most likely not be repeated.

We were excited and confident things would go smoothly. Six weeks before my due date I had some premature contractions and they told me to stay put. But this time I wasn't afraid.

Paul was in Miami directing a "Miami Vice" episode, and Lucy came and stayed with me for a week. I savored my last quiet time with Ari. I was relaxing in the warm light of our special world that I knew would change when the new baby arrived. My obstetrician and Paul and I had decided that instead of automatically scheduling a caesarean, I'd go ahead and try to have a normal delivery.

Jake's birth was a great triumph. I delivered him naturally, on October 25, 1984, which brought both Paul and me great joy. Even my obstetrician was excited. I remember Dr. Brooks telling me that he thought of me as one of his most shining moments because they'd saved my uterus and now I had a second healthy baby.

Ari was three and a half and basically well prepared for the arrival of her baby brother, whose name was going to be either Sam or Jake, we couldn't decide. I had read her books about new babies and we had talked a lot about being a big sister. Nevertheless, once we got home, she became very angry, blaming me for bringing home this squalling baby, who had completely overturned our lives. For six weeks she only wanted her dad. He was back home then and the two of them did everything together.

Paul has a separate office behind our house and they would spend hours painting and drawing. I would be lying in bed feeding Jake and they would appear with beautiful pictures they had created. We'd hang them on the kitchen walls. Other times Paul and Ari would leave on long nature walks. They would bring home precious treasures and tell me of the amazing aloe plants they had discovered or an unusual feather or flower they had found. We were a regular family learning to live with new members and new rules.

CHAPTER
❧ 2 ❧

It was ten months later, just before Ariel turned four in the spring of 1985, that Paul was offered the job of directing his first feature film, *Band of the Hand*. It was being produced by Michael Mann, for TriStar.

When Michael was a script consultant on "Starsky," he and Paul had known each other. Michael went on to produce "Miami Vice," and, remembering Paul's strong directing style in his work on "Starsky and Hutch," asked Paul to direct three episodes of the series.

Michael was pivotal in Paul's transition from acting to directing. *Band of the Hand* was being shot in Miami, so right after Ari's birthday in August we packed up the family and rented a house on the beach for the three-month shoot. It was a great opportunity for Paul and it seemed like it would be a great adventure for the rest of us.

From Miami, at the beginning of September, I took the children to visit my parents in Puerto Rico. We had just returned from that trip when Ari started to have stomachaches and cramps. She was in a great deal of pain.

I went to a pediatrician in Miami who said she probably had picked up a bug in Puerto Rico. When she didn't get better in a few days, I went to another pediatrician who did a blood test and said that although her hematocrit, which measures the level of red cells in the blood, was low, it was still within the normal range. He suggested we see a gastroenterologist about her stomach.

I called our pediatrician back in Los Angeles and we went over the few facts we knew. He said to keep her on a diet for diarrhea and that it should clear up in a week or two at most. I wasn't particularly anxious, but Paul and I both wanted to figure out what was going on.

Then one Sunday Ariel's lips went white. I'll never forget it because it made her look so fragile and ghostlike. She began to tire so easily. When I would pick her up from the little nursery school she was attending she would fall asleep as soon as she was strapped into the car seat. It was only a half-day program and it was unlike her to be so fatigued.

But it was the chalky white color of her lips that scared me. Friends like Lynn would call from Los Angeles and ask how we were.

"Ari still seems to have the bug she picked up in Puerto Rico and it's so strange," I said. "Her lips are white—like the lipstick you used to wear in college."

"What are the doctors telling you?"

"They don't know. They still think she has a parasite and this should clear up if we watch her diet, but I'm worried because she seems so weak."

"Elizabeth, I'm sure once you start getting some food into her she'll bounce back. Kids are so resilient at this age."

"I don't know, Lynn, sometimes this feels serious. Paul and I are both getting scared. She wakes up in the night screaming in pain because she has to go to the bathroom. Sometimes it seems so much worse than a stomach virus or diarrhea. We're going to see a specialist tomorrow. I'll let you know what happens."

Paul was in the middle of a shoot, which meant he was gone from six A.M. until midnight six or seven days a week. He was under intense pressure because this film was his first big break as a director. He would get away when he could, but it can cost $50,000 a day to make a movie and as director Paul couldn't be absent from the set very often. He couldn't just say, "I have to go now to be with my family." In addition to the responsibility of a huge daily budget, a director has about two hundred people on the set depending on him to make all the decisions. Therefore, most of the worrying about Ari was falling on my shoulders.

I was reading more and more articles about AIDS in the newspapers, but neither Paul nor I had any friends with the disease, and the epidemic still seemed remote. There was a lot of discussion then about whether people with AIDS should be allowed to work in restaurants. I remember feeling bewildered and baffled by this new disease that I felt I didn't know enough about. Should I be worried about catching it? But thoughts like that were fleeting and peripheral. I thought if there was something to really be afraid of the doctors would warn us.

The sudden stress in the family was especially hard on Jake. He was just having his first birthday, Paul was gone, I was preoccupied with Ariel, Graciela had brought her daughter Cindy to Miami with us for one month, but she had just returned home to be with her own family, and Maria Lopez, our new housekeeper, had just arrived. They were all hard transitions for Jake. I had called Lucy in L.A. to see if she could come and spend a few days with me, but it was impossible.

In October, I took Ariel to see a specialist in pediatric gastroenterology. The specialist was convinced that Ariel had picked up a parasite or bug in Puerto Rico and said the best way to identify it was to get nine or ten stool samples in a row. Since we lived so far from the lab and hospital, he suggested that we check into the hospital for three days. I could stay in Ari's room, and after the samples were analyzed, we could pinpoint what was wrong. I told Ari that we were going to the hospital, but we'd just pretend it was a hotel—like Eloise at the Plaza—and turn the experience into an adventure. We bought cute clothes and new ribbons for her hair.

The hospital was decrepit and depressing. Going through the admissions process was frightening for me. I maintained a cheerful front for Ariel, but was not happy inside.

After we were admitted they drew blood immediately. All of her blood work had been done with finger pricks, but now they were drawing it from her veins and she became hysterical. I was horrified to see vial after vial being filled with Ari's blood. It's a sight I could never get used to, but the first time it happened I felt stunned.

At ten o'clock that evening, doctors came rushing into our room to say her hematocrit had dropped to twenty, which was dangerously low. She would have to be transfused immediately because the blood needs a certain number of red blood cells to carry oxygen. The doctors said they had no idea what was wrong with Ariel, but for the next three days, they watched her as if she might die.

It was at that moment that I once again saw her life as precarious. I could feel all my dreams and plans start to crumble. My many fears began to return. Without even knowing what was wrong, I was fighting for her life all over again. It was torture for Paul not to be able to be by our side.

The first priority was to stabilize her hematocrit. We waited for the hematocrit numbers to come up from the hospital lab, the soon-to-be-daily wait for the right numbers. The numbers told us how well she was doing. When they were high, we felt like we had something to hold on to. If they were low, all I could do was pray for higher figures the next day. Once again, I felt utterly powerless.

I knew that if her hematocrit kept dropping we would need more blood. The blood supply was supposed to be safe from AIDS, since blood banks had been screening their donations since earlier in 1985. But I was still afraid that the screening might not be completely reliable and that Ari might be transfused with infected blood and get even sicker.

I had no close friends in Miami except my new friend Janet Goldstein. Paul was working night and day. It was as if Ari and I were alone on an island. I had to be brave so that she wouldn't get scared, but after she fell asleep I would find the head nurse, a wonderful woman named Debbie Delaney, who would put her arms around me while I cried and cried and cried.

My friend Rena Kramer, whom I met when I first came to L.A. and her daughter, Sara, who had been one of Ari's first playmates, had been planning to visit us while we were in Miami. Rena came even though Ari was sick. I needed a friend beside me. The night before we left the hospital, Rena and I managed to go out for dinner. The three days had stretched into a week and this was the first time I had left the hospital. I was scared to leave Ari for even a minute, but I needed fresh air.

We went to an outdoor Italian restaurant. I was sitting at the small table talking with Rena, when something happened to me that had never happened before—it was like an out-of-body experience. While I was sitting in the restaurant, I saw a vision of myself and there was a wickedly dark cloud over my head. I was way up high and in a flash, I shot up through this cloud into a bright blue sky. I tore through the darkness into the light. It was an incredible visual experience and was over in seconds.

I had no idea what prompted it. I am sure I did not miss a syllable in our conversation. It wasn't frightening, just startling. It was so strange I didn't tell anyone about it; I had no idea what it meant. It was the first of a number of strange visions, dreams, or experiences that would enter my life. I wanted to believe it meant we'd shoot through the darkness of Ari's illness. A few minutes after, the hospital called to say Ari had awakened and was frightened without me. We rushed back.

How I yearned to be on the beach again with Ari. My mother had taught me how to love looking for seashells and now I had been teaching Ari. We'd walk the beach and look for treasures together every day before she got sick. Ari found luster and beauty in the broken chips of shells, the scraps most people would ignore. We looked at the way the shells caught the light and imagined the tiny creatures that had lived inside. I had always loved nature, but Ari helped me experience its awe.

Ariel was finally released from the hospital and by the time we left Florida in November she was stronger, but not well. There was color in her face and lips, but she still had bouts of diarrhea and would wake up in pain. Her doctors in Florida diagnosed Ari as having hemolytic uremic syndrome, a blood disorder that usually leads to renal failure.

When we returned to Los Angeles, we began to see Dr. Richard Fine, who was the pediatric nephrologist at UCLA. He worked with his wife, Shawnee, who is a clinical nurse with a specialty in pediatric nephrology. Richard Fine used to kid me when we first met because I looked like anything but the wife of a television star. I wore sneakers and simple cotton dresses that were comfortable, but in no way chic. The Fines soon came to feel like family to us. Richard was paternal but not in a condescending way, and I had complete trust in him. He and Shawnee were reassuring and I relied on them completely.

Over the next few months, from January to April 1986, we were doing test after test, trying to diagnose the underlying cause of Ari's illness. We all knew something was wrong but there would be periods of a few weeks when Ari would be on a plateau and relatively stable, living a mostly normal, four-year-old life. She happily went to nursery school each day, and had a playdate every afternoon with one of her friends, either Amy or Francesca or Sara or Taylor.

Paul was in post-production on *Band of the Hand*. So as it had been in Miami, the demands and pressures on him were intense, but he would try to be home by early evening and we'd all have dinner together. I would fill Paul in every night about what had happened during the day. He was anxious and frustrated about the doctors' inability to find a diagnosis.

Paul and I had told Ari there was something funny with her blood and that was the reason she was so frequently tired. We told her that the doctors were going to keep doing tests and that they would find a way to make her better.

I had great faith in doctors but now they seemed stumped. Throughout my life I had assumed that doctors had answers for everything. The first time I confronted the fact that they didn't, my vulnerability soared.

Different people do different things when they feel vulnerable. I take action so I don't feel helpless. I began to reach out in other directions during this time to find answers to a puzzling situation. One of them was to Jim Blechman, M.D., whom I call my homeopathic doctor. Jim was trained in Western medicine, but he also uses alternative forms of treatment like homeopathy, herbs, and acupuncture. He believes there are times when natural healing can be a valuable adjunct to, not a substitute for, conventional medical treatment. When you're with Jim you feel both comforted by his tranquillity and protected by his strength.

I took Ari to see him, but she reacted to Jim as she did to all doctors—as a potential threat. Ari was discerning. She was the kind of child who would either really embrace you and let you in or keep you at a distance. She did not immediately embrace the world. She first evaluated and then made up her mind. But you always knew where you stood with Ari. So although she liked Jim, her experience in Miami made her wary of doctors.

Jim thought Ari had some low-grade virus and he put us on some homeopathic drugs to help build up her blood count. He was puzzled when she didn't respond as rapidly as he anticipated and although we didn't make much progress medically in those early months, I found it easy to trust Jim.

Every week, Ari had to be taken in for her blood test. It was always terrible because she would shriek and scream in terror each time blood was drawn.

They would draw the blood and then we'd have to wait until that evening to find out if everything was stable. My anxiety would build and build as the day went on until by evening I was a bundle of shaking nerves. Usually, I was the one who had to call for the results. I dreaded this. The phone became the enemy. Finally I would get enough courage to call. The doctor would be out and then we'd have to wait for him to call back. When the phone would finally ring, Paul and I would get into skirmishes over who would answer it because we knew it was the doctor calling back with results of the lab work. My fear was palpable.

Sometimes we'd be in the middle of dinner when the call would come. I would look at Paul and say, "*You* have to answer it!" I'd look at Ari and I was filled with tears that I held inside.

Paul would stare at me with a look that said, "You answer it!" He wouldn't say anything because neither one of us wanted Ari to know how panicked we felt.

The phone would ring a second or third time. I'd look at Paul and shake my head to say, "No, I won't answer it." Then Paul would get on the phone and give me some sort of signal while he was listening to let me know everything was okay.

My friends became increasingly important. They were the ones who were always there for me if I fell apart in the middle of the day. I could reach Paul if there was an emergency, but it was my women friends I could count on when I felt all was going wrong.

One afternoon I stopped by to see Lynn, who was now working as a production executive at MGM. Ari had blood drawn that morning and the results were to be ready that afternoon. I was petrified. The fear was always in me that if the numbers were low, we would have to go back to the hospital.

I was sitting in Lynn's office calling and calling. Each time the line was busy I'd become more and more nervous. When the secretary finally answered and put me through to Dr.

Fine, I could hardly breathe. I heard his voice. I heard him say everything was stable. I knew we wouldn't have to go back into the hospital this week. I burst into tears. So much anxiety had built inside of me that all I could do was shake and sob when it was over. It was horrible for both of us.

Thank God Lynn was right there. She was a rock for me. Our friendship goes all the way back to pledging sororities together at the University of Wisconsin. In college, we had that prom queen innocence about us.

When we started at Wisconsin in 1965 it was a party school with 40,000 students and we fit right into the good times. But by the time we graduated in 1969, buildings were being blown up to protest the Vietnam War and the National Guard was on campus. Over the years, Lynn and I have lost our innocence together. We lost our innocence in the heartbreak of our first loves. We lost our innocent idealism in the antiwar protests, and we lost our happily-ever-after innocence when our first marriages ended in divorce. But this was more difficult than anything we had faced before.

And so when I cried, she held me and reassured me that somehow, some way, they would discover what was wrong with Ari and then, with the wonders of medicine, make her better.

At the same time we were trying to find answers to Ari's medical questions, we were planning for the future by looking for a school where she could start kindergarten in the fall. The thought of her not getting better never entered our minds. My own bias as a teacher was toward public schools, but I was willing to look into private education. I looked at one school and then stopped.

Crossroads is a private school that goes all the way through twelfth grade. Although it emphasizes traditional learning and academics, it is very creative and encourages, or dares, children to find something that excites them. I remember when we had an interview with Mimi Baer, the director of the lower school, she asked us if we were tired of interviewing for schools. When I told her we were only applying to Crossroads she seemed dumbstruck, because the admissions were so competitive.

Six months after we applied we were accepted. It was a vote for the future. As a teacher I knew this was an exceptional school. It was only eight blocks from our house, so it was a neighborhood school as well. It was perfect. As soon as we read the acceptance letter we got right in the car and I showed Ari where her school was going to be. We were both thrilled.

As time went by and things still didn't improve, Ariel was tested for all sorts of unusual diseases, including lupus, a blood disorder I had never heard of. That test came back negative. There was talk of doing a liver and kidney biopsy but that was postponed.

A few weeks later Richard Fine said he wanted to test for leukemia. Leukemia? I knew Ariel didn't have it, but Dr. Fine said he wanted to do an aspiration of her bone marrow and check for any malignancy that might be lurking. We would have to be briefly hospitalized.

Dr. Fine was still protecting us from his worst suspicions. Both he and Shawnee secretly felt that Ariel should be tested for AIDS, as a precaution. They knew about my blood transfusions, but the prevalent medical thinking at the time was that you needed to have direct contact with blood or semen to catch the virus. There was nothing about breast milk as a source of transmission.

Shawnee convinced him, and they debated how they should approach us, since doctors need legal consent to test for AIDS. Since they didn't want to confront us with the HIV test, they decided to run tests that might rule out AIDS as a diagnosis.

When the test for leukemia came back negative, I felt we had won another diagnostic round. I felt relief. Richard Fine wasn't as cheerful. He knew what we didn't—Ari's diarrhea was a symptom of AIDS. He had had a gastroenterologist look at her colon and take a biopsy of the colonic tissue to see why she was having this intermittent diarrhea. We also found out they had tested Ari's T-cell levels while she was hospitalized. Out of all the tests, the only one that pointed out anything new pointed toward AIDS—her T-cell count was low.

T-cells are the white blood cells that defend one's immune system against attack. The HIV virus infiltrates these cells where it then replicates in every new T-cell that is produced. The infected T-cells then die off. So as the disease progresses, T-cell counts make a long, slow decline, robbing the immune system of the very cells it needs to fight off infections.

Dr. Fine had asked the hematologist to take a look at Ari's blood work.

I was unaware of his mounting fears. I still believed that once we diagnosed Ari's illness and treated it, everything would turn out fine. But no matter what I believed it was a stressful, scary time. I needed support. I was already facing issues I never thought I'd have to face.

The other person I reached out to at that time was Rabbi Jonathan Omer-Man, who is a blend of therapist and spiritual teacher and describes himself somewhat poetically as a man who works with people who have lost the story of their lives.

Working with Jonathan is a process of empowerment, of regaining control after tragedy or upheaval throws your life off its course. I had started seeing Jonathan when we returned from Miami and had no idea how much I would need him as time went on. Jonathan said I was like a steel wire that was lying in a twisted mess on the ground. But he said the wire was capable of great strength once it was unraveled and pulled taut.

On the surface my life still made sense. But on an inner level, I was faced for the first time with a situation that I couldn't control. The old ways weren't producing any answers; I had been raised to feel that I was a person who could make things happen, but I wasn't able to now.

By the spring, Paul and I needed a break. Mustering up the courage to leave Ari and Jake, even briefly, was a big deal for us. We were still anxious about Ari's health, but she seemed to be relatively stable. We knew we needed to spend some time alone. Paul had finally finished *Band of the Hand,* and this seemed like a good time to pay attention to each other. We decided to go to Hawaii.

We stumbled into paradise tired and stressed, but began to feel rejuvenated quickly. We met new people who would become very important to us in the months and years ahead: Steven Spielberg, who was then married to Amy Irving, Richard Dreyfuss and his ebullient wife, Jeremy, and Ron and Carol Herman. We told them that our daughter hadn't been well, but that we were optimistic that everything would be fine once she was finally diagnosed.

Being in the luxurious beauty of Hawaii, loving each other, and laughing with new friends was such a welcome relief. We convinced ourselves that a happiness we could hold onto was just ahead. We came back in mid-May and two weeks later I got a call from Dr. Fine.

"Look, I don't want you to be anxious about this, because I am sure it's not possible, but the hematologist who has been studying Ari's blood work passed it along to the infectious disease people and there are a few things in the picture that make them feel it would be smart at this time to test for AIDS."

"Okay, all right," I told him. By then Richard and Shawnee were almost a part of our family. I had complete faith in them. "We've tested for lupus. We've tested for leukemia. We'll test for AIDS."

I don't think I was any more anxious about the AIDS test than I was for anything else. How could Ariel have gotten AIDS? I wasn't worried about her transfusions in Miami because she was already sick by the time she got them. Just as her doctors had ruled out lupus and leukemia, they'd rule out AIDS.

But Paul was livid when he heard that Dr. Fine wanted to test for AIDS. It seemed preposterous to him. He called Richard Fine, furious that the illness had been going on for six months without any resolution or improvement. Although Ariel wasn't getting any worse, she certainly was not getting any better. Paul was petrified by the thought of AIDS. But once he vented his frustrations he finally agreed to let them do the test.

We went in and they drew the blood. I had to sign a form that gave them permission to test for AIDS.

Paul was home when the phone rang the next day. We were in our bedroom. He answered it and I saw him nod and mutter something like "Uh huh," and when he hung up he said, "They've got to run it again. It's shown some kind of positivity. It's probably a mistake and we'll know in two days."

It was two days that felt like a lifetime. I don't remember talking to Paul about it. If one of us had started talking about it the other would have said, "Look, this is silly, we don't even know. It's a waste of time to even speculate. In two days, we'll know what's going on and it probably is going to be fine."

I remember telling a few friends that the test was being repeated because there was something quirky in the results and it was probably a false positive. I was truly in shock. I only went through the motions of acting positive for Ari's sake.

The two days slowly but eventually passed. Richard Fine called that morning in late May. "The test has come back positive. You all have to come in tomorrow to be tested."

At first no words came. And then I blurted out, "How could this have happened? How could this have *happened?*"

"We don't know. We need you all to come in and be tested. I'm so sorry, Elizabeth."

Ari had been diagnosed. Ari's illness now had a name. Ariel had AIDS.

I remember walking into the bathroom and screaming as loud as I could. Ari and Jake must have been out of the house because I would never have fallen apart in front of them. I was screaming and crying. I don't remember how long I stayed there. I don't remember anything.

Paul walked into the bathroom, but we couldn't touch. We couldn't even look at each other. He turned and walked out. I was still crying. He walked back in. He said, "You have to pull yourself together." I thought, *Why? My life is over. Why should I pull anything together? Why should I bother going on? The most important thing in my life—my daughter—is going to die.* That's all I could think at that moment. So why go on?

I became more and more hysterical. Finally, Paul sat down by me on the edge of the tub and just said, "We don't know. You have to get control for Ari and Jake, Elizabeth. You have to—now *do it.*"

From that moment on I had no choice but to become intentionally schizophrenic. What I felt and what I was thinking were one thing, and what I presented to my children and the rest of the outside world was another.

Unbelievable as it may seem, it began that very night. I had been a volunteer in Tom Hayden's office and had coordinated a cocktail party for that night for one of Hayden's environmental issues. Since I was expected to speak, I felt there was no way I could show up. Lucy came with me. Ari's diagnosis had turned Lucy into a basket case. She was shaking and distraught, but I was still too numb.

It was as if I became my own understudy. There was someone to go out onstage and fill in for me; she knew all of my lines and she even looked the part. But the real Elizabeth Glaser was somewhere else, somewhere in a dark, dark hole that felt way too deep. Somewhere else, so afraid, that she couldn't let anyone see it.

The next morning we went in to UCLA and were all tested. Richard Fine called back later. "We have to run the tests on Elizabeth and Jake again," and by then we knew what that meant. It meant we had tested positive. It meant they didn't want to give us positive HIV test results unless they had confirmed it twice.

Paul and I went back to UCLA and sat numbly in Dr. Fine's office with him and Dr. Richard Stiehm, the pediatric immunologist who would become Ari's doctor. We sat like statues. We were in shock. There was little emotion. We nodded in agreement to words that made no sense.

They explained that there had been a lot of infected blood at Cedars-Sinai Hospital in the early years of the epidemic because it is located on the edge of West Hollywood which is predominantly gay. They asked me if I had ever had any sexual relationships with anyone other than Paul. I laughed because the question seemed so stupid. I hadn't even kissed anyone else except my husband since the day I met him.

Dr. Stiehm said he thought I had been infected through my blood transfusion and had passed the virus on to Ari during breast feeding and to Jake in utero.

Paul and I sat there. In our worst nightmares, we could never have imagined the devastation of that office visit. Our entire world had been crushed. Ari, Jake, and I might all die. It was too much to comprehend. Still, today, it is too much to comprehend.

There was business to take care of. They said that Ari should start on gamma globulin treatments right away to shore up her immune system. She would not have to be hospitalized for them but could get the infusions at the UCLA clinic by sitting for four hours with an IV in her arm. Dr. Stiehm said that we shouldn't tell anyone about our diagnosis because the experiences of other families with AIDS had not been positive.

"The world is not ready for your family," was how he put it. He advised us to tell not even our closest friends.

But nevertheless, he said we needed to either tell her nursery school or take her out of it. The Centers for Disease Control (CDC) guidelines, at that time, said that a child with

AIDS should not be in nursery school without first getting permission from the school.

It was surreal. Along with this hideous medical diagnosis came instructions on how we needed to handle the rest of the world.

Dr. Stiehm told me that I could test positive and carry the HIV virus without being symptomatic or showing any signs of the disease. In other words, there was a big difference in being HIV-positive and having full-blown AIDS.

I asked Dr. Stiehm, "Can you tell me where I stand?"

He said there were certain things that could be looked for. My anxiety was building.

"Well," I said, "take me into an examining room and examine me right now. Will you do that? Can you do that right now?" I needed all the information I could get right then.

He checked between my toes and fingers for thrush, which was a rare fungus. He checked for swollen lymph nodes. He found no symptoms. He said I would need an adult doctor and recommended that I see Dr. Michael Gottlieb at UCLA, an immunologist who has been in the forefront of the epidemic since it began.

Although Jake had tested positive, his other tests were all normal. Because he was only eighteen months old and Ari hadn't become sick until she was four, I think I felt that Jake still had time. Immediately, one hundred percent of my focus shifted to Ari.

I told Dr. Stiehm that day that I could not live without telling my friends. They were the mortar that held our lives together. They had also been following Ari's illness since Miami, and their support and concern had been crucially important. Paul and I decided we had two choices. We could tell some friends or we could pick up, sell our house, and begin our life all over again someplace else where we knew no one. But Paul and I both knew it made no sense to leave.

We went home and I looked at my children and felt what I still feel every time I look at Jake: "I love you so much, and I am so scared that I may lose you."

The life that we had known was over. From now on nothing could be taken for granted—no moment and no action. If I had thought I had responsibilities taking care of Ari before, now I felt that burden constantly, and magnified an infinite number of times. At the same time it's a duty I never once considered shirking. As far as my own physical condition was concerned, I knew I had to stay strong so I could save my children. Our first steps were perhaps the hardest.

One of the first calls I had to make was to my parents. I looked at the phone and found one excuse after another not to pick it up. I would wait until the children were asleep. I would wait until I had something to eat. I would wait until I could get the words out of my mouth without bursting into tears.

I hated the thought of what this call would do to their lives. They were in their late sixties and happily retired in Puerto Rico. They lived in a house they had designed and built themselves that overlooked the ocean. These were supposed to be prize years they had worked so hard for all their lives. Now I had to tell them their only daughter and grandchildren had the potential for developing a disease for which there was no known medical treatment or cure, a disease that no one recovered from.

I finally picked up the phone and dialed. I sat on the bed. My mother answered.

"Hi, Mom, it's me."

"How are you?"

"Well, we're not good."

"What's wrong? I don't like the sound of your voice. Is Ari sick again?"

"It's worse than that, worse than anything anyone ever imagined. Ari has AIDS, and Jake and I are HIV-positive. We just found out. Paul is the only one who isn't infected."

"Oh, God, Betsy. There must be some mistake."

"There's no mistake. They did all the tests twice. I got it from the blood transfusions when Ari was born."

"But how could she get it? You got the transfusions after she was born."

"But I nursed her and Dr. Stiehm says you can get it from breast milk. Jake got it before he was born. I'm so scared. I don't know what to do."

I cried and cried over the phone and my mother tried to comfort me. She said she would come right away if I needed her, and I said I did but to wait for a few days until we regained some equilibrium. She came a few weeks later.

Another decision we had to make right away was about Ari's school. There were only three weeks left until Ari would be leaving nursery school for kindergarten. I felt it would be too big an issue for the school to handle in that short amount of time. Dr. Stiehm had said, if I didn't tell them, I'd have to take her out. So the lies began. I told the nursery school director that Ariel's doctor, Dr. Stiehm, felt that it would be good for her to have a quiet summer so she could regain as much of her strength as possible before the start of kindergarten. If I concentrated hard enough I could almost make myself believe it.

Taking Ari out of preschool was a decision that caused me great anguish. She had been at Circle of Children for three years. I wanted her to experience everything wonderful that she could, right now. I hated to take her out of an environment that brought her such delight. What difference could another twenty-one days make? She had been infected since birth. What could happen in the next three weeks that hadn't already happened? I wanted so much for her to celebrate finishing nursery school with all her friends. But now we knew Ari had AIDS, and nothing could ever really be the same. We took her out of school.

The doctors told me what to do and at that time I was following their directions exactly.

Ari had been enrolled in a summer day camp. It was like an outdoor preschool, a few hours each morning. I needed to find out if they would accept a child with AIDS without inquiring directly. Gene Seymour, a doctor and one of Paul's best friends, contacted the director of the day camp for us and asked if they would accept a child who had been diagnosed with AIDS. The answer was a flat no. We took her out of summer camp.

I told Ari what I told everyone else, that her doctor felt she needed to rest and become stronger so she would be ready for kindergarten in the fall. Ariel was very accepting. I tried to compensate by taking her to the park with Jake every day and doing all our favorite activities. Leaving nursery school was much harder on me than it was for her, because I pretended that nothing was really wrong, and she believed it.

Paul's nephew, David Kantar, was to arrive on our doorstep two days after we were diagnosed. His mother, Connie, is Paul's sister and we go to the Kantars' house in Maine every summer. David was dropping out of school for a year and he was coming to spend the summer with us. Would

David still want to live with us? Would he be afraid? Would his family be afraid? I mean, we knew from the papers that people were afraid of AIDS.

We called Connie and her husband, Billy, and told them about the diagnosis and asked them if they still thought it was okay for David to come. They thought it over, called us back, and said, "David is still coming."

It was a relief to think that there would be someone else around to lean on, but the reality was he was only a twenty-year-old young man. David got off the plane, walked into our house, sat down with us at our kitchen table, and I was hysterically crying. He was thrown into a crisis that was unimaginable for someone so young. But his love was unwavering and he made a tremendous difference to our family during that time.

Paul and I decided to confide in only a handful of friends, some whose children were playmates of Ari and Jake. For these friends, finding out that we had AIDS was like finding out that for years their children had been in imminent danger. Had they already been contaminated? Nothing is rational when it comes to the safety of your children. I wondered whether I would react any differently if I was in their place. We were nervous but we assumed everything would be fine. We were wrong.

I told our friends in person, one by one. I would call them and say, "You've got to come over, right now. I have got to talk to you, right away."

We couldn't talk in my house in front of the children, and we couldn't talk in theirs so we would take a walk around the block or get in the car and drive. I never did any of this without a cigarette—I only smoke when I'm nervous—so sometimes we would have to first stop at the liquor store to buy some. Inevitably, the matches that were slid across the counter with the pack always seemed to have "AIDS" printed on them.

When I told my friend Rena we drove over to Ocean Avenue and parked under the tall palms that edge the park. I lit a cigarette and began. I said, "The most horrible thing has happened. Ari has AIDS, and Jake and I are HIV-positive. Paul doesn't have it."

Rena, like my mother, thought there must be some mistake. That this was all a horrible mistake. Unfortunately, I said between sobs, it wasn't a mistake. She was very comforting, and as I continued to cry, I made Rena, and later everyone else, promise not to tell anyone except their husbands.

When Rena and I drove back, Paul came out and sat on the doorstep with us. He said this was going to be a test of courage for all of us, that it would measure the limits of our morality and integrity and strength. It was moments like these, when I felt I didn't have the strength to go on, that I could turn to Paul and he would help me to see a larger picture. He would talk about the growth and learning that would come from all of this. Paul was able to find wisdom in crisis right from the start.

The secret . . .

The secret.

When we told people about having AIDS we forced them to enlist in a conspiracy of silence. The quality of our lives now hinged on the ability of our friends to keep quiet. Were word to get out, we knew we would be treated like plague victims for no reason.

All of us were very afraid and confused. This was completely new territory for us and for our friends. At first, everyone reacted very sympathetically: "Oh, this is terrible, this is so awful. We love you and will do anything we can to help you." Our friends who didn't have children who played with Ari or Jake were easily straightforward in their support.

It was a very different decision for the parents of our children's playmates. For four years our children had gone from babies who had drooled over bottles and pacifiers together, to toddlers who ate and bathed together, to preschoolers who swam and took baths together. Now these friends were scared that their children might become infected with a virus we knew little about. The rationale that "what might happen probably already had" didn't work. The initial reaction of "How can we help?" was followed a few weeks later by great fear and many restrictions. We watched as the quality of our life disappeared before our very eyes.

I had been going to see a yoga teacher since we came back from Miami because of all the stress. The exercises were relaxing and yoga helped me feel centered and in control. I went back for my next session three days after we were diagnosed. When my teacher offered me a glass of water I panicked. Should I drink it? Could I drink it if she didn't know?

I told her about our diagnosis, asking her to think it over and let me know if she could continue to see me.

She called to say she never wanted to see me again. I was devastated. This was someone I thought might be thinking on a higher spiritual plane than the rest of us. Forget it. It was the first concrete example that people would want nothing to do with me and my children because we had this disease.

Around this time I also called my old therapist, a wonderful man named Dr. Harry Brickman whom I had seen off and on for years. When I had stopped seeing Harry Brickman, Paul had started going to him and so Dr. Brickman knew our family very, very well. Harry was over at our house within hours. Paul and I talked and cried and talked and cried. We talked about life and we talked about death. It was very overwhelming. I told him how afraid I was for Ari and that I really wanted to get a support system in place for her right away. I asked if he could please make some calls and see if he could find a therapist who would be willing to work with her when and if we thought it was appropriate. He called back a few days later and said that the psychiatrists he had spoken with said they would be unwilling to work with my child because she had AIDS.

Forget the yoga teacher with her body oils and breathing techniques—these were doctors! Psychiatrists didn't want a child with AIDS in their practice because, if word leaked out, they were afraid they would lose too many other clients. People were responding so fearfully that I started to feel dangerous myself.

One day I took Ari and Jake to a small park in the neighborhood and I remember thinking, "Everyone is staring at me. What are they thinking? What if they all know?"

I would push Ari in her stroller down Montana Avenue in Santa Monica, feeling like a leper. Every time I went into the supermarket, I envisioned everyone slowly and silently moving away as if they had just seen a rattlesnake.

I had been told to see a doctor right away, and made the appointment with Dr. Michael Gottlieb, the immunologist mentioned in Los Angeles as soon as you said the word AIDS. He moved to L.A. in 1980 after completing a fellowship at Stanford and started working at UCLA doing immunological research. Curious about a rare form of pneumonia that was turning up in gay men, Gottlieb published what turned out to be the first report on the epidemic in June 1981, and has been on the front lines of the epidemic ever since. By the time I became his patient, Gottlieb's practice had become focused solely on AIDS. The summer before, he had been the doctor who finally confirmed to the world that his patient Rock Hudson had AIDS. He was also the co-founder of the American Foundation for AIDS Research (AMFAR).

I went alone to my first appointment with Gottlieb. Paul was working, but I would have gone by myself even if he had been free. My mom had recently arrived from Puerto Rico and wanted to come with me, but I refused. I wanted—and needed—to hear whatever Gottlieb had to say by myself. My mother felt rejected and it was a difficult moment for both of us.

I couldn't bear the thought of having anyone else with me if Michael Gottlieb told me I was going to be dead in two years. I had to absorb the news by myself before I could share it with Paul and my parents. Since we had been diagnosed, I had been thinking only of Ari and Jake. As I drove down San Vicente Boulevard on my way to UCLA, I tried to calm myself and think as positively as I could.

I felt as healthy and as strong as ever and hadn't been sick since I was seven years old. Maybe they'd got the wrong girl. I was too much of a fighter and Ariel had just as much spunk. We would show them that we could beat it. We would pave the way for Jake. There had to be a way for us all to make it. Paul could not bear to lose his family one by one.

By the time I got to Michael Gottlieb's office, I had rallied as much courage as I could and was ready to hear whatever he had to say.

He did a complete physical exam and drew blood and then did a chest X ray and a few other baseline tests. The news from Gottlieb was grim. He didn't tell me I was going to die, but he said there was a thirty-percent chance I would become very ill within the next three years. He told me I had asymptomatic HIV infection, which meant I carried the HIV virus in my blood, but didn't show any symptoms of AIDS. I did have a low T-cell count, 210, and one of my lymph nodes was slightly enlarged.

Even though he had treated hundreds of AIDS patients

by the time he met me, Gottlieb was both patient and compassionate. I had so many questions: Am I going to die? How long can I live with this? Will I definitely get AIDS? And if I don't get AIDS, what about ARC (AIDS-related complex)? Will this be a long, drawn-out process, or will it come quickly? What can I do? Exercise more? Take vitamins? I needed to grab onto something, *anything* Gottlieb had to offer.

Michael answered my questions as best he could, though I quickly discovered how little was known. "Frankly, Elizabeth, we don't have a great deal of information. There's been so little research. You may live five years or ten years. It's not impossible."

I didn't really realize how desperate my situation was at the time. Now I see how little doctors had to offer AIDS patients in 1986. Aerosol pentamidine didn't exist back then but is now widely used as a prophylactic treatment for pneumocystis pneumonia, an infection that killed many people with AIDS in the early stages of the epidemic.

Drugs were just beginning to be tested despite the fact that the epidemic was five years old. It had taken that long to make the government care. Gottlieb was one of the first doctors in the country to use AZT (Azidothymidine) in clinical trials. He had been testing it for six months and was encouraged by the results and felt medicine was just on the threshold of finding treatments for AIDS.

Gottlieb discouraged me from reading the newspaper. "Don't become an AIDS junkie," he said. "If you have questions, talk to me. Sometimes the deluge of information on television and in the media is very damaging. If you are sitting in a room and something comes up on the news about AIDS, don't run and turn it up because a lot of what you hear will be misleading or wrong."

Just as I had waited for Ari's red blood cell count, now I became a player of T-cell roulette. When you are diagnosed with the HIV virus, your T-cell count is one of the first things doctors check because they believe it's a direct way of measuring the progress of the virus. Gottlieb explained that a healthy person might have a T-cell count of 1200, but it can range from 500 to 1500. When I was diagnosed, I had 210. When Ari was finally diagnosed she had only *4*. The lower the numbers go, the more vulnerable a person is to opportunistic infections like pneumocystis pneumonia or Kaposi's sarcoma or any of a dozen other diseases.

When I walked out of Dr. Gottlieb's office I began replaying the visit in my mind, trying to absorb it all. I had my first inkling that I was not going to see things eye-to-eye with the medical profession.

"Wait a minute!" I thought. "Why didn't he tell me I had a seventy-percent chance of doing just fine over the next three years? I could play with those odds." I decided that first day that I was not going to let myself be held hostage by this virus. If I felt fine, then I was fine. Gottlieb had told me that I could keep doing whatever I enjoyed. After five years of caring for AIDS patients and being sneezed on and coughed on, he knew that AIDS was not spread by casual contact. He said there was no reason I couldn't cook dinner for friends and eat with them in their homes. He saw no reason for Ari and Jake to change the way they interacted with other children.

But my friends weren't doctors, and words of reassurance were often no match for their fears. The first people my friends turned to with their questions about AIDS were their own pediatricians. In May of 1986, answers were in short supply and there were no guarantees.

CHAPTER

❧ 3 ❧

What most of our friends remembered were the stories that made headlines, like Ryan White and the Rays.

Ryan was the teenager from Kokomo, Indiana, who was barred from attending junior high school after he was diagnosed with AIDS in 1984. The following year, Ryan's family sued in federal court to get him admitted to school. While appeals were under way, Ryan was linked to his classroom through a special computer-telephone hookup. His quiet courage and determined valor had made an indelible impression on the country and inspired others who were fighting the same fight. But it didn't resolve the issue.

Clifford and Louise Ray received the diagnosis just a few months after we did that their three hemophiliac sons were infected with the AIDS virus from transfusions with a blood clotting factor they needed to stay alive. They turned for help in their rural community of Arcadia, Florida, to their church and their school. The message was the same from both—stay home.

The Rays took their case to court and won the right to send their boys to school a year later. Then the death threats started. During the first week of school, their house was burned to the ground. Having won the legal battle but losing the war against hysterical fear, the family moved.

What could have stopped the fear and hysteria was strong

leadership from the Reagan administration. But in those early years of the epidemic, that leadership was absent. Those of us who fought AIDS had to fight on two fronts, medical and social. AIDS may one day cost me my life, but community reaction right away cost me the right to live the rest of my life the way I choose. That was my first fight.

Most of our friends mirrored the vulnerability of the nation. They wanted to stand beside us, but they also wanted assurances that there was absolutely no risk to their children if they continued to play with Ariel and Jake.

My pediatrician said there were no reported cases of AIDS being passed by casual contact within families where one person was infected. But he added that only about one hundred families had been studied so far. Even saliva had not been conclusively ruled out as a means of transmission by the summer of 1986. It would still be nine months until the Surgeon General went on television and said flat out that you can't get AIDS from saliva or kissing. There were still many people, when we were first diagnosed, who thought you could get AIDS from sneezing or mosquito bites. The friends we had turned to found they could not stand by us.

This was the climate of fear of mid-1986. At the beginning of the year, a *New York Times*/CBS poll found that forty-seven percent of Americans believed you could catch AIDS by sharing a drinking glass. Twenty-eight percent thought toilet seats could pass the virus and twelve percent of all Americans thought that they could get AIDS by touching someone who had it. Similarly, a *Washington Post* poll completed about the same time found that thirty-four percent of those Americans polled felt it was unsafe to "associate" with a person with AIDS, even when no physical contact was involved, and another twenty-two percent were uncertain.

People with AIDS lost jobs, were thrown out of schools and apartments, were discharged from the military. Hospitals refused to treat people and even, on some occasions, refused to send ambulances for someone suffering with AIDS. There had been reports to counter the fear, but hysteria spreads a lot faster than reason and is hard to control. People wanted reassurances when what they were reading in articles were disclaimers like "appears to pose no risk."

It was a time that would almost be unimaginable if we hadn't lived it. It is what all families battling AIDS had to face then. You are told you and your children may die. You are told that there are no answers now. And then as you are struggling not to completely fall apart, you realize that very few people are going to reach out to help or comfort you.

In fact, most are afraid of you. The doctors say there is no reason for fear—but this means nothing because your neighbors and friends are not your doctors. Since you don't know how much time you have left, the quality of that time becomes even more intensified. You become determined not to lose out on any more of your life than you have to.

Lucy called the house one day and Paul answered the phone. "Where is she?" Lucy asked.

"Elizabeth's out back. Ari and Jake are playing with each other," Paul said; then he paused and with deep resentment in his voice he said, "I guess they'll just have to get used to that." And they did. From that time on, they developed a bond of deep love and caring because, initially, none of Ari's and Jake's friends were allowed to play with them.

We felt so alone. We felt no one would reach out to us and take our hand and make it better. We wished for an angel, an angel who would help us get through it all. But at that time it seemed we had no angels watching over us.

My attitude was, "You can't be my friend unless you accept my family." A lot of our friends wanted to stay friends with us and after talking with their pediatricians and internists, they formulated their own rules. It was a nightmare for us.

At first, no one would allow their children to come and play at our house. Some friends refused to let my kids come to their homes at all. Some said Ari could come to play at their homes as long as she played outdoors and with supervision. Some said their children could continue to play with mine, but only at the park. Some weren't comfortable with any contact and dropped out of our lives.

Whenever the children played, we watched them like hawks. It started at the park. Most friends started outside. Ari and a friend would be playing and whenever the kids moved, the mom, my friend, would adjust her position to see "everything" that was going on. If they happened to hug each other, that would create panic. My heart would race, because I was afraid park play would now be off limits as well.

We'd thrash it out. I'd say, "Are you afraid?"

She'd say, "Yes."

I'd say, "You want to quit?"

She'd say, "No," and we'd go on.

In time park play was expanded and with a certain amount of pressure from me we would try a playdate at the other child's house. If the kids were in the bedroom, we would be in the bedroom. If they were in the kitchen, we would be hovering over them. When they went to the bathroom, we followed them there, too. We were all fighting to maintain our reason and protect our families.

I called my parents in Puerto Rico. We needed a support system we could rely on. I was afraid that we would never be invited to anyone's house again. Paul and I talked at great length about asking my parents to move to Los Angeles. We knew it would be a huge sacrifice for them to uproot their entire life, leave their home and friends, and move to a new city where they knew no one. But we decided we needed them desperately.

When I asked them, they said they would come. I have the most wonderful and loving parents anyone could have. It was a tiny glimmer of sunlight in a very threatening sky.

One of my friends wanted to invite Ari to her daughter's fifth birthday party, three weeks after our diagnosis. Both she and her husband wanted Ari to come, but felt it would be unfair for them to make that decision for the parents of the other children who would be at the party. This was always at the heart of the dilemma for so many of our friends. "It's okay with us, but how can we choose for our friends? What will they say if they find out later on that we knew Ariel had AIDS but didn't tell them?"

So Ariel was not invited to the party. I was devastated. Each rejection was further sealing my family off from the world. This was the third party she had been rejected from. They were her best friends. It was breaking my heart.

But then, the day before the party, an invitation arrived on our doorstep. My feelings skidded out from under me and I cried and cried because I was so happy. I had quickly become dependent on all my friends. In that first month even the smallest gesture felt like an extraordinary act of kindness.

I went with Ari to the birthday party and stuck to her like a magnet, making sure she didn't poke her fingers in anyone else's food or drink from their juice. It was so bizarre to worry about danger in something so commonplace.

I now had to ask permission to be included in our friends' lives. It was like playing "Mother May I?" "Mother may I come to your house with my children?" When the answer was yes, we would take a victorious step forward. When it was "No, you may not!," we would remain frozen in place.

It was the same old Santa Monica, but my children and I were suddenly viewed as dangerous. In the beginning, I felt as spooky as everyone else. When I went to the house of someone who didn't know, I was on pins and needles. What if they offered me a drink from their cup? Should I take it? Or if they wanted to share something for lunch, or if they didn't wash the fork well enough? Would I be doing something wrong? Our world felt claustrophobically small and our own home became our fortress.

One of the first inklings of hope at that time came from Jim Blechman, Ari's homeopathic doctor. I remember going to see him just after that stupid yogi rejected me. He had been Ari's doctor but now he would become mine as well.

Jim began to do acupuncture on me to relieve the stress. I started to see him once a week and he became a friend, counselor, and doctor. He saw me as a strong person who could become even stronger if I pulled together my inner strengths. He talked to me about being a warrior. I felt like one. When you move through the world as a family with AIDS you have to be as "hyper-alert" and as vigilant as a point man.

Paul was locked into a demanding work schedule once more. He had just completed directing a segment for Steven Spielberg's television series "Amazing Stories" and was now directing a TV pilot. Paul was a part of all these struggles with our friends, but he was one step removed from it because of his work. I was the one who arranged Ari and Jake's play-dates and schedules and coped daily with all the stress of working through the questions and fears of our friends.

It was only in Jim Blechman's office, at that time, that I was really able to lie down and share my suffocating fears for my children's futures and my own. To share my disappointment in my friends, and my sadness for my daughter who might lose all her best friends. We would talk and then he'd put acupuncture needles in me and I would fall asleep. It was my only sanctuary.

Jim had also suggested that I see a woman named Aetla Cirocco who was a healer. I gave her a try because I trusted Jim. Aetla is a woman in her mid-fifties who has a chunky Scandinavian accent. Thirty-four years ago she had been diagnosed with a brain tumor and given six months to live. Aetla believes she can heal with her hands and her energy. She is a powerful positive force.

I've always had an ability to detach and watch what is happening to me with reasonable humor. I looked down on myself and thought, *Oh, my God, here you are lying on a table with this woman who is making circular motions over you with crystals in her hands.* I couldn't believe I was participating in this, but I couldn't deny that it was very relaxing and enjoyable. So I said to myself, *Why censor any experiences if they don't harm anyone else?* Maybe this would be beneficial. None of my traditional doctors had any answers, so I reached out to alternative ways of healing.

Aetla put her hands on me the first day she met me and said, "I work with many AIDS patients and I don't say anything carelessly. You are going to live. This disease is not going to kill you." I told her I certainly hoped she was right and continued to see her for many, many months.

What was important for me at that time was for someone to offer me the option of survival. It helped me to say to myself, "I might not die. I don't feel sick and I don't feel like I am going to die." There are always survivors.

I remember one day, right in the beginning, I came home and found a crack in the flaky skin between my toes. My mother was there and I became hysterical.

"My toes are going to fall off, this means I am going to die!" I got on the phone and called Michael Gottlieb. "I have this crack between my toes, is this something horrible, what does it mean?"

"It means you have athlete's foot, Elizabeth," he said. "Put a spray on it."

Athlete's foot. Okay. I could deal with that. Initially, everything that wasn't right was so ominous. A cough. A cold. A stomachache.

I started to feel paranoid. One day there was weird stuff floating in our pool. Paul and I stood there and looked at the cloudy, white goop. Could our pool have turned into a giant petri dish?

"It wasn't there yesterday. Paul, you don't think we're growing the virus, do you?"

"I don't know. It's weird. You'd better ask someone about it."

We stayed out of the pool for a few days but the white film did not go away. I finally called Dr. Stiehm, who laughed. This was the only easy question I had ever asked him.

"Elizabeth, listen to me. You cannot grow AIDS in your swimming pool!" It turned out to be congealed suntan lotion which we swept away.

One of the telephone calls I dreaded most was to Crossroads, where Ari had been accepted. Both Paul and I desperately wanted Ari to be able to start kindergarten that fall. It was one of the few direct links we had to the future, and it meant so much to Ari. Paul and I had never met Paul Cummins, the school's headmaster, but we knew he was the one to talk to. We decided I would go talk to him alone.

Paul Cummins had no idea why I'd walked into his office, which was crowded with books and colorful with posters. I sat down on the sofa near his desk and he sat across from me. He seemed both confident and relaxed. I was petrified and I took a deep breath before I began.

"We have applied to your school, we have been accepted, and we were planning on having our daughter, Ariel, start kindergarten here in September. But I just found out that she, my son, and myself are all infected with the AIDS virus."

I started to cry. I was sure he would send me away and tell me to find another school. Paul Cummins walked over and put his arms around me. "You are part of our family. We want you here." He held me as I cried.

My anticipation of rejection was so overwhelming that when it was finally released, I dissolved. When I could pull myself together enough to talk, I said to him, "Are you sure you mean what you are saying?"

"Yes," he said. "Of course I'm sure. We don't yet have a school policy on AIDS, but we'll get one in place. I am so sorry for you."

Paul Cummins was the first person we didn't know who reached out to my family without any hesitation or fear. He said he had been appalled by the stories about children with

AIDS around the country being mistreated in schools. He was convinced that AIDS was not spread by casual contact and he felt that a child with HIV or AIDS deserved to have as normal a life as possible for as long as possible.

I left his office feeling both relief and joy. As long as I could see that not every door was going to be closed to us, I could hope. If I'm able to hope, I'm able to live.

I was trying to put some of my feeling from that time down in my journal.

So here we are, the all-American, happy beautiful family blown apart. It is as if a hurricane came through our house and nothing was spared except Paul. All the lights are out and nothing is in the right place. Who will straighten it out? I know I have to but I don't know where to begin. If I give up today and they find a cure for AIDS tomorrow, that would be tragic. I have to fight this war against time with every ounce of strength I have. Maybe this won't all end tragically. Maybe they will find a cure or at least a stabilizing drug.

It's strange that everything around me still looks the same.

Compared with AIDS, I thought, nothing else could ever scare me again. Other disasters like earthquakes would at least wreak havoc on everybody, not just me.

But when I jumped out of bed one night during a small quake that first summer, none of those thoughts went through my head. I was going to get the children and stand under a doorway just like before. But the quake was over before I got to their rooms. What amazed me was that I even responded with fear at all. If I could react that way, it meant to me that I hadn't given up hope.

As time went by, good things started to happen. Early one Friday evening, the doorbell rang. Ariel and Paul were upstairs painting pictures. It was Amy, one of Ari's playmates inviting Ari to dinner. My heart turned cartwheels. No one had just stopped by our house since this all began!

Ariel hadn't played inside at Amy's house yet, so this felt like a breakthrough. I asked Amy if her mother, Hilary, was with her. She told me her mother was out doing errands and her grandmother was baby-sitting.

My heart sank. Her grandmother didn't know Ari had AIDS. She didn't know that our children weren't allowed to play indoors together.

I scrambled to explain. "I think it's a wonderful idea, but let's double-check with your mom to make sure she doesn't have something else planned for tonight." The two little girls were standing on the doorstep squealing, "Please, please, please, pretty please . . ."

"Come on," I said. "We'll get on our bicycles and ride over to your house and see if it's okay." I hated to put Hilary on the spot, but the situation had forced my hand. When she heard about the invitation she hesitated momentarily and then with a warm smile said that it would be okay.

I was so happy I started to cry. It was a Friday night and I pedaled home to get the challah Ari and I had made for Shabbat.

My friends and I were all so acutely anxious. I am sure that some friends felt I was pushing too hard, but I couldn't help it. I was scared every day. I never knew when a friend might change her mind and say, "Sorry, I made a mistake, I don't want Ari here."

One day I had breakfast with Rena to try and resolve the issue of whether our daughters could play inside together. We chatted on aimlessly for a while and then I brought up the subject.

She said the girls could play together inside if I agreed to two conditions. Her rules were that they could not drink from the same glass and they couldn't use the same towels in the bathroom, but otherwise, everything could be the same. I was delighted. After so many big compromises, small ones like these were easy.

About six months after telling our closest friends I decided to reach out to someone new. Suzanne Buhai was a friend I hadn't told because she and her family lived farther away and we saw each other less frequently. Her daughter, Sophie, was the same age as Ari. I have always felt close to Suzanne. She had lost a child at birth several years before and has the spirit of a survivor. She and I were alike in many ways and I was curious about her reaction to our diagnosis.

My friends had often asked me, "What would you do, Elizabeth, if you were in our shoes?" I never had an answer for that but I sensed my reaction might be like Suzanne's.

She was wonderful. She didn't feel threatened at all. She knew a lot about AIDS and said our children could play together as they always had. She was the first person with small children who said there is no reason for any of us to behave any differently. What she gave me was hope. If there was one Suzanne, there could be many others.

One weekend Paul and I went on a white water rafting trip with Carol and Ron Herman, our new friends we had met in Hawaii. They knew nothing about our diagnosis. It was particularly strange to be with them and all these other strangers who could see only the privilege in our lives and none of the pain. For most outsiders, we were a family to be envied.

I tried on the rafting trip to leave my concerns behind me but I just couldn't. I found myself floating down the river thinking depressing thoughts. I would worry about Ari and then I would worry about Jake. Then I would worry about what would happen if I cut myself on a rock and started to bleed and had to tell all these people not to touch my blood. I would force myself to acknowledge I was only driving myself nuts and say, "Elizabeth, you must live now. Otherwise you are wasting your life."

Shortly after we were diagnosed I had a dream unlike any I had ever had in my life.

I was on a tall cliff overlooking a bay. The cliffs were like the ones in Santa Monica over the ocean, but the town was ancient and reminded me of Jerusalem. It had winding cobblestone streets that were no wider than a wheelbarrow. Like a kiln, the sun had baked the buildings into hard, white clay. It felt like a peaceful day and I squinted at the sun. Suddenly I saw a gargantuan dragon emerge through the clouds.

The dragon was cold, large, and menacing. It was ice-blue and white, the same colors as the clouds and sky through which it slowly moved. The dragon blocked the sun and began its descent toward the water. I suddenly realized the dragon was looking for me. Our eyes locked and I was scared. The dragon did not roar or breathe fire, nor was it poised to attack. It was just an extraordinarily powerful presence.

The dragon hit the water, creating a great wave, and I knew it was real.

As it disappeared beneath the water, a large, ice-blue man with a cold stare rose up over the waves. He was as gigantic as the dragon. He was neither friendly nor angry, but he dominated the sky. I turned and fled into the town behind me, trying to hide from the dragon. I ran as fast as I could, careening through the confining streets which I knew the dragon was too big to enter.

The dream ended. The dragon could not get into my world unless it chose to crumble everything.

At first the dream terrified me. I tried to hide from the dragon because I was afraid it was going to kill me and I didn't want to die. But the dream made me begin to face my fear.

Jim Blechman, my homeopathic doctor, said the dragon could be my immune system. Jonathan Omer-Man, my spiritual teacher, said that the dragon might be the angel of death. My psychiatrist, Dr. Brickman, said that maybe the dragon represented the omnipotent medical establishment. I talked about it with each of them because the dream was unlike any I had ever had. It was another thing I felt I needed to understand.

I finally found my own explanation. For me, the dragon symbolized the virus. As I thought about the dream, I knew I wanted to have it again. I wanted to face the dragon and say, "I will stand before you with my fear. Even if I am afraid, I will not run away. My feet are planted firmly on the ground. I don't have to kill you and you don't have to kill me. I can face you because I am as strong as you are. You and I are in a battle and if you don't take me, I want it to be because of my strength, not because I am hiding."

The dream forced me to find the strength I already had within me and it forced me to confront my life. I think the dragon was saying, "I am not going to go away. If you want to meet me, you will have to delve into the deepest part of your soul and find a strength equivalent to mine." I accepted the challenge and knew that I would never again run and hide.

While I was battling my virus, Paul was coming to grips with his own private war—a battlefield on which he might lose all those he loved, but on which he would survive. It was a difficult struggle for him then and it still is now. He started meditating and doing his yoga. He looked inside to find answers to very hard questions. He worked as much as he could, as that gave him the strength to keep going. Sometimes it is hard for me to believe that my life is real but trying to imagine being Paul is even more difficult.

By mid-July, Ariel was doing well. Dr. Stiehm was pleased with her blood counts and liver functions. People would often say to me what a spectacularly beautiful child she was. We still appeared, to so many, the picture-perfect family. Sometimes it would make me weep.

Each morning, I would sit with Ari and pick out the special hair ribbons or bows she would want to wear. We would stand in front of the bathroom mirror and I would brush her hair one hundred times to make it shine. It was as easy for her to be feminine as it was for me to be a tomboy. But I loved sharing it with her. As her hair glistened, silent tears would fill my eyes and my heart would break knowing that I might lose her. It became impossible for me to ever feel really happy without feeling achingly sad.

In August, we had a small celebration at home for Ari's fifth birthday. Our nephew, David, was there and the Seymours came over with Josh and Amanda who were like a big brother and sister to Ari and Jake. Ari always beamed when she was around Josh. Gene and Judie Seymour were unflinchingly loyal toward us. They hadn't told Josh and Amanda yet about AIDS, because they thought it would be too overwhelming. So when Josh and Amanda came over and played, it was truly just like old times.

Graciela came over for Ari's birthday and Maria was there too. We had one of Ari's beautifully designed cakes. She always wanted flowers and rainbows and this year, a unicorn. After dinner we all sprawled around on the floor and played games.

The next day we were getting ready to leave for vacation. It was a day of contrasts as were so many. The good part was taking Ari to get her ears pierced. It was a birthday treat and a way of celebrating being a big kindergarten girl. Ariel felt so grown-up. I felt glad because each rite of passage that we got to share felt like a victory. I tried to memorize each image.

That same day, however, we had to go in to UCLA for her infusion of gamma globulin. At the clinic she sat in a big chair, similar to a dentist's chair. She would cry so very hard as they tried to find her vein, which sometimes took three attempts. Every needle prick was a horror and I worshiped the nurses like Lesa Grovas, who succeeded. I hated the nurses who missed on the first try. Ari got through it as she always did, and we went home to pack.

We left the next morning for Maine. My own cherished memories of summers at Camp Fernwood make it so meaningful for me to go to Maine with my own children. I went every summer for seven years as a kid. It was probably the most perfect time of my life. You played sports all day with all your friends. There was a special spirit at camp. You were a part of a large family; you learned to rely on yourself but you also learned to rely on other women and enjoy having adventures together. Ever since Fernwood, I've always had strong women friends.

This time, returning to Maine was especially poignant because we had been diagnosed three months before. We stayed with Connie and Billy, Paul's sister and brother-in-law. They are gentle and down-to-earth and anything you do with them is fun. Having raised four children of their own, they are used to the commotion of kids. It was also a great relief not to be worrying about Ari's friends and mine as well.

Connie loved nature as much as Ari did. We would go on walks and never get very far because everything was so interesting right where we were. We looked at weeds and wildflowers, the way the moss grew on a tree, and all the little creatures that jitterbugged out from under a big stone when you turned it over. Jake would have little patience, but he'd follow Ari and she'd show him. Although we would never be a normal family again, there were moments when life seemed full of goodness and hope and was blessedly ordinary. Maine was confirmation that I could still find beauty and love in the world as I had before.

Paul was about to begin directing *The Running Man,* a movie with Arnold Schwarzenegger, for which he had been hired two weeks into production. The directing career he had dreamed of was finally taking shape. Because of the film, Paul came home from Maine a few days before we did. Neither of us realized how difficult that would be. When he walked into the empty house he immediately thought that this is how it would be if we were all dead. When we came home he was still frightened and worried. It had sabotaged his strength. I tried to convince him that we were the ones who were going to make it.

"Honey, there are survivors of everything. Some people survived the concentration camps. People survived Stalin, some escaped from Pol Pot. There are always a few who make it. If we can stay strong until the war ends, we may be one of those survivors. Sooner or later, someone is going to survive AIDS and there's no reason why it can't be us, if we think positively, stay strong, and keep fighting."

I needed Paul to stay strong because his strength, right from the beginning, has also been crucial to my own emotional survival. Being strong completely alone is, I think, much, much harder. But if you know that someone else is standing right next to you and is reaching deep inside himself as well, it gives you determination and courage.

I have never been a quitter. Much of my strength comes from an inability to ever give up or let go of the possibility of a miracle. I don't see myself as a victim, and in order not to feel victimized by my life, I have to stay strong.

My parents, Max and Edith, told me I could do anything I wanted to in life and I believed them. They raised me to have a strong sense of values and purpose. I was born on November 11, 1947, in New York City and grew up in Hewlett Harbor, a small town on Long Island. My brother, Peter, was born when I was three.

My first rush of success came when I was about five. I was proud of being a fast runner, and one afternoon, Dad challenged me to a race across the front lawn. I beat him and was thrilled. I began to think I could do anything after that. It wasn't until I was a teenager that I realized he'd let me win.

In grade school, I always won the 50- and 100-yard dashes. I loved the races that were short and fast. Aggressive and highly competitive, I liked to go all out and push myself to my limits. Some things never change.

Back then, I was a very good "Betsy," because I've always had the spirit of a cheerleader. My role in the family was to be the happy one. We were close and talked a great deal, but feelings were not always easily expressed and I learned that good girls did not get angry.

Compared to my friends' parents, mine were great adventurers. They taught Peter and me to live for today. Life was not a spectator sport to be watched from the sidelines. We went traveling in Cuba, skiing in New England, sailing on

South Shore Bays of Long Island, and snorkeling in the Caribbean. We drove down the Eastern seaboard to the state parks and camped out. In our family, time together was more important than anything money could buy.

My father was vice president for the General Cigar Company and was gone a lot during the week. My mother stayed home until my brother and I were in school full-time, and then she became director of urban renewal for the Town of Hempstead. She built low-income housing for the poor, and everyone in the community looked up to her. I could not have had a better role model. My parents believed in teaching children values by living good lives, and we were raised to believe that it was our responsibility to take care of people who had less than we did.

My parents made me feel confident and proud of myself for who I was. They believed in me completely. Achievement in my family was never measured by grades and I felt as though I was a great success, even though I got mostly Cs at Woodmere Academy, the private school I attended.

What I remember from school are the sports, not the classes. I was a superb athlete. I played field hockey and volleyball in the fall, basketball in the winter, and tennis in the spring. I was a tomboy and a jock when it was still unusual for women to be in shape. Cathy and Leslie were my best friends, but most of my other friends were guys. Joel, Michael and Harold are still wonderful friends today.

When I was little, my dad and I used to watch the New York Giants football games together on television. Y.A. Tittle was the quarterback and he was magic. There would be just seconds left with the Giants behind and it would look like it was over and then Tittle would go back, back, back, throw the long ball, and they would win the game. It would be incredible and we'd be screaming, "He did it, he did it!" Moments like that inspired me as a child, and made me believe that anything is possible if you try hard enough.

As soon as we unpacked from Maine we began getting ready for school. Ariel was excited about finally being old enough to go off to kindergarten. We went shopping for school clothes and she picked out a lavender backpack which looked adorable slung over her shoulders. Shopping with her was a snap if you headed for the ruffles, laces, and bows. We came home that day and put on a fashion show for Paul. In the whirlwind of back-to-school activities I remembered from my teaching days how much I'd loved getting my classrooms ready for the first day of school.

Crossroads had a meeting for all the incoming parents. The seven-year elementary curriculum was explained and the others tried to imagine what their children would be like when they were twelve. I tried to keep focused on the moment. Seven years seemed like a lifetime to me. I barely let myself look seven days ahead. People were friendly to us, but of course no one knew. Even though our secret was safe, Paul and I felt fragile and vulnerable, pretending we were just like everyone else.

Kindergarten began on September 10. I hadn't slept much the night before and got up early to make Ari a special breakfast. She wore her favorite pink dress with bunnies and had purple bows in her hair. Every parent has mixed emotions of pride and sadness when their first child is old enough to start school, and I was no exception. I was proud of Ari, and happy that she was getting to live just like everyone else. We had made it to another milestone.

I walked her up to her classroom, she gave me a kiss good-bye, and then went in and found her seat. I had tears in my eyes, but so did all the other mothers. But unlike the other women, I was both grateful and scared. Grateful to be in kindergarten but frightened that we'd never make it to first grade.

At 10:15 P.M. that night the phone rang. It was Paul Cummins, the school's headmaster. His voice was pained. He said there were some problems at school and he wanted to meet with us the next morning.

What could be wrong? Ari had only been in school one day. Paul and I were so scared we lay in bed in silence. Inside we were shaking. Finally, he rolled over and held me and we both fell asleep.

The meeting was at our house at ten the next morning. Paul Cummins brought Mimi Baer and Charles Boxembaum, the president of Crossroads' board of directors. Paul and I tried to be composed but the tension was as bad as it had been since the day we were diagnosed. How many more trap doors were going to spring open in our lives?

Paul Cummins began by saying, "We have backed ourselves into a corner and we don't know how to get out of it."

I was confused. "What are you talking about?"

"We really want to pass an AIDS policy. But we're afraid that if we present a policy to the board of directors out of the blue they're going to ask why we're concerned with this now. They'll want to know if there's a child with AIDS in the school.

"We can't lie to the board. But if we tell them the truth, then we run the risk that the level of fear may rise so fast that the policy will be defeated. Your privacy would also be put in jeopardy because they would be curious for more details."

Through the best of intentions, Crossroads had found itself in an untenable position and my family was to suffer. Paul and I looked at each other and shook our heads. No angels here. He spoke first.

"So what are you saying? What should we do?"

"I don't know that we have any choice," said Paul Cummins. "On a personal level, you know I want to do anything I can to help you and Ari, Jake, and Elizabeth. But as the headmaster of the school, the only viable option I see is that you take Ari out of kindergarten until we have our policy passed and then re-enroll."

I fought back the tears and the anger. "But what do we tell her! She's already started. Today is only her second day!" Crossroads symbolized everything I had been holding onto.

"We can probably get the policy passed in a few weeks, a few months at the most. Maybe you could keep her in school for the rest of the week, and then have her start public school on Monday."

That's what we did. By the end of the meeting, Paul and I had created another lie. We told Ari and our friends that we were transferring her to public school because Dr. Stiehm felt the all-day kindergarten program at Crossroads was too demanding and might jeopardize her steady recovery. Later in the year, if she had regained enough strength, we would send her back to Crossroads.

I felt sick, all the old anxiety ricocheting around inside me. But Ari handled the news without fuss and everyone else accepted the story. Ari had friends in the Roosevelt kindergarten class she would be attending and that helped a lot. Her friend Amy would be there and that made the transition much easier.

The public school guidelines in Los Angeles at that time required that the school be told if there was a child with AIDS in attendance, but they did not have to know who the student was or which grade he or she was in. Dr. Stiehm's former nurse, Kit Dreyfuss, was now the nurse for the Santa Monica public schools. She moved into full gear and set everything up for Ari over the weekend so she could start school there on Monday. It seemed impossible but she did it. Without Kit I don't think we would have made it.

So Ari started school all over again, upbeat and cheerful. Her own inner strength and resiliency were remarkable to me.

I, however, was very tired from the strain of just getting through each day. It seemed there were never any uneventful days in our lives.

I had asked Dr. Gottlieb's office to send my medical records to Jim Blechman, but they came to our house by mistake. I read them and was shocked. My condition sounded so much worse than Gottlieb had ever acknowledged. I thought that maybe I was dying. It was horrible to read what had been written. I called Gottlieb immediately and he apologized for the mix-up. He told me to try and forget what I'd read. There was no way I could push it out of my mind.

In the months since we were diagnosed, Michael Gottlieb was becoming not just a physician to me, but also a steadfast friend. He understood that sometimes what I really needed when I came to see him was a safe place to feel terrible.

Every six weeks I would come in with my brave expression firmly in place, and Michael and I would chat for a few minutes. He would ask me about my health, go over my numbers, and then ask me how things were at home. The tears would build up so fast inside of me my head would strain from the pressure.

"It's awful. Ari can't go to someone's house. I don't know if Crossroads will be able to take us back. They don't want Jake in school for four more years. What am I going to do?" Michael never told me to stop crying, he never told me it would be okay, and he never told me to be brave. He just slid me a box of Kleenex.

When I left his office I felt defused. The tension was spent and I was able to continue doing whatever needed to be done. Ari had to switch classrooms one more time at public school, and she was understandably unhappy about that. She was hysterical on her *third* "first" day, and I stayed in the classroom for an hour with her.

When I finally was able to leave her at school, I just drove around in a mindless, monotonous circle. I wanted to quit, to run away. I wanted to have it all be over. It felt like too much for anyone to bear. But I couldn't allow myself to fall apart.

Now that Ari was finally settled in school I had to start figuring out a program for Jake. There wasn't any time to relax. Dr. Stiehm didn't think children under five should go to preschool unless the school knew the child had AIDS. This was the CDC guideline.

Paul and I disagreed with him. We thought that logic might apply to a day-care situation where there were many children. But I was looking into a "Mommy and Me" program where Jake and I could go together. We didn't feel if *I* was there I needed to tell anyone, and that gave us another twelve months to try to find a nursery school that would accept him.

What was I going to do if all of Jake's friends were in nursery school and he wasn't? What if every school I told said he couldn't come? What would I tell people? He was healthy and normal, so why wouldn't he be in school? Would Jake have to grow up in isolation? Would I have to teach him at home? I thought about starting a preschool for children with AIDS. But if everyone was hiding like me, how would I ever find people?

It's the incredible isolation that AIDS brings with it that wears you down. You're fighting for your life behind walls of fear and you're fighting to achieve the normalcy most people take for granted. It's a fight that should never have to be fought.

I asked Michael Gottlieb for advice about Jake's preschool situation. He canvassed some other doctors around the country who were working in pediatric AIDS, and those doctors thought it was fine for Jake to go to school without the school's knowing, especially if I was there.

Gradually, I was learning that you can't always rely on doctors to tell you what to do. I had to make my own decisions. I had sought as much ethical, medical, and scientific information as I could and in the end I had to take responsibility for my own decisions and my own life.

Paul and I told Dr. Stiehm that we were not going to follow his advice, that Jake and I would go to "Mommy and Me" without their knowing his condition. I respected his opinion, but this time I didn't follow it.

My parents were supportive and concerned, and having them around the house and in the neighborhood was wonderful. But there was really nothing they could do to help. It was the same with our friends. Lynn or Lucy or Susan or Hilary or Rena would always listen to me but what could they actually do to change anything? The best thing they could offer was normalcy, and even that eluded us at first.

Jonathan Omer-Man, the rabbi I was working with, would often meet me at the beach near our house. This was completely unorthodox for him, but it seemed to work. We would sit by the sand, watching the sea gulls and sometimes the seals. I would cry a lot and he would put his arms around my shoulders and just let me sob. At times I would be ferociously, raging mad.

I told Jim Blechman how demoralizing the school situation had been that fall. He always has unusual and important insights, and that day he told me that I carry the power of the black dragon. As he explained, it's a force that no one can contend with. It's like the dark force the Japanese refer to when they talk about the Ninja warriors. In nature it's the fury of a hurricane or the surge of a volcano. It is an awesome power that can be either beautiful or terrible, so the challenge is to harness the power for the maximum good. Blechman told me that for the rest of my life, I am destined to be a warrior. But I have to learn how to take off the heavy armor without leaving the sword behind.

I think a lot about the people in the concentration camps. They were people probably much like me who, through circumstances totally outside their own control, were put on a train and taken away from everything they had ever known. They knew, as I know, that it was likely that they all were going to die because so many died before them.

I've been a good person, and don't feel I "deserve" what has happened. *Why me?* I thought. There is no answer to that. I've learned that you often have no say in what happens to you, but you can choose how you bear the consequences. Perhaps, as someone wrote, it isn't what we expect out of life that's so important, but what life expects out of us.

Just after Ari finally got settled in kindergarten, Paul woke up at two in the morning. His heart was beating so fast he was convinced he was dying. I was overwhelmed. What if he really was sick? What if he died? I was too scared to contemplate that thought so I told him I would be so angry if we all beat AIDS and lived and he died!

That next morning we talked to our internist, Paul Geller. He said Paul would be fine. It was the stress and anxiety that were making him sick. Geller told us the rapid heartbeat wasn't dangerous per se, but that too much stress is bad for anyone. We knew that, but what could we do? Our life was one big stress. But Paul was smart, and he knew he needed to find his yoga and his meditation again, and so he did.

By midpoint that autumn, we realized that it was unlikely Crossroads would get its AIDS policy in place before the end of November. I kept wishing for things that never seemed to happen. I wished someone would invite Ari over to their house for a sleepover. I wished one of Jake's friends would invite him for a playdate. It would be lovely if Paul and I were invited to a dinner party.

At that point in our lives, coping with fear was far worse than coping with AIDS. The societal pressures were enormous and enormously claustrophobic. I wanted immediate acceptance from our friends and some of them needed time. It made me harsh, demanding, and tyrannical at times, but I couldn't help myself. I was too scared to be polite and I am sure my harshness alienated people.

Our friends were struggling too, although they were understandably reluctant to share their anguish with us. Often they would pretend that everything was okay, but I became as instinctive as a blind woman who can sense the changes around her that she cannot see. We were all just doing the best we could.

The gamma globulin infusions Ari was getting at UCLA seemed to help keep her strong and she looked beautiful. Many people knew that Ari had been so sick in Florida and they would always ask how she was doing and we hated to lie. So we cut many of our old acquaintances out of our lives.

We just never called or initiated anything, and slowly they stopped calling us.

Keeping the secret made us feel as though we were moving through a jungle that was loaded with land mines. You never knew when a step or a snapped twig was going to make the world blow up in your face. The fear of rejection or exposure was with us at all times. Each day wasn't a crisis, but the potential was always there and it bred such tension and sadness. Our house was a fortress. We only felt safe inside.

Most people have nightmares when they sleep, but when you are a family facing AIDS, the nightmare begins fresh every day. Sleep is the only time when I feel just like everyone else. Often I wake up in the morning having forgotten for an instant about AIDS, but that lasts for only the blink of an eye.

In the fall of 1986, the doctors still had no answers. Naively, I thought we were ahead of the game. Since none of us were sick or deteriorating, I felt that maybe if we could just stay strong, doctors would find a cure. Ari was already five years old, while most children with AIDS died by the time they were two.

Of course I was angry. I felt I had every right to be angry. But what good was it going to do? Would it make Ari well? Would it make Jake live longer? I couldn't stop myself from being angry, but I could keep that anger from being trapped inside my body, where I knew it would eat me alive. I never tried to deny the anger—I just made sure there was a way for it to flow right through me.

I would think of the image of a room with two doors. If the anger came in one door that slammed shut and locked automatically, then there was no way out. The anger was trapped. I tried to be sure there was always another door so the anger could get out.

I finally learned that, if I was not going to stay angry, I had to learn to forgive. I had to forgive the blood donor. I had to forgive the doctors. I had to forgive the hospitals, the schools, and I had to forgive fate. I had to forgive God, if there is one, and I had to forgive my friends, who had to forgive me.

Right away Paul saw that we would have to forgive everyone, that we would let the anger pass right through us. He helped me to learn this. It was hard, bitterly hard. Anger is a poison that will seep into your system and want to stay.

But I still get angry.

When I get really angry, I get angry at God. I'm not even sure if I believe in a God. I don't think I do. But sometimes this God, whether he is there or not, seems to be the only person I can get angry at. Sometimes when I am alone in my car I scream, "If you are there, God, I hate you! I hate you for making this my life. I hate you for letting Ari get sick. I hate you for not making it all go away. And I hate you because I don't really think you are there." My throat hurts when I'm done from shouting and crying. But I usually feel calmer after, and though I walk into my house with red eyes, at least I have had some release.

There are other feelings to contend with besides just anger. So many conflicting emotions tear at me. I would feel a painful jealousy whenever I saw people who seemed to have normal lives and healthy children. "Oh, my God," I would think. "I wish I were that person. I wish I were anyone but myself right now."

I would feel an excruciating envy toward strangers and my friends who could have what I never could. And then I would feel very, very sorry for myself.

I had to learn to let go of *all* of these emotions that deadened and depleted me. I am never going to be able to have what other people have. One of the struggles for me that whole first year was with envy. I still struggle with it, but much, much less. Christmas and other holidays can be bad times. If someone's child is graduating from high school or college, or in a school play, I am reminded that this is something I may never get to experience. But at some point you begin to accept that this is your life and that, no matter how hard you wish, there is nothing that will change your reality.

When Ari was about a year old, I had joined a temple. I hadn't belonged to a temple since I was a little girl but I had known since my trip to Israel that when I started a family I would also start a new Jewish life for myself and my children. It had nothing to do with believing or not believing in God, but with wanting to feel a part of the special Jewish heritage, a family larger than my own. Although I never went to services much, when Ari was older, we started having Shabbat on Friday evenings.

We would often spend Friday afternoon baking challah together. We would knead the dough and then read books or draw pictures while waiting for it to rise. The dough would then be divided into thirds and we would braid it. Ari loved the braiding and I loved watching her do it. Then we would put the bread in the oven and wait for the aromas to fill the whole house.

At sunset we would light the Shabbat candles and move our hands over the flickering flames three times. Then we covered our eyes and said a prayer because you're not supposed to look at the candles directly until they have been blessed. I can remember Ari standing on the dining room chair, her small hands pressed hard over her eyes. We felt linked in a tradition that Jewish women have shared for centuries and this brought me solace.

Jake sat in his high chair, moving Cheerios around with his fingers, making car noises, a somewhat passive observer, but I'm sure somewhere deep inside he still has memories of his sister and Shabbat.

On the lucky evenings, Paul would be home to join us, but that was rare in those days, as he was still filming *The Running Man* in Pomona, California, and for six weeks he would come home only on Saturdays. That year I did a lot of single parenting. That is just the way it is when you're making a movie, and luckily, we already knew that. Once a week, Ari and I would get in the car and drive an hour and a half to see him. We would stay about an hour and then turn around and drive back. Jake usually stayed home, but sometimes he would come too.

For Paul, *The Running Man* was an escape back into a world completely different from our own. It was very frustrating for him to have no one know what he was going through, and eventually Paul felt he had to tell the truth to at least one person on the set.

Tim Zinnemann was the producer of *The Running Man* and he became Paul's friend and confidant. He, his wife, Meg Tilly, and their children became a very important bridge between Paul's work and home life.

The other link was our nephew, David Kantar, who had decided to stay with us for the year. He became Paul's assistant on *The Running Man* and, initially, the only person on the set who knew our secret. That year, David and Paul found a very special relationship, which I imagine helped both of them to grow.

Crossroads passed their AIDS policy by the end of Ari's first semester in kindergarten. We were told that Ari could begin in January, but we opted to wait until first grade. Ariel was so happy in Mrs. Watanabe's classroom that we decided to let her finish out the year at Roosevelt.

After such a disastrous start in September, she was having the happiest year imaginable. She had made new friends whose families didn't know about the diagnosis. It was easier not having any restrictions when the children played together. Of course, then I always had to be present on her playdates. This was a big responsibility, but I wasn't going to complain about that. The hard part was to be constantly pretending that we were just another regular family. It was always exhausting.

The other parents were terrific and we formed a very cohesive group. I tried to enjoy every second of normalcy I had. I volunteered at the school two hours a week. I loved being in a classroom again, and Ari's being there made it perfect. Watching her make new friends, and work and succeed at her kindergarten challenges, was pure joy.

Even though we weren't at Crossroads, the school was still very involved and Mimi Baer was helping us find a nursery school for Jake. One of the schools that she recommended to me was First Presbyterian Nursery School in Santa Monica. I made an appointment to have a tour with the director, Mary Hartzell, but told her nothing about our reality.

Mary impressed me immediately as a smart and spontaneously affectionate woman. She has a gentle manner that invites you in. Mary is in her forties and the mother of three. Her wavy hair gently frames her face. Her open spirit is almost Midwestern in its friendliness, but she has an Ivy League mind that is impatient with pretense.

Mary's first love, like mine, is teaching. We found it easy to strike a rapport because we both thrive in the world of stubby scissors and block corners. Mary gave me a tour of the school and was optimistic about there being room for Jake come January, which was when I wanted him to start since he'd be three.

But I knew Mary Hartzell might reject us as soon as she knew the truth. The first preschool I looked at for Jake turned me down. The director never said it was because of AIDS and I actually don't think that was the reason. She said the waiting list was too long. If someone isn't willing to bend the rules, then you just may not get in.

I begged and pleaded with her, but she was not willing to let Jake leapfrog over others on the waiting list. She also felt it would be unfair to other parents in the school to have Jake there without their knowing he was infected, so maybe it was the AIDS issue in the end.

Anyway, that spring, when I returned to meet with Mary Hartzell a second time, I was filled with drag-your-feet dread. But Mary handled the news with equanimity and said she would still be delighted to have Jake enroll as a student at First Presbyterian.

Mary is an example of the fact that leadership and courage are the antidote to the fear and discrimination that hysteria breeds. Mary had already crafted an AIDS policy with her school's board of directors, but it was still not in place. Based on our Crossroads experiences, Paul and I weren't going to count on anything until that policy was passed.

The policy said that a child with the HIV virus could continue in, or be admitted to, the school. The policy also had a section on confidentiality. Mary said that only she and Jake's teachers would know that he was the child with HIV. The other parents would not be told unless our secret was revealed in some other way.

We started the wheels rolling at First Presbyterian and then waited until their next board meeting for things to be finalized. This was months away and therefore months of underlying anxiety. But Mary was certain there would be no problem. And so we felt fortunate that Jake might now have a school.

We had finally, and gruelingly, achieved normalcy again. Even our friends who knew were back as an important part of our life. It seemed as though we had all been on an emotional outward-bound trip together. We had survived, and were stronger and closer because of the journey.

There was a certain false stability during that winter and spring of 1987. I was lulled into believing that we could go on this way forever and that it was possible for us to live with AIDS. I felt strong and Jake and Ari were doing very well. The only medical treatment Ari needed at that time was her gamma globulin infusions every three weeks. I could never totally relax, but I was breathing a little easier. I let myself hope that life could go on at this level of compromise indefinitely. Ari would not get any sicker, and Jake and I would be able to maintain our level of strength as well.

From the time we were diagnosed in May 1986, through the first half of 1987, the entire focus of my energies was on stabilizing my family, stabilizing our social relationships and our place in the community.

I tried to find a way to create the highest quality of life for ourselves, given the bleakness of our medical realities. Normal, ordinary life was to be the light that would shine in the darkness. I wanted us to be able to live as we always had for as long as we possibly could.

My physical relationship with Paul had found its balance as well. When we were first diagnosed, we both thought, *No big deal.* We had been having the normal sexual intimacy of a married couple for five years without knowing I was HIV-positive, and since Paul was not infected, why not just continue?

But in a few weeks that sense of security passed, and Paul and I decided we needed to talk to our doctors about safe sex and unsafe sex. Michael Gottlieb helped both of us set parameters we could feel comfortable with, which we've maintained ever since.

Of course there were times when we both were afraid, afraid that we were making poor choices, but the doctors would reassure us that we were doing fine. We would work hard to believe that in our hearts as well as in our heads.

CHAPTER

❧ 4 ❧

Summer was in full swing. Paul had finished editing *The Running Man* that spring and we had decided we would make our annual summer trip to Connie and Billy's house in Maine. Screen doors slammed and we were swimming, boating, hiking, or picking wild blueberries on Pleasant Mountain. At night we would make a fire and toast marshmallows, then smush them together with chocolate and graham crackers in perfect s'mores. Simple and intense delight.

But Ari started to seem weak and I sensed for the first time that she was beginning to fail. It was harder for her to eat and that became stressful for everyone. Her appetite diminished and she complained of stomach pain. She had to have food to stay strong and we would battle incessantly as I tried and tried to get her to eat.

In past summers she had always been eager to go in the canoe and be by the water, but now that eagerness was gone. She wanted to stay indoors. She would make up little skits and dance with Jake, but she tired easily and I knew she was sliding downhill.

I remember the day because it was Ari's birthday, August 4. She was six years old and having terrible stomach pains. She looked thin. Lynn called to wish her happy birthday and to talk to me. I was standing at the top of the stairs and tears were rolling down my cheeks. "Lynn, she's slipping away from me and I can't do anything about it." As a mother, I knew instinctively that I was losing her. The doctors were saying that her numbers were fine and it didn't look to them like anything was wrong, but as a mother I knew I was losing her.

I called Dick Stiehm in Los Angeles. "We've just got to get AZT now," I said. "We must have AZT. She's starting to fail."

"It's not ready for children," he replied.

"What do you mean it's not ready for children? It's ready for me!" Although I hadn't needed to start taking it yet, I knew it was available as an option.

"AZT hasn't been approved for pediatric use. It's just not ready."

"We've just got to find a way to get it and use it."

"Elizabeth," he said, "we don't even know the dose to give her. We can't just experiment. This is a toxic drug. It could kill her."

"When will it be ready?"

"In the fall."

I took a deep breath and prayed we could hang on until then.

By the time we got home, Ari was thinner and weaker, but Dr. Stiehm felt she would still be able to start school. He wanted to start her on AZT, but the drug had still not yet been approved for pediatric use.

In 1987, AZT was the only treatment that seemed to be effective against AIDS. It blocked the onset of symptoms in people who hadn't yet gotten sick and it slowed deterioration in those who already had. I could take AZT as soon as I needed it, but my child couldn't. I was outraged and incredibly frustrated despite the promise that the drug's approval was only weeks away.

Just before the start of school, Crossroads hired a new elementary school director named Joanie Green to replace our beloved Mimi Baer, who had resigned. I was sure I would feel uncomfortable with the new director, but Mimi assured me that Joanie would be warm, easygoing, and accessible. This was an understatement. Joanie Green turned out to be magnificent.

Joanie came to Crossroads from a teaching job in New Jersey. On her first day in the new job she was taken out to lunch and told by the assistant director, "We have a child coming to school in September with AIDS." Joanie later told me that she was speechless. She had left her comfortable and predictable life back East and was suddenly confronted with a challenge that was larger than anything she had bargained for. She felt overwhelmed and then, a split second later, challenged by the simple yet significant idea of making a difference in one little girl's life.

Ariel had her heart set on beginning first grade at Crossroads in September 1987, and so did I. For any family these passages are milestones, but for mine each was evidence that we could still live like everyone else.

It didn't work. Although Ariel looked beautiful with her shiny hair and luminous blue eyes, she frequently had outbursts of ghastly pain. It was often so painful that she would cry and scream when she went to the bathroom. It was frightening to Ari. The teachers, who knew the cause, and the other children, who didn't, were scared too, because they didn't know how to help. Indifferent to all this, Ariel wanted to go to school every day. She was a valiant fighter but was only able to finish two weeks of first grade at Crossroads.

I didn't see Ari's limitations as an outsider would. I didn't realize how sick she might appear to other children because to me she was always beautiful. Maybe Ari should never have started school at Crossroads, but we were all determined to try. I wanted Ari to have as many opportunities to be just like everyone else as she could.

When she left school, we told Ari that she could go back to first grade when the pain went away and she felt stronger. We all believed that would be within a few weeks. Paul and I had to believe that or we would have given up right then and there.

Neither Joanie nor I could face the possibility that Ariel might never return to school so we charged ahead like bulls. Joanie began coming to our house three times a week to tutor Ariel so she could keep up with her class.

Joanie's decision was her own, not something Crossroads asked her to do. This was a gesture of love from a woman with a bountiful soul. Joanie had just begun a stressful job, but decided to take time from it in the middle of the day to help Ariel feel included in her school. Joanie was one of the real angels who had come to help.

Even though Ari was not in the classroom, Joanie convinced her that she was still a first grader. She made Ari feel important and treated her with incredible dignity. Joanie compensated for Ari's limitations by reinforcing her strengths. Joanie always praised Ari for what she could still achieve, which was always our basic philosophy at home.

Throughout September, October, and November, we made school in our den. Joanie, with her bright eyes and big smile, would come to our house as if there was absolutely nowhere else on earth that she would rather be. She and Ari would read and do math together. The first-grade teacher also sent home all the art projects so Ari could keep up with the class.

Jake was still at home at this time. He had been accepted at First Presbyterian Nursery School and although their AIDS policy was in place he wasn't going to start until after Christmas, when he was three. That became a problem because he always wanted to be included in Ari's lessons. Our housekeeper, Maria, or I would have to take him outside to play while Joanie and Ari had school.

Joanie became a wellspring of courage for me. She was calm and confident and shared my conviction that Ari was going to get better. Her sensitivity allowed her to understand Ari in a way that many people weren't able to. Most people only saw the part of my daughter that loved bunnies and soft gentle things. She did, but she also had a ferocious spirit, great strength, and a zany sense of humor, all of which Joanie appreciated. Joanie told me she always felt she gained a hundred times more than anything she gave.

Pitched into a life-and-death struggle, our lives became serious and intense. That kind of pressure is exhausting and you need a release. By coming into my kitchen and making me laugh and telling me stories about her own life, Joanie was recess for me. I needed that as much as Ari needed school.

Joanie worked well with Ari because she understood her playful spirit and how much she loved a dare. Joanie would say in her best schoolteacher voice, "Ariel, I know you are not going to be able to do this. This is a math problem for a third grader, not a first grader, but let's try . . ." Ari's eyes would shine at the challenge as she attacked the problem. No one could tell Ari there was anything she couldn't do.

Math was hard for Ari. She preferred Joanie's lessons on

reading and drawing, but her favorite activity with Joanie was their nature walks. Since Ari tired so easily, we could only walk around the block, though she was always eager to get as far as the huge aloe plant that grew in the alley by Adelaide Avenue. Ari would pick pieces of aloe to give to friends as gifts. We also knew where rosemary and thyme grew alongside the bluff, and Ari loved the smell of the herbs rubbed between our fingers.

"I love being so close to Ari," Joanie told me. "But it just makes it so much more difficult watching her when she's in pain."

Often during her lessons Ari would be in staggering pain. I explained to Joanie that we were doing everything possible to ease her suffering.

"You know, Elizabeth, it's the only time I ever see her afraid. Her eyes seem to lose their fire, and suddenly it's like I'm looking at someone else. It's the only way I can tell, by looking in her eyes. I get so infuriated at how helpless I feel."

I think I was the only one who could do anything for Ari at these times. I would just hold her and we would get through it together.

As the pain increased, Ari and I became more and more like one person. No one knew why she was in so much pain; all we knew was how real it was. In her worst moments, my eyes would start to fill with tears and I would say, "Oh, Ari, I wish I could take all your pain into my body. I wish I could make it all go away." She would look right into my eyes and very slowly answer, "But you can't, Mom." We both knew it was true.

It was extremely frustrating to see her hurting so and have the doctors unable to offer any remedies or therapies. As a parent, my deepest and most primal instinct is to protect my child. When I can't, I feel a monstrous powerlessness that transcends any emotion I've ever known.

Paul and I still don't know to this day whether the stomach pain was a prelude to the pancreatitis she was soon to get or whether it was something else still not yet understood about how AIDS affects children. Ari's doctors had no explanation.

As the pain got worse, we would cherish the good moments more than ever. Paul would take Ari to the end of the block to feed the pigeons and at night he would lie beside her in bed and make up wonderful, fanciful stories. Ari's favorite was about a little round stone that was found in a stream by a child. Then the child loses it and it is discovered by a bird who brings it to many different and magical places, but in the end the stone is found by a special little girl.

We went back to Crossroads with Ari one last time. It was for the Halloween party. Her friends were very excited about having her join the class again, and we made a big deal about shopping for her costume. Ari dressed as a flapper in a fringed outfit with beads and as many other baubles as she could find. While she was tired and weak, she was looking forward to going to school for a day.

Ari was excited about Jake taking part in Halloween as well. During this fall, Jake and Ari had become closer than they ever were. Since they were both home, they were spending a great deal of time together.

We would create puppet shows together, and Ari would teach Jake what to do. They would disappear into her room and return transformed into dancers or goblins using all of Ari's dress-up clothes. Ari watched out for Jake with the instincts of a playful mother. I know it was during that time that Jake came to love his sister with a depth none of us would really understand until much later.

That Halloween at Crossroads, a witch came to the classroom, told ghost stories, and made a punch that they called a fantasy witch's brew with eyeballs, beaks, and toadstools. It was Ariel's final day in first grade, and she pulled it off with her own inimitable pizzazz, as a flapper in pink satin with silver moccasins.

It was at the same time, in September and October, that some parents at Crossroads started getting curious. Joanie, in her role as elementary school director, had to frequently sidestep questions about Ariel's long absence from school. Rumors were raging and several parents came into her office and asked point-blank, "Does Ariel Glaser have AIDS?"

Joanie would tell them matter-of-factly that the school's policy of confidentiality prevented her from discussing the medical condition of *any* Crossroads student. But each time we found out that someone was asking, our anxiety soared.

By 1987, AIDS had become an issue of greater national concern. Momentum had been building since October 1986, when Surgeon General C. Everett Koop released the results of his AIDS investigation. Koop bluntly and forcefully said the government had to launch a massive sex education campaign in schools.

Incredibly, by the end of 1986, the United States was the only major industrialized nation that had failed to implement *any* educational efforts to halt the spread of the disease. In other words, the government refused to do the one thing that might stop the epidemic—teach people how not to become infected with the virus.

In his report, Koop called for the widespread use of condoms, and said that mandatory testing was meaningless unless it was backed up with legislation to ensure confidentiality and protect against discrimination. He also said talk of quarantining AIDS victims was ridiculous. But there were people in power, oftentimes led by Senator Jesse Helms, who apparently wanted to discriminate rather than educate, and I felt that these people posed a constant threat to HIV-infected people.

President Reagan ignored the report and denied Koop's requests to meet with him. Reagan's first speech about AIDS did not come until mid-1987, when the epidemic was six years old and had killed more than twenty thousand people. He gave the speech at an AIDS benefit dinner in Washington and in it called for an increase in HIV testing but little more. Education and research were never priorities in his administration.

Money, at least for adults with AIDS, was becoming increasingly available because unlike the White House, Congress realized that AIDS was a crisis of cataclysmic proportions. Senators Edward Kennedy and Orrin Hatch, a liberal Democrat and a conservative Republican, were co-sponsoring a bill authorizing a billion dollars in AIDS spending for 1988. Congressman Henry Waxman was leading the fight in the House.

What was lacking was leadership from the top. With the White House clearly indicating its attitude toward the AIDS crisis by its silence, conservative fundamentalists attacked and ridiculed Koop, who at that point was the only Reagan administration official willing to deal with the epidemic without fear or prejudice.

America was certainly becoming more familiar with AIDS as it took the lives of many in the arts, entertainment, and fashion industries. Since Rock Hudson's death, Liberace had succumbed to AIDS as had Michael Bennett, the creator of *A Chorus Line*. Perry Ellis, the fashion giant, was also reportedly killed by the disease.

But by late 1987, Paul and I still felt the risks of going public clearly overshadowed any gains. We had never even questioned our decision to stay in hiding because, as awful as it was for us to shoulder the massive weight of the secret, we felt we could not risk the possibility that our children might experience any of the hysterical fear that still surrounded AIDS in many parts of the country. To be banned from school or have play with friends restricted was out of the question. Quality of life today was all we had to offer our children. No burdens were too great for us in protecting Jake and Ari. In many ways for me and Paul, it would have been easier to just tell the truth. But not for the kids. So we guarded our secret with all our energy.

Joanie Green had always felt that, if our story became public, the other parents at the school would rally in support. But right now they were asking questions, dangerous questions. We were afraid. In case the news broke unexpectedly, we decided we needed a "contingency plan" and sought out someone to help us create it.

Paul and I had met Josh Baran over the years at political functions and through mutual friends. He ran his own public relations firm. When we decided a contingency plan might be wise, we needed to find someone who would help us create it.

Josh was friendly with one of Lucy's best friends and a new friend of mine, Jody Uttal, and it was Jody who suggested we approach Josh.

He's a very savvy and intelligent publicist and was a perfect choice to help us. Josh's past history showed he wasn't afraid of sensitive or somewhat challenging issues. Josh has represented everyone from the Dalai Lama to Diane Keaton, but most of his work is devoted to issues of social concern, like abortion and censorship. He is not intimidated by complex issues, he thrives on them.

We approached Josh, who graciously volunteered his time to help us develop strategies to protect our story. With his help, we prepared for the worst. If our story became public, we had a press release ready to go. We also wrote a very personal letter that would be mailed out to all Crossroads parents with a packet of relevant AIDS information and articles. As I wrote the letter, my heart felt like it had been hit by a torpedo. It was the first time I had put my story on paper. I wrote, in part:

Now each one of you will have a choice to make and each choice will affect both our lives, yours and ours. You may choose to teach your children that despite all the medical evidence, a need still exists to protect your family from Ariel and her family. Or you may choose to teach your children that prejudice, fear, and ignorance are the real dangers and that your family can help our family by offering love, compassion, and friendship.

Life today for us is very fragile. I am afraid of losing my children, a fear I hope none of you will ever have to face. I am also afraid of losing the quality of the life that is left us. Maybe that will happen, maybe it won't. I am also afraid of looking each of you in the eye tomorrow, not knowing if I will see love or hatred.

For just one moment, imagine you are me. I ask you to look for the strength that each of us needs to step into tomorrow.

With great sadness and great pride, I remain, Elizabeth Glaser

The letter was locked up in Joanie's office. It sat there waiting for a catastrophe. Josh Baran became crucial to protecting our secret. He was like an early warning detection system. He picked up scuttlebutt in the Hollywood community. He chased down rumors and was able to confront or deflect them. If any calls came into his office, or if someone on his staff heard something, he simply responded by saying that the Glasers don't give interviews and whatever rumors they heard were wrong.

Ultimately, Josh says, he knew the secret was doomed. "We all knew in our gut that this would come out eventually. It was inevitable. People love to gossip and too many people knew some of the story." But Paul and I didn't feel that way and we certainly didn't know he felt that way, because he never would have said it to our face.

At one point, a story appeared in a London tabloid that

was inaccurate, but close enough. The story said that Ariel had gotten contaminated blood at Cedars-Sinai Hospital, and that, fearful of AIDS, we had her tested, but she was not infected. We were afraid that a newspaper here might try to do a follow-up story, but fortunately for my family, none did.

It had been nearly a year and a half since our diagnosis, and Paul and I were beginning to tell a few more people. But each time we did we were increasing our risk. The alternative was to lie, but the isolation of living a lie is devastating. Being with people who didn't know the truth was exhausting. We were constantly avoiding questions. We found ourselves redirecting conversations over and over again. People would ask about Ari, and the pain of lying was immense. By the end of an evening, we'd be exhausted.

It became simpler either to tell people or not to see people who didn't know, so we edited many people out of our lives. I imagine they thought we didn't like them anymore. We stopped going out, except with the few friends who were pledged to secrecy. It was difficult to be our friend. We were all living in an America that ostracized and rejected people with AIDS.

Over the years, my friend Lucy had worked her way up from a free-lance script reader to a vice president at Warner Bros. and had recently married Doug Wick, an independent film producer. Doug's parents have been lifelong friends of the Reagans; his dad, Charles Wick, was head of the U.S. Information Agency in the Reagan administration.

One evening when Lucy and Doug were at a cocktail party they heard someone say that Paul Michael Glaser's family had AIDS. In her deadly, low-key way, Lucy emphatically told this person his statement was not true. She implored him to tell her where he heard it, and it turned out his source was an agent in town. Tracking the agent down the next day in his office, Lucy made him understand the magnitude of the harm he was inadvertently inflicting. Our friends worked as hard to protect our privacy as we did. We were like an army protecting a state secret. Everyone was on constant alert.

By November of 1987, *The Running Man* had been released and received very well. Paul had more free time now as he was waiting for his next job. Every day he would go up to his office over the garage behind our house to work, taking a break to "do lunch" with colleagues in the film industry.

While he was working at home he always made special time for Ari. They would spend hours and hours up in his office drawing and painting in their own private world. They continued to take long strolls to feed the pigeons. When Ari was in pain he would hold her as I would, embracing her small body with the strength of his much larger one.

When he needed to escape it all, Paul began going to the golf course where he could lose himself in the beauty, peace, and concentration that the rolling green fairways demanded.

At night, we would climb into bed exhausted by the strain of just being us. If we talked about our fears, we felt overwhelmed. If we talked about our hopes, it felt like pie-in-the-sky dreaming. So usually, we didn't talk at all.

Some nights I would just lie there and think how trapped Paul must feel. How hard it was to live with us and how impossible it would be to leave. If he walked away, everyone would think he was such a "bad" guy. How could he leave his wife and children when they needed him so much? But I knew he must have wanted to run away at times. Run to a life that seemed more like everyone else's. Part of me would have wanted that, so part of him must have also. But he never said it, and we never shared what we were thinking. It was too scary. On a good night we would fall asleep in each other's arms, embracing anything that felt peaceful and loving.

Ari was getting weaker and weaker that month. We had been waiting for AZT all that year and each month it wasn't ready. Paul and I were holding our breath and silently praying that something would change the course of our lives, working hard to keep our family life optimistic. But one Sunday right before Thanksgiving, Ari had terrible, terrible stomach pains.

We went to the emergency room at UCLA and after hours of fear and many blood tests, we were told that Ari had acute pancreatitis. They immediately admitted us to the hospital for a week, but we ended up staying a month.

Even though Ari had been weakening, it was a shock to be back in the hospital. It had been two years since Miami. I hardly ever left Ari's side and when I did, Paul was always there. The hospital felt strange, alien, and frightening. I couldn't feel any optimism around us, and I knew I needed to have that in order to keep going.

Jake barely saw me. My parents were there for him, and they also came to the hospital almost every day to help with Ari. They were devoted to us and were always on call.

Paul and I went back and forth to UCLA like runners in a relay race. I would rush home for two hours while Paul would stay with Ari. Then I would rush back and Paul would come home to be with Jake. We lived like that every day for a month. One of us slept in Ari's room every night, usually me.

Ariel was in withering pain from her pancreatitis. As she became sicker, our relationship became more intense and unlike any I have ever had with another human being. She and I became one even more powerfully now. I was feeling every ounce of her pain, every grimace. It was as if our hearts beat in the same body, like they did before she was born.

On that first trip to the hospital, Ariel had to have a sonogram. The machine would show immediate pictures of her stomach and might possibly help us identify some of the causes of her ongoing pain. The sonogram could point out liver or kidney problems as well. We had to go downstairs to a room that was chilly and austere. Ari was scared. She hated having strangers with grotesque machines probing her. I could feel her anxiety.

She was lying on the examining room table and the technician was getting ready to administer the test. I was on the other side of her. I leaned over Ariel and made her eyes connect with mine. With all the creativity of a good teacher and all the determination of a frightened mother, I drew Ari with me into a world of make-believe: a world in which there was a magic little girl and bunny who could face danger and make wonderful things happen. It was a world filled with pastel flowers, billowy white clouds, and extravagant rainbows.

Ariel's eyes were riveted to mine. Several times during the twenty-minute story, I knew I was weaving an unusual and magnificent tale. Ari knew it too, and we journeyed deep into a world that was far, far from our own.

When the test was completed, the technician turned to me and said, "That was an amazing story. Your relationship with your daughter is very unique."

Maybe it was unusual to the technician, but it wasn't unusual for either Ariel or me. I was all instinct and adrenaline. Nothing could fog my focus because the survival of my child was at stake.

When you are totally involved with one person, it is almost impossible to really be there for anyone else. The only other time I had felt obsessed like that was when I fell madly in love with Paul. Then it had seemed like nothing else mattered except Paul. Now I felt the same intense focus with Ariel.

Since most of me was always with Ari, I was never completely emotionally available to anyone else. Ariel became all that really mattered to me and I know in the process I shortchanged people I loved like Paul and Jake, my parents, and friends.

Jake rarely had me alone. When Paul reached out with a hug or a kiss, I was often unresponsive because even though Ari might not have been in the room, I was sending all my love to her at all times. I often wasn't aware of anyone else's presence.

My rationalization was that there would be more time in the future for Jake, Paul, my parents, and friends. With Ariel, it felt like the hourglass was running out. Deep in my bones, I believed there was a way to keep my daughter alive. I just had to find it, even though I didn't know what to look for. So I spent all my time reviewing in my mind where we were and what choices lay ahead.

Part of my response was panic; I was operating on instinct. Part was the natural desire Ariel and I had always had for each other's company. And if she were to mention a new pain, I thought I should be with her so that I could tell the doctors. The answer was out there somewhere, and I was convinced that if I spent every moment with her I could find some solution in time and Ari would not die.

Ari was in the hospital for Thanksgiving. My brother, Peter, his wife, Janet, and their twin boys had already arranged to come for the holiday. Paul stayed with Ari so I could join my parents and brother for Thanksgiving dinner. Thanksgiving? How could anyone with a life like mine be thankful for anything? I tried not to ruin the dinner for everyone, but all I felt was despair, not gratitude.

I wanted more than anything to give Ari, and us, something positive. Any little happy moment was a treasure. Lucy had been to the hospital and told me she had dined with her friends James Taylor and Kathryn Walker the night before. Ari had a huge crush on James Taylor. She watched him on "Sesame Street." I asked Lucy if she thought James might stop by the hospital to visit Ari, but he was leaving town the next day and wasn't able to. I was disappointed, but knew I was grabbing at straws anyway.

This first hospital stay was very difficult and a painful learning experience for all of us. I had not yet found my role with the nurses and doctors. We were not yet a team.

Entering a hospital is like entering an alien world. The language is different, the atmosphere is different, and everyone could be divided into two groups: anyone who approached Ari with something potentially painful became an enemy; anyone who helped support us quickly became our cherished friend.

Paul, Ari, and I fought to maintain our optimism and humor. We always talked about going home. The goal was to get out of the hospital and getting home was the prize. Ari had lost a great deal of weight for her little frame. She was thin and weak but her spirit was still resolute and strong.

We'd go down to the playroom every day where she would draw beautiful pictures for Jake. One day she made a collage of Jake's name and covered the big letters with little colored rocks. On the bottom she wrote, "I love you, Ariel." He still has the collage on the wall in his room: his name and Ari's love.

We fought back against being at UCLA by making Ari's hospital room a vibrant and colorful place. We wanted it to feel like a home. We decorated the walls with her artwork and anything else we could find. There were flowers and balloons, quilts and pillows, toys and stuffed animals (especially her gray bunny) from home. Her old friends and her new classmates at Crossroads sent her pictures and letters which were displayed as well. Every night we played a tape of classical music to put her to sleep. It didn't look like any other hospital room at UCLA.

My parents came often and so did our friends, although the only friends we allowed to visit were those who knew the real story.

When we were in the hospital we felt more vulnerable than ever about being discovered. Paul was more visible and people were always paying attention to him—other families on the floor, other visitors. We kept our profile as low as we possibly could and friends knew to do the same. We were so nervous that we registered Ari under my maiden name of Betsy Meyer. The nurses would come in and call her Betsy, and we would all laugh.

Friends who didn't know the real story and wanted to come by were told that Ari was too tired and that we needed quiet. We were terribly afraid a friend who didn't know might find out she had AIDS from the "infectious disease" sign on her door or by seeing one of the nurses wearing gloves for no apparent reason.

Those gloves made me crazy. Somehow they symbolized all the uneducated and fearful misunderstandings about AIDS. It was not until our second hospital stay, four months later, that I realized I had the power to deny those hospital personnel access to our room.

It was *our* room and by that time no one who was wearing gloves or masks inappropriately was allowed in. As bravely as I could, I told them either they removed the gloves or they didn't enter Ari's room. Sometimes gloves were necessary, for example, when blood was drawn. Then I never said a thing. I had talked to our doctors at length about what precautions needed to be taken and so I knew I was not asking anyone to put themselves in jeopardy.

We became very dependent on Nancy Potash, the head nurse in pediatrics, who was unfailingly supportive and reliable. Nancy is clearly in charge, but she does it without acting cold or tough. She maintains her authority without losing any of her compassion. The first time I met her, she had walked into Ari's room while I was crying.

"I don't know how I am going to get through this," I said to her. "I just don't know."

"We'll get you through," she told me. Since then that's become the mission statement for her nursing unit: "We'll help you make it through."

What I learned gradually about hospitals, and what most people don't realize, is that ultimately the patient is in charge. I could pick up and leave; I could tell the doctors or nurses that I didn't want to do something they were urging me to do. I learned during our first hospital stay that, ultimately, Paul and I had control over Ari's treatment.

What we could not defend Ari against was the pain. When

the pain hit nothing else mattered or made any difference; not the pictures on the wall or a Mylar balloon floating from an IV pump. We felt helpless and insignificant as we watched Ari suffer.

I saw the impact this had on Paul. It was excruciating for him. We all realized how much he was really hurting. There were times when he would back off and seem distant, not because he didn't care, but because he was summoning the strength and courage he needed to go on.

There were other times when his anger over Ari's suffering would erupt in rage. He would scream at the nurses, the doctors, or anyone else who happened to be around. But after he exploded, he would always apologize and express the warmest feelings. He was never angry at the individuals; he was angry at the circumstances. He was angry at AIDS and we all knew it.

Ariel's pain was caused by her acute pancreatitis, which itself was caused by her immune deficiency problems. Her pancreas was inflamed, which meant she couldn't digest food, which meant it became impossible for her to eat. Ari's inability to eat further inflamed her pancreas, which intensified the pain. She was in a vicious and relentless cycle.

The only alternative to painful starvation was intravenous feeding. We were told we could take Ari home if we allowed her to have a catheter called a broviac surgically implanted in her chest or abdomen so food and medicines could flow into her intravenously. We could feed her at home if we mastered a system called Total Parenteral Nutrition (TPN). The TPN would then be connected to Ari's broviac and infuse her with the proper caloric and nutritional balance over a ten-hour period each night.

Even though the broviac surgery was relatively minor, we were afraid. Despite everything, she had never before faced anesthetics, knives, and surgeons. But we knew Ari couldn't eat. Her normal life was being stripped away inch by inch.

Her surgery was successful, but the trauma depleted her. She never really got strong again, but I remained hopeful and every day waited for her condition to improve.

The day Laurie Reyen, the TPN nurse, came to Ari's room to explain the system was the first day since our whole ordeal began that I wanted to give up. I wanted to resign from life and say: "This is too much. I've had it. I'm not strong enough." Ariel's old life was drifting past us like smoke. No matter what we did, no matter how hard we tried, we could not hold on to it.

I was scared and overwhelmed by TPN. I knew why we had to feed her intravenously, but I did not see how I could possibly learn such an extraordinarily intricate and tedious procedure. Laurie Reyen was so calm and quietly competent that I felt even more helpless in her presence. But she insisted this was something I could master.

Before I could begin there were at least sixteen steps I had to learn, and if I made a single mistake along the way, I had to start all over again. When I realized that in order to do this I would almost have to become a nurse, I felt an over-powering sense of despair.

As Laurie was teaching me, tears would begin to fill my eyes. As the tears would fall down my cheeks, I would silently wipe them away, only to be told by Laurie that I now had to start the sixteen steps all over again because I had de-sterilized the process.

Laurie never pushed me. With a rain-or-shine reliability she came back day after day to help me learn the feeding system that would enable me to take my daughter home. Each time when I felt I just couldn't go on, Laurie reminded me that other mothers did this and so could I. Nevertheless, I found the process overwhelming and the responsibility frightening. If, while I was preparing the TPN setup for Ariel, I contaminated any part of it with my own germs, she might develop an infection and get sick and die.

When I close my eyes, I can still see how the sterile swabs have to be unwrapped, and then dipped into a Betadine solution that gets swished through alcohol. Next I drew medicines into the syringe so I could inject them into the solution bag and then I had to add vitamins and medicine to counter the acid in her stomach. I also had to learn how to clean the bag so I didn't inject germs into the solution along with the medications.

I was taught how to put the IV tubing into the bag and set up the IV pump, how to clean the catheter and hook up the pump. I was taught how to make sure the pump was running correctly. I had to learn how to punch in the correct numbers to turn off the infusion in a certain way the next morning, so Ariel wouldn't get low blood sugar. After I unhooked everything, I had to immaculately clean the connections where the bag and the IV were hooked together to eliminate any possibility of infection. It was a mountain of knowledge to integrate.

At the same time we were learning about TPN, we were told that Ari could finally have the long-awaited AZT. The National Institutes of Health (NIH) doctors now had enough information from the clinical trials to suggest a dosage. By the end of 1986, AZT was finally being tested in a pediatric clinical trial program.

The study, which involved thirty-five children, was being conducted at NIH in Maryland, at Duke University in Durham, North Carolina, and at Miami Children's Hospital in Florida. Because the testing was all back East, if I had wanted Ari to participate, we would have had to all move or be separated for months at a time. Neither was an acceptable alternative for us.

When the AZT study was completed a year later, more was understood about the side effects of the drug and the proper dosage for children. Ari was probably the first child in the country not enrolled in a clinical drug trial to use AZT, which in late 1987 was still the only drug known to be effective in treating AIDS.

I told Paul I felt like we were pioneers in the first wagon train heading West. We had no maps to follow on our journey, the road was rugged and dangerous, but hopefully it led to a better life at the other end. Paul and I sat in Ari's hospital room, squeezed each other's hand, and said, "Westward, ho," desperately holding on to something positive.

We were optimistic about the pills of AZT and hoped that after a brief period on TPN, Ari's pancreatitis would subside enough and she would be able to eat again. It never happened.

Ariel was a bare echo of her six-year-old self. She was weak and had lost a lot of weight. Walking was becoming increasingly difficult for her. We left the hospital on the first night of Hanukkah which that year fell on Wednesday, December 16. My fragile family lit the first candle and prayed silently for a miracle to happen.

CHAPTER
❧ 5 ❧

Christmas came a week later and for Jake's sake, we tried to have fun with my parents, but I felt hollow. The holiday season felt oppressive and the music mocked what we didn't have. There was no joy in our world and our nights were anything but silent. Ari often cried out in pain over the hum of the machines that were pumping food and medicine into her to keep her alive.

After the first three or four weeks at home, I was beginning to remember the steps and keep up with the TPN routine. When I knew what I was doing, it only took forty minutes at night to prepare the TPN setup and about twenty minutes in the morning to dismantle it. But in the beginning it took me at least two hours every evening.

The nighttime instructions were four pages long. If I made one mistake, I had to start all over again. It was terribly frustrating, and at first Paul would sit in the room with me while I would hook Ari up. If I rubbed my eye without noticing, he would catch me and I would start all over. I wanted him to watch because I was afraid that if I made a mistake, Ari would get sicker. At first Paul's commitment was to watch me, but as time passed he learned as well and equally shared the work.

We kept the feeding machines and pumps out of sight when they weren't in use because we never wanted Ari's bedroom to look like a hospital room. Ari was fed this way for eight months, and in time, Paul was also able to do the entire setup in forty minutes.

One of the remarkable things to me about Paul is that he never shied away from this kind of responsibility. He may have hated it and felt enraged that he had to do it—but he always came through, whether it was changing a diaper, mixing Ari's food, or cleaning up her vomit. I was, and am, very lucky that Paul was willing to share the many medical responsibilities we had at home. And the wonderful thing was that as in everything else, Paul did it with his own style. He would create amazing ways to hold twenty-two long Q-tips in one hand. The first time I saw it I had to laugh. Paul has a special way of teaching me how one can bring creativity to almost anything. We each brought our own personality to the job at hand.

One day shortly after we got home, I remember I was adding heparin, an anticoagulant, into the bag. Something happened and both the catheter and syringe flew out of my hand. The catheter dropped on Ari's beloved gray bunny. Our eyes opened wide. Ari and I were both very protective of gray bunny. I just looked at her and said, "We Glaser girls are going to have to change our style!" My fast-forward approach to life was useless when it came to TPN.

Learning the TPN system marked another turning point for me. It taught me to cut off my tears. Wiping my nose or my eyes was a luxury I could no longer afford when I was in the midst of the process. I rapidly learned how to be very sad but not cry. I learned how to sever myself from my emotions by throwing a mental switch inside myself. Months later, this training would give me the ability to go to Washington and talk about my life in a matter-of-fact, practical way.

TPN also honed my ability to concentrate. Ari might have had the worst day of her life, I could be terrified that she was going to die, Jake and Paul might be in nasty and argumentative moods, but Ari still had to be fed. I couldn't cry, scratch, or sneeze. I couldn't let my mind wander for a moment. I cut myself off completely from whatever else was happening in our lives. I learned to focus.

When AIDS destroyed my sense of control, I was forced to realize how illusory the whole notion of control is. It creates a false sense of security. I now think most people spend too much time worrying about where their path is going to take them instead of living where they are. None of us know when lightning will streak across our path or when the next curve in the trail will bring us to a rainbow. I have had to face that illusion in the cruelest way, but the lesson is valuable for anyone.

There are no guarantees. I take one step and then I take another. The fear of taking the first, hardest step often stops people from ever trying to move in a new direction.

Paul and I had to choose whether to nurse Ari ourselves or have her stay in the hospital where someone else would care for her. The first step is never easy, but once we started the process, we adapted to it.

Lesa Grovas, our favorite nurse from UCLA, came to our home a few nights a week to give Ariel her albumin, which was protein, and Lasix, which acted as a diuretic. She gave Paul and me a break as well. She was there for us as much emotionally as she was medically, and she had a good rapport with Paul. He would tell her how it was killing him to watch Ariel fade.

The TPN made Ari uncomfortable and bloated all over her body. She looked less and less like our cherished daughter. And as she deteriorated she slowly stopped walking. Then it became hard for her to hold a paintbrush. Paul would just sit next to her and do the paintings himself as she would nod encouragement.

We asked Dr. Stiehm why this was happening, but he had no real answers. Ari was sick with a serious and deadly virus, and she was becoming more debilitated each day. The AZT we had hoped would make a difference seemed to have no impact on her at all.

Since even talking was hard for her, we learned to communicate with our eyes. Her eyes were always alive. They could share pain. They could scream in anger as her frustration intensified, but they could also show wonder and excitement, humor and love. Sometimes I couldn't understand what she was trying to tell me and her eyes would shoot darts that pierced my heart. But when her eyes spoke to me with love, I would answer with words of love and hope.

Throughout January and February of 1988, Ari became weaker and more confined. We were on a downhill path. The one thing that really brought her joy was a tape James Taylor had sent her. When he couldn't visit her in the hospital, he had recorded five songs in his living room and sent them to us. Ari's favorite, "Jelly Man Kelly," was included and the tape began with James saying "Hello Ari, this is James Taylor." He went on to talk to her about his animals and what he could see from his apartment window. It was very special and meaningful to all of us, especially Ari. Every time he said, "I hear you are very funny and pretty," she'd smile.

By February she stopped walking completely. I carried her everywhere. I did everything for her. She was as dependent on me physically as she had been as an infant. She was unable to speak, but we both remembered the words that had already been said.

We would still go for long walks. Because she was unable to sit up, I would put her in the stroller, cushioning her with pillows and wrapping a blanket over her legs. We didn't need words to share the peaceful beauty of nature. Despite the pain and the weariness that she always felt, she never failed to respond to the beauty around her.

I would push her on our favorite route in the sunshine with the air smelling of eucalyptus. Ari would thump on the frame of her stroller with her palm to get my attention. I tried to figure out what she needed. "Ari, does something hurt? Do I need to fix your pillows? Do you have to go to the bathroom?"

Ari would thump and thump again and then I would see it. "Oh, do you want me to get you that puffer flower?" A smile would fill her eyes as I snapped up the dandelion and breathed onto it, both of us marveling as the feathery little seeds drifted to the ground.

I became so consumed with making the quality of Ari's life valuable that, in many ways, Jake lost out. My parents did things with him and so did Paul, but because Jake was only ten months old when Ari got sick, I did not have the experiences with him in his first few years that I did with her.

Luckily, Jake had started nursery school in January and his life was actually becoming more normal as Ari's became less and less. Now he was gone all morning, playing with other children and making new friends.

Jake made his best friend in his first few weeks at school. Tommy Solomon was a very handsome and active three-year-old. He and Jake became fast friends and I met Tommy's parents, Annie and George.

I had decided not to tell any families at the nursery school about Jake being HIV-positive but after spending an afternoon with Annie I broke that rule right away. Annie is a tall and striking blonde with a contagious personality, and it is impossible to keep her at arm's length. We told Annie and George, and they became a safe island in Jake's new world.

There are moments I can remember when Ariel, who was barely able to do anything, would be propped up on the couch in the den. We always made sure she never spent the day in bed because we never wanted her to feel like an invalid. We dressed her, carried her downstairs, and made her comfortable. Jake would come and sit next to her and she would muster up all her strength to reach her hand out to hold his. They would sit there quietly as brother and sister, offering the best they could to each other.

The first few months of 1988 were very demanding. Our friends and family were all that kept us going. They would call every day. We were at home alone much of the time, but we never felt isolated. Lynn, Lucy, and Susan called every day. Jody, Claudia, Rena, Hilary, Havi, Carol, Susie, Suzanne, Mom and Dad, everyone who knew also checked in constantly. And the friends who only knew that Ari was ill from some strange kidney and liver problem called too.

Ari's friends were her tiny thread to the world. Amy and Francesca, or Sara and Taylor, would come to visit at least once a week. Because she was so compromised, we had to be inventive. Taylor would come and watch TV on the couch with Ari. Amy would visit and we'd do art projects for Ari. Amy would ask her what color markers to use. She would pick a pink one and look at Ari to ask if it was a good choice. With a glance of her eyes or a nod of her head, Ari would approve or disapprove.

Francesca would come and we would always play "Old Maid." I would hold Ari's cards and Ari would let me know which one of Francesca's to pick. We would all end up laughing because inevitably Ari would win.

These weekly visits meant so much to Ari. Her friends were with her and she knew it. They never judged her and so she never had to judge herself. Jake also enjoyed playing with Ari's friends. Like so much else in my life at that time, seeing all the children together would simultaneously break my heart and bring me joy. It seemed very brave for my friends to continue to bring their children when Ari looked so awful. But neither the parents nor the children ever complained, at least not in front of us.

Paul had gotten another job. The producer Richard Zanuck had hired him to direct a big-budget action-adventure film at MGM called "Blue Lightning." Saying yes was a big decision because the film was going to be shot in Miami. We spent about three days trying to decide what he should do. If he said yes, it meant the family would either be separated or have to move to Miami. If we decided to go, was it possible to move Ari that far and set everything up again without any friends or family?

Finally, after changing our minds so many times that we both felt dizzy, I just said, "You have to do it. We'll get to Miami one way or another." We knew there was no way we could be separated. Paul couldn't imagine being away from the children and I couldn't let him give up the directing career he had worked so assiduously to attain. I called Dick Stiehm and asked him if Ari could be moved to Miami and he said he thought it was possible if we really had to. I'm sure he felt it was a preposterous idea, but he didn't try to talk us out of it.

In March, nearly two years after our initial diagnosis, Ariel got pneumonia and we were back at UCLA again. Once we were admitted, there was a constant barrage of tests. Dick Stiehm suggested that as long as we were there, we should do a magnetic resonance imaging, or MRI, to evaluate if there was central nervous system damage. An MRI is like an X ray, only it utilizes magnetic energy. The MRI showed that her brain had severely atrophied. Like a balloon losing air, her brain was deflating. The doctors said it was irreversible. It was one of the central nervous system complications of AIDS. It was devastating information for me. As far as I could see it left no room for getting better. Now we knew why Ari couldn't do all the things she used to. It wasn't because she had a serious virus, it was because somehow the virus had compromised her central nervous system. Paul and I could barely fathom it.

Ariel was the sickest she had ever been. After we had been in the hospital for four days, Dick Stiehm solemnly sat us down and told us he did not think Ari would last much longer. He said she had probably forty-eight hours to live. We weren't prepared for this.

He said Paul and I would have to decide whether or not to put her into intensive care. We looked at each other and without saying a word knew what our answer was. If there was no hope, if the central nervous system couldn't be restored, we certainly did not want to turn her over to technology and watch her life played out in beeps and blips on instrument panels.

With great pain in our hearts, Paul and I agreed that we would not put her in intensive care. We would fight for her life, but we would not prolong her death. Deciding to withhold the treatment that might extend a child's life has to be the hardest decision a parent can make.

It was a decision that tore us apart, but it was the only choice we felt we had once we saw the results of the MRI. If her central nervous system deterioration was now irreversible, if her brain was atrophied, it felt selfish to hold on to her any longer. We had to decide what would be best for Ari, what would bring her peace. So we decided to stay by her side, as always, and let nature take its course. She was never alone for a moment. Ari was breathing weakly, but she hadn't given up.

We called our friends. Lynn got to the hospital first. We told her the doctors thought Ari was going to die and could she call our other friends and let them know. She went through the motions of staying calm. She got a handful of quarters and started making calls. She later told me she had no recollection of dialing any numbers or how she began, but within hours our closest friends were all standing beside us. Everyone believed the end had come. Everyone but Ari.

It was pure hell for her, but she fought back. Her eyes did not say, "I'm ready to die." They said, "Get me out of this." If Ari could have had a temper tantrum, she would have. Instead, her eyes were having a temper tantrum.

Our friends would take turns coming. Lucy lived very close by and was there almost every day. I found out later she had usually cried in the parking lot before pulling herself together to visit. That's how bad Ari was in those days. I never would have guessed how Lucy felt from how positive and supportive she was in the room.

Despite the fact that Ari had been very sick for months, I never believed she was going to die. I could not imagine it and was totally unprepared for it. It was not until the doctors told us that there was absolutely no hope that I confronted the possibility of Ari's death for the first time.

I remember when Lucy came to visit that Saturday. Paul stayed in the room so I could go outside on the fire escape and have a cigarette with her. The sun seemed too bright, the day, all wrong.

I lit one cigarette and then another. I was shaking and not yet able to talk. I looked at Lucy as tears welled up in my eyes and with outrage and disbelief I said, "This isn't possible, Lou. I have done everything I can to make our life in Santa Monica normal and valuable and real. Our friends are back in place, the schools are settled, Paul and I are doing everything we possibly can. I've worked so hard and Ari is still going to die? She is still going to die! It makes no sense! How is it that she is still going to die, Lou?"

Lucy clutched my hand, crying with me. It was in that moment of honest desperation that I realized I could no longer sit quietly in Santa Monica. A mother's job is to save her child; it's a basic animal instinct. But I was failing.

"Lou," I said, "I have to do something, what can I do? I have to do something to save my child! I have to get to the President!"

"Okay, okay," she said. "If you have to get to the President, we'll get you to the President."

I lit another cigarette.

"If Ari dies, then Jake is going to die. I can't keep sitting here in Santa Monica making a cozy little life for my family if we are all going to die! No one cares if we all die from AIDS. Something is very wrong. You have to get me to Reagan."

I finished my cigarette and we walked back into Ari's room. I had a new strength because now I was so angry that I had stopped being a victim. Up until that point, I had focused only on Ari's condition. I knew what was happening in our little world, but I knew very little about the larger picture. I had learned to be very assertive and challenged our doctors, but I had only a minimal understanding of the broader AIDS issues around the country. I knew we couldn't get AZT for Ari when she needed it, but I hadn't really gone beyond that to try to figure out why.

That night Jim Blechman, our homeopathic doctor, came to UCLA and visited Ari. He held her hand and looked in her eyes.

"Elizabeth, she isn't going to die. Look at her. There is still too much fierceness in her eyes."

He was right. It was a miracle. Ari gradually began to get stronger. She pulled out of the crisis. No one knew why. We were all astonished, yet part of me always knew she had it in her.

On Monday, Dr. Stiehm came back to find us alive and on the mend. I am sure he was shocked, but also genuinely happy. I looked him in the eyes. "I think I'm ready to try and do something about this," I told him calmly. "There are some serious problems here with AIDS, aren't there? I want to try and make a difference. Is there anything I can do? Do you think there is a way I could do something and still keep our privacy?"

"I am sure there is," he said in his even, steady way. Dr. Stiehm is such a calm man it is hard to even imagine him blowing his car horn in frustration.

I said to him, "I have to find out what I can do. Will you help me?"

He said he would.

"What do you think I can do? Is there any hope?" I asked.

And then Dick Stiehm talked about the possibility of finding a way to block transmission of the virus from an infected mother to her child. "Do you think it's possible?" I asked.

"Yes," he said.

"Could I have more children?" I asked, holding my breath.

"Maybe," he replied. It was a thin ray of hope dangling before me. I grabbed. I didn't think I could have more children, but now Dick was saying research offered the possibility of answers that might change that. It offered the possibility that we could learn more and maybe help me and my children. What else mattered? I jumped in with both feet.

"I think I can get to President Reagan. But I have to know what I am talking about."

"You have to talk about the children," he said.

I didn't really understand what he meant, but he was certain I should move ahead. He told me he had been waiting for me to reach this decision.

Dick Stiehm was the very first person I talked to about my new idea. I hadn't even mentioned it to Paul. If Dick had not taken me seriously, or if he had not had the confidence and foresight to realize more could be done, I probably would have stopped right there.

I was saying the words, I felt it in my heart, but I had no idea how to move ahead. If he had said, "Elizabeth, I think you should just concentrate on Ari and your family because they really need you," I would have agreed with him. But as I would come to learn, Dick Stiehm is one of the unique people in the world. Figuratively, he took my hand without hesitation, and said that he would help me walk my path. It made all the difference.

I knew Ari's illness was progressing much faster than my own, but I didn't really know there was such a thing as pediatric AIDS. I thought AIDS was AIDS. I knew there was a lot that seemed wrong with the way the epidemic was being managed and much seemed unfair, but I didn't have the ability to label any of the problems.

I had many questions about Ari's illness but the answers were always, "We don't know why. We don't know when. We don't know how." I had been unhappy about that but I had accepted it. Now I wanted to know why we didn't know more.

Ariel came home on a Friday. That night I said to Paul, "I want to try and do something about this, about how unfair everything seems to be in our life. Do you think it's okay for me to become actively involved in trying to change things? It might put our family's privacy in jeopardy, but if I don't do something, we may all die."

We were sitting at the kitchen table. We were both still somewhat numb from Ari's bout with pneumonia. Paul was silent for a long time and then with great gentleness and deliberation he said, "I'll support you in whatever you have to do. I don't want to be an active part of it. I just can't speak publicly about something I feel is so personal, but if you feel you have to do something, I'll certainly stand behind you."

For Paul it was a brave and hard decision as well. He knew it would put all of us at risk. If our story came out, we were never sure how the industry would react to him. Would it hurt his career? Would people not want to hire him? Would they feel he was a wounded animal that should be cut from the pack?

I also felt strongly that whatever work I did should be mine and not Paul's. As an artist he needs to focus on creating, either as a director or as a writer. But I felt the time had come for me to step into another arena. Paul offered me the love, support, and confidence I needed to move ahead.

I gave my husband a big hug and felt a smile spreading across my face. I knew this was the moment when I was taking that hard first step. I didn't know it at the time, but it was a step that has kept me in motion ever since. Symbolically, it was the step that said, "No matter what happens, I will try my best. I will try and take some control of my future."

It was as if I had suddenly awakened and realized that there was no one waiting to make everything all right for us. I had convinced myself that at some moment when our lives seemed utterly hopeless an angel would suddenly appear to set everything right. Well, there weren't going to be any angels of that kind. If anything was going to be done, I was the one who would have to do it. This was not a role I wanted; I simply had no choice.

I called Josh Baran, our friend and publicist, and invited him over the next night. I felt there was no time to lose. I sat him down at the kitchen table and got out a legal pad and a pen.

"Josh, I want to do something."

"What do you want to do?" he asked.

Once again, a desperate mother's voice said, "I don't know, exactly, Josh. I want to save my family, but I think to do that I have to change the world. So much seems to be wrong in this battle against AIDS."

"Okay, how do you want to go about it?" he said without missing a beat.

"I have no idea, but I don't think I can do it privately. I can't raise enough money. I think I have to do it federally. I have to do it on the highest level. I want to get to Reagan."

"Right, Elizabeth, we can't futz around here. If you're going to do something, you have got to go for the biggest thing you can. You don't have time to have little bake sales and seminars and fund-raisers that raise $5,000. We really have to reach the top people." I like the way Josh thinks.

"If you are going to do this," he continued, "you'll have to educate yourself. You can't do this just knowing about your own life."

"Okay. So where do I start?"

"Get a copy of . . . *And the Band Played On,* Randy Shilts's book on AIDS, start reading the newspaper every day, and start talking to people."

We began making lists. We started with the doctors, first Ari's and mine; Dick Stiehm and Michael Gottlieb. Then we added the Surgeon General and Admiral James Watkins, the man in charge of President Reagan's Commission on AIDS. We sat at the kitchen table, writing name after name. Many people we'd only heard of but didn't know. The next column was for the politicians. Tom Hayden, Alan Cranston, and Henry Waxman, one of the most powerful members in the House on health issues, were added, along with Ted Kennedy and the Reagans.

Then we made a heading for celebrities. Whom did we know? I had taught Cher's daughter in elementary school. Jane Fonda was approachable because I had volunteered for her husband Tom Hayden. Paul knew plenty of people, and Lucy knew Steven Spielberg and had promised that she would ask her husband, Doug Wick, to try and arrange a meeting with the Reagans. I had to see everybody I could think of.

Josh knew how hard it was to deal with Congress and the Senate and how tough it can be to raise money. I, on the other hand, didn't really know what I was getting into.

Each of the four people I talked with in those first few days gave me the sense that I could accomplish something. Their confidence allowed my mind to think big. If Lucy had told me how hard it was to get to President Reagan, or that she wasn't sure she'd be able to do it, I might not have been as enthusiastic and energetic. I didn't want to hear about what I "realistically" could expect. I didn't want to think realistically. I wanted to save my children, and I knew only bold strokes could accomplish that.

Monday morning I set up appointments with Stiehm and Gottlieb. I went to see both men and asked them for their assessment of AIDS as an issue. What needed to be done?

Where was there room for improvement? Whom did they think I should see?

The answers to all the questions were staggering. There was room for so much more work. It became clearer and clearer as I talked to Dick Stiehm that to save my children, I needed to concentrate specifically on pediatric issues. Because I'm infected, I'll never lose sight of the adult issues, but my activism needed a focus, and children were it. Now when I looked at Ari at least I knew I was trying to do something that might make a difference. I started setting up meetings.

A few days later, during an appointment with Michael Gottlieb, he paused and said, "Do you want to meet with the Surgeon General?" He knew C. Everett Koop was going to be in town a few days later and thought he might be able to schedule a meeting. The answer was, of course, "yes." He was on my list.

I was scared. Was I ready to meet with someone as important as Koop? Did I know enough? I had never imagined that such a significant meeting could be set up so quickly.

I was on edge for two days, waiting to find out if the meeting could be arranged. Koop's schedule was tightly packed, but he said he'd see me for twenty minutes if I came to his hotel and drove with him to his next appointment in Beverly Hills.

This was the first time I told my story to someone I didn't know. Never before had I told a complete stranger that my family had AIDS. Even getting dressed up in a white skirt and green sweater seemed so strange. I was stepping back into the normal world from which I felt I had been evicted. After all those weeks in the hospital, I wasn't sure where I belonged anymore.

I was getting dressed to go out. My mother would drive me downtown. I would meet the Surgeon General! I kissed Ariel good-bye. She still could not walk or talk or sit up, but she was alive. To an outsider she must have looked so sad, but to me she was always my precious daughter. I kissed Jake and gave Paul a big squeeze. My heart was pounding as I got into the car with my mother.

All I really knew about Koop was that he was a pediatric surgeon and very smart. He became my hero when he said in a special on HBO that AIDS could not be transmitted by tears or saliva. It was a huge step in teaching the public that AIDS is not spread through casual contact.

I was filled with anxiety as we walked to his car. All he knew about me was that I was a mother whose children had AIDS. When we settled into the back seat I began by saying something like, "Six years ago, after giving birth to my daughter, I hemorrhaged and was transfused with seven pints of blood. . . ."

Koop listened compassionately. Yes, he was a pediatrician and the Surgeon General but, he explained to me, he was also a parent who had lost a child. "It is the worst fraternity in the world to be in, but I understand what you are going through."

I told him that his recent statement had made a monumental difference in our lives. I said to the Surgeon General, "I don't know what I am going to do or what I can do, but I want to tell you that I am here, and if you can use me in any way behind the scenes, do." I also told him I thought I could have access to the White House.

Without even knowing it, I had learned my first Washington lesson. When I told people I might have access to the White House, I didn't realize the impact that would have. The people I spoke with saw me potentially as "a player" even if they hadn't yet decided whether or not to take me seriously.

Access to the White House impressed people—but more important, it motivated them. Maybe they thought I could make a difference. I imagine that is why the Surgeon General called Admiral Watkins and part of the reason why he saw me.

I could never have imagined our meeting going so well. Koop's understanding and compassion helped ease the tension I felt about talking about my life to outsiders.

If I had really known what I was up against, I would have been even more intimidated. Since I didn't, I left that first meeting feeling excited and optimistic.

In the next few weeks I had several more meetings. I met with a representative from Congressman Henry Waxman's office and then I met with Senator Alan Cranston. After I told my story I would say to each of them, "I don't know how I can help yet. You know more about this than I do.

What should I be doing?" They said they didn't really know but that they'd keep me in mind.

What I hadn't learned yet was that nothing happens if you wait for them to tell you what to do. Things change when you go in and say, "This is what needs to be done." But I was in process and I was learning how to talk to people about my life. Soon I would start to learn about how to try and make things better.

I also had to reiterate to each the need to keep what I had told them completely confidential. Tom Hayden was supportive as well but then asked me to testify at a hearing on AIDS. I said, "Tom, you've missed the point. No one can know who I am!"

After the meetings I would go back home and care for Ari. She was stable, but immensely compromised. After three months, we stopped giving her AZT because it wasn't doing any good. She was still in excruciating pain and now had a morphine pump as part of her technological arsenal that continually infused her with the painkiller to blunt some of her agony.

At the same time I was having these meetings, I was reading . . . *And the Band Played On.* I forced myself to pick up the book at night. As I read more and more about AIDS, I became more and more frightened about my own health. Even though I was HIV-positive and not classified as having AIDS, it was still hard to separate the two.

I was reading about people who died with T-cell levels much, much higher than mine. Each time I turned a page, I felt more vulnerable. I read about night sweats and swollen lymph nodes. I read about cancers and pneumonias. I read about diarrhea and weight loss and debilitating exhaustion. I was plunged into a world of grotesque horrors that can be the reality of AIDS.

I started to feel sick. I started to feel scared. I only had 210 T-cells—could they do the job? Finally, at page one hundred, I put the book down. I was losing more ground than I was gaining. Randy Shilts has written an important book, but I couldn't read it.

As the weeks wore on, my nursing skills kept expanding. I learned how to draw blood so I wouldn't have to take Ari to the hospital for tests. I labeled each vial and drove it to the lab at UCLA. Paul and I had mastered the TPN system, setting it up in even less than forty minutes. I had started carrying a beeper so Maria, our housekeeper, could reach me at any moment. If Ari needed me I wanted to be there and, if there was a medical emergency, wearing the beeper gave me the security of knowing that I was tethered to her every single second of the day. Even when I left the house she was with me.

We never really slept without interruption. Ari was on machines all night and even on the few nights a week when we would have a nurse come in, part of me was always listening for a cry or an alarm bell. One way or another, we were all plugged into the system.

CHAPTER
❧ 6 ❧

By mid-May of 1988, six weeks or so after my first meetings in Los Angeles, I made plans to go to Washington, D.C. I had spoken to many people and had already learned a great deal. Dick Stiehm had helped me formulate a simple and straightforward plan. I would try to get more money so there would be more pediatric clinical trial units (PCTUs as they were called).

The Surgeon General's office had made arrangements for me to see Admiral Watkins, the head of President Reagan's Commission on AIDS, as well as Dr. Tony Fauci, who controls much of the AIDS money as head of the National Institute of Allergy and Infectious Diseases (NIAID).

I had several other meetings set up on Capitol Hill and at the National Institutes of Health. I wanted to find out who was doing what, if anything, in pediatric AIDS and if there was anything I could do offstage to help. I also wanted to know if there was something on the medical horizon that might benefit Jake. I assumed that we were doing everything that could possibly be done for Ari, which was basically nothing, but since Jake was still healthy, I thought maybe there was a way to intervene early and prolong his life indefinitely. Maybe we could offer something to Jake that we had been unable to offer Ari.

Paul was getting ready to leave for Miami for preproduction on "Blue Lightning," but luckily he didn't have to leave until after I got back from Washington. That made me feel better, but leaving Ari was very difficult for me. We had never been apart during the times she was really sick. She was so compromised that I wasn't even sure she would realize I was gone. That made it both easier and harder to leave, even with Paul and my parents there.

Preparing for my departure seemed so absurd. In the bizarre reality of life, it was almost humorous to think that I was going to Washington, D.C. Truthfully, I knew I was like a tiny ant climbing a fortress wall, but I couldn't stand still. When I got ready for Washington, I put my blinders on and plowed ahead. Even if I accomplished nothing, getting out and trying to do something, however foolish it seemed, gave me strength to keep going.

As it turned out, Michael Gottlieb was going to Washington the same day I was. We took the same flight and stayed in the same hotel. Driving into Washington from Dulles Airport, I admit I was excited at being completely away from the family, though frightened to be too far away to be called in an emergency.

The beauty of the capital was enchanting. The buildings are magnificent, the avenues are wide, and the trees are lush and green.

That night, the Washington sky was ominous and untamed, and I loved it. As I stood at the front desk of the Willard Hotel, I realized that I had never checked into a hotel by myself; I had always been with Paul or a girlfriend. It was odd to even notice such a minor experience but as excited as I felt, I also felt weightless and terribly alone. I was all dressed up with someplace to go, but suddenly I didn't know what the hell I was doing there. Was I charging at windmills on a quest to nowhere? What if they didn't take me seriously?

When I walked into my room I was feeling overwhelmed and depressed. The first thing I saw was a basket of spring flowers. The card said, "Dr. Glaser, knock 'em dead. Love, Lucy and Doug." Their thoughtfulness and humor helped me find mine. I smiled and remembered I was not alone. My friends and family in L.A. were all rooting for me. I looked in the mirror and said, "Okay, Elizabeth, let's go."

I went to bed, mentally rehearsing the preparations I had made for the trip with Dr. Stiehm. I wanted to find out why there was such a delay in getting AZT out for children. I wanted to find out why the federal budget for clinical trials in pediatric AIDS was only $3.3 million, which would fund only four or five clinical trial units for the entire country. These PCTUs are the drug programs that test new drugs and are usually run at research and teaching hospitals like UCLA. At that time all three were back East. The West Coast could offer nothing to a family like mine. Dr. Stiehm felt there was a need for more PCTUs and I wanted to find out if there might be a way to expand the program.

My first meeting the next morning was with Admiral Watkins. He has the poise and bearing of a military man yet he is unpretentious and enormously warm and kind. He has a reputation for integrity, discipline, and hard work. Watkins is a conservative, but his work is uncluttered by any ideological baggage.

Polly Gault, his chief of staff, is a smart and irreverent dynamo who gets everything done with gusto. It was my first big Washington meeting and I found myself comfortable and relaxed.

When I met him, Watkins, the former chief of naval operations and member of the Joint Chiefs of Staff, had been working on the AIDS issue for a year. I was impressed with his devotion and dedication to the project. He was due to complete the commission's report in a few weeks and hand it over to the President in June.

I told him I would like to help identify the pediatric issues which would be included in his report. I offered to assist in any way I could behind the scenes and said there was a possibility of my meeting with President Reagan in the future.

James Watkins and Polly Gault told me they had interviewed many people like myself who were living with AIDS during the commission's year-long investigation. They said they would double-check to see if the issues I was talking about had been specifically addressed by the panel's research.

After the meeting I felt both good and bad. I was certainly pleased at how comfortably the meeting went, but on the other hand, if they had interviewed so many others like myself, what difference could I make?

That evening, Tim Westmoreland came over to the Willard Hotel to meet me and Michael Gottlieb. Tim works for Los Angeles congressman Henry Waxman as counsel to the

House Subcommittee on Health and the Environment. He has earned the reputation of being the most knowledgeable staff person on Capitol Hill about the AIDS epidemic. Tim has the expertise of an insider without any of the arrogance. He's been involved with the epidemic since it began and, though dedicated to turning indifference into action on AIDS, Tim informed me that no more money could be found for another sixteen months.

I looked at Tim, trying to maintain my composure as my heart pounded and my eyes filled with tears. "Tim, sixteen months from now my daughter will be dead. Nine months ago she finished kindergarten at the top of her class. Six months ago she was too sick to continue in first grade. Three months ago she stopped being able to walk and now my daughter can't sit up or even talk and you're talking to me about something that might happen sixteen months from now? My life can't fit your time frame. Tim, I'm sorry. It's inhuman." I tried to control my anger. I knew it wasn't Tim's fault, but my desperation and exasperation were out of bounds.

Tim was stunned. "I . . . I just don't think I have heard any of this before."

Michael Gottlieb was incredulous. The tension was mounting at the table. "Tim, do I understand what you are saying? You're the most knowledgeable person on Capitol Hill about AIDS and you're telling me that the things Elizabeth is telling you about pediatric clinical trials and AZT are things you've never heard before?"

Tim paused. "No one has ever talked to us about these issues before."

Michael lowered his gaze and shook his head and very softly said, "I don't believe it . . . I just don't believe it."

At that moment, I was as scared as anyone could be on her first trip to the capital. Besides trying to get extra funding, my goal in coming to Washington was to find the most competent and informed person who was speaking out on pediatric AIDS. Instead, I found there wasn't anyone. I could not believe that Tim Westmoreland was hearing about pediatric issues for the first time from me. Could it be that there was *no one* who was actively lobbying on behalf of children with AIDS? If that was true—and I had no reason to doubt that it was—then we were in big, big trouble.

No one was fighting for the children.

No one.

I felt a mantle of responsibility descend over my shoulders. It was a frightening and unforgettable moment.

When I had started meeting with people informally in Los Angeles several months before, I was hoping, at most, to be able to add momentum to an issue which was already up to speed. I wanted to find the coach of the pediatric AIDS team and say, "Hey, I'm ready to get in the game." Instead, I now found out there was no coach, no team.

I saw myself as a mom, a teacher, and a museum director from Santa Monica, California. I knew I was smart, but I had not bargained for this. How could I be the team captain when I hadn't even learned how to play the game?

I walked out of the meeting knowing it was foolish and hopeless for me to have come to Washington. As we were saying good-bye, Tim asked me to come to his office the next morning. He said he'd try to get me in to see Henry Waxman.

Thank God Michael Gottlieb was with me. We had dinner at the hotel; otherwise I would have just gone up to my room and cried myself to sleep. Though he was not new to this, Michael shared my amazement and shock. He has been fighting AIDS in the trenches since the war began in 1981. No one had to tell him how horribly wrong things were. Michael could draw a map of the battlefield with his eyes closed. I was seeing it for the first time.

The next morning, I walked over to see Tim. It was the first time I had walked around Capitol Hill since I was a child. It was as grand as anything I had ever seen. For months and months my world had been hospital, home, Ari, pain, machines, fear, secrecy, Paul and Jake.

Now I was in a new adventure. I said to myself, "Open your eyes, Elizabeth, and see the world." Walking through the rotunda and the marble halls, I noticed every other woman was serious, briefcased, and dressed in the Washington uniform of a suit with pearls and low heels. I wanted to be like them but I felt like an alien. Life still made sense for these people in a way it would never again for me. I suddenly thought of Ari back home . . . I was doing this for her. And Jake. And every other child in their situation. That was why I was here.

Tim and I chatted for a while and then he said, "Look,

you should talk to Maureen Byrnes on the Senate side. She works for Lowell Weicker on the Senate Appropriations Committee, and I think you need to meet her."

Tim picked up the phone and called Maureen. "Maureen, there's a woman in my office right now and I want you to see her. It's very important. Can you give her ten minutes?"

She said she would if we came right over so Tim rushed me down to the subway that runs beneath the Capitol between the House and Senate sides. Two years later I still love being on that subway. It has to be the best "E" ticket ride ever. It takes you from one bastion of power to another and the only scenery involved is intense and sometimes famous faces. Tim scooted me up to Maureen's office and then left.

Her office was a cubicle that resembled the small, partitioned space you would find at a travel agency. I clutched. How was I going to tell her anything and not have all the other staffers hear? What if I started to cry? What if she started to cry?

I sat down beside her and pulled my chair as close as I could. In something that was less than a voice and more than a whisper, I began by saying, "My name is Elizabeth Glaser. I'm from Los Angeles . . ."

Maureen was suddenly confronted with my life before she even had time for her second cup of coffee. I knew we only had ten minutes so I had to talk fast. "Tim says we can't get any more money into the budget for sixteen months, but it can't wait that long. There just isn't time to do things the way they've always been done."

Maureen's eyes filled with tears. "Look, I'm really glad Tim brought you over here. Let me talk to Senator Weicker about what we can do. Washington works the way it works and you happened to catch it at a time when budgets are very tight, but we'll try."

Like Tim, Maureen is part of the quiet but very bright corps that makes Washington work. These are people whose names are never known and whose pictures are never in the paper but their importance should never be minimized.

After meeting with Maureen, I went to see Barbara Masters, Senator Cranston's staff aide on health. She told me to meet her in the center of the rotunda. "How will I know you?" she asked.

I took a deep breath and, much to my embarrassment since

I grew up in New York, said, "I look like I'm from California. I have on a white skirt and green striped sweater. I look like a tourist." And I did. No one wears white in Washington before Memorial Day.

I told Barbara my story again. She said Senator Cranston would help by writing a letter to Senator Weicker supporting allocation of funds for more PCTUs. A letter didn't seem too significant to me, but I was grateful for any help I could get. When I finished, I went back to see Tim.

Tim introduced me to Henry Waxman who has been one of the original leaders on the issue of AIDS. In a very brief conversation, Henry expressed his concern and support for the issues I was raising and promised to help in any way he could. When I left his office, I had to go to the National Institutes of Health. I asked for directions, and it turned out Mrs. Waxman was going in that direction and could drop me off.

When I got in the car, even though I was determined not to, I started to cry. The day had been intense. Telling my story over and over was emotionally exhausting. I had never done it before. I closed the car door and I couldn't stop the flood of tears. Janet Waxman didn't know what to say. As I explained why I was there, I became overwhelmed by how little I felt I was accomplishing, how foolish it all seemed.

Then in the midst of my tears, she had to stop and pick up her children at school. In an instant, I had to compose myself again. I couldn't be crying in front of her children. I flicked the switch and found a smile that was not mine to put on. Janet Waxman dropped me off at NIH and I walked over for my first meeting with Dr. Phil Pizzo, filled with more emotions than I had time or energy to sort out.

Phil is the head of pediatrics at the National Cancer Institute (NCI), which is part of NIH. Dick Stiehm had felt Phil was one of the most important people I could meet with. After years of work in childhood leukemia, Phil began the first study of AIDS in children at the NIH in 1986.

I hadn't been in a hospital since Ari won her bout with pneumonia, and even though she survived that crisis, hospitals still mean more sadness to me than hope.

Riding up in the elevator, I began to sweat and fight back the tears that were rising in me. My heart was beating out of control and I felt like I was in a cage.

Dick Stiehm thought I should meet Phil Pizzo to find out

if he knew anything that might be beneficial for Jake. Phil was on the cutting edge of research in pediatric AIDS. But when I met Phil I was perplexed, because all he wanted to talk about was Ariel. After I went through the whole course of her illness, he was so persistent and thorough in his questioning that I felt like I was being cross-examined. I was getting impatient. This made no sense. It wasn't why I had come.

I finally said to him, "Dr. Pizzo, I appreciate your interest in my daughter's case, but I didn't come here today to talk about that. I have accepted her situation. I'm here to talk about my son. I want to know what we can do differently for Jake so he doesn't have to suffer like his sister."

"But if you could get something for Ariel, something more, what would you want?"

"I would want something that would improve the quality of her life. Even if it were only that much," and I held my fingers apart a tiny bit. "But I know there is nothing that will help."

Phil paused. He was calm and deliberate. I looked for a clue in his dark brown eyes to his baffling insistence on focusing only on Ariel. Slowly and quietly he said, "We are using AZT intravenously here in a study and we are having some very unusual and positive results."

I was so surprised, it was hard to even breathe. There wasn't a sound in the office. In the softest voice I ever heard come out of my mouth I asked, "Do you think it's worth trying it on Ariel? Her brain is completely atrophied and I don't want to put her through anything unnecessarily."

I waited. My whole body was in suspense.

"I think it is worth a shot," said Phil.

"For how long?"

"Try it for four weeks. If there will be any improvement, you'll see it by then. If there is no change, then quit." There was a long pause until he said, "But I wouldn't give up yet."

My heart was racing. "But what does that really mean?" I was stunned by this development. "If she gets pneumonia in the next four weeks, do we put her on life support systems?"

"Yes. During the next four weeks, do everything you can to keep her alive."

This was not what I expected to hear. My head was spinning. Was there actually something we could have been doing for Ari that we were not? The AZT she had taken orally had no impact on her whatsoever. But Phil said there was a possibility that she hadn't absorbed any of it because her digestive system was so impaired. She wouldn't have to swallow intravenous AZT, and that might make a difference.

He looked at me intently. "I will do everything I can to get you this drug, but we don't control it. Burroughs Wellcome controls it."

I knew what he was saying. Burroughs Wellcome is the drug company that manufactures AZT, and it had come under increasingly harsh criticism from AIDS activists and PWAs (Persons With AIDS) regarding the availability of the drug as well as its price, which many believed was grossly inflated for larger profit margins. Burroughs Wellcome controlled the drug and called the shots, and it was a very powerful company.

So far, the trip to Washington had felt like a failure. I was flattened with fatigue and thought I had accomplished nothing. But quite unexpectedly, Phil Pizzo was offering me hope. It didn't come as an appeasement or guarantee, but as a sincerity I could trust. When I left his office, I felt an excitement so intense that it almost made me shake. I was afraid to hope again.

There was still one more meeting before my day was over. I was scheduled to see Dr. Tony Fauci at the National Institute of Allergy and Infectious Diseases (NIAID).

This was a crucial meeting. Tony Fauci was the closest thing the country had to an AIDS czar. Phil walked me over to Fauci's office and we began immediately because he was expecting a television crew to show up shortly for an interview.

I asked him if he felt more clinical trials were needed in pediatrics and he seemed ambivalent. I said, "But tell me, what do you really think? I can't go around asking for more if you don't think you really want them." NIAID was in charge of the PCTUs and he ran NIAID.

Fauci didn't give me any answers. In that first meeting, he was cool, remote, and ambiguous. I don't remember much of what he said because I don't think he said much of anything. He seemed to avoid answering my questions directly, and I hadn't yet learned how to politely demand an answer.

I had hoped Tony Fauci would say, "Great. Here are the problems we need you to fight for us." But he didn't. So I struggled to remember whom I was fighting for. The truth was I couldn't tell if anyone really cared. Was I making these problems up? No one else seemed very bothered by them. Was I blowing everything out of proportion? Impossible. I had lived with these problems. I was fighting for myself and all the other mothers of children with HIV or AIDS. It didn't matter what anyone else said or thought. The only important question was: What's the next step?

I had dinner that night with Rita Braver and Bob Barnett, friends I had not seen for twenty years. Rita covers the Justice Department for CBS News and her husband, Bob, is a lawyer. I had known Rita at the University of Wisconsin, and we had not seen each other since college. When I was pregnant with Ari and confined to bed, I watched a lot of television. That was when I discovered Rita again on CBS.

We all met at The Palm. I ordered an extra dry martini with two olives. I needed that drink and savored every sip. We raised our glasses and said how wonderful we all looked and how great it was to be together.

I hadn't decided if I would tell Rita and Bob anything, but as dinner went on it became increasingly difficult. Simple questions like, "Why are you in Washington?" were hard to answer. Whenever Rita tried to steer the conversation to my family, I steered it away. Rita was too good a journalist not to be curious about what I wasn't saying.

Midway through the meal, when Bob had to make a long business call, she turned to me and said, "Look, I don't know why you are out here, and I don't want to pry, but if you would like to tell me, I'd love to know. If you don't, let's just keep talking about who's who and what's what."

It was tempting. I said, "Rita, I really want to tell you this, but I know our relationship will never be the same. Part of me thought it would be great to have one last night together just like old times. I want you to know right up front that this is going to be really awful. I am living everybody's nightmare." For the final time that day I told my story and for the final time I cried.

When I flew home the next day, I knew I had changed nothing. It hit me with full impact and I sat on the plane weeping as all the feelings I had kept inside while telling my story over and over in Washington came spilling out. I had spoken about my life to more strangers than ever before and I was emotionally drained.

Something had to be done, but I didn't know what it was or how to do it. The bureaucracy seemed so monumental and so monumentally slow-moving. In my naiveté, I had hoped people would say, "Oh, yes, we see, here is the problem. We'll take care of it for you, and thank you so much for bringing it to our attention." I realized that even if the government did care, it would probably never move quickly enough to help my family.

In my heart, it was hard for me to imagine how intravenous AZT could possibly make any difference at all in Ariel's condition. I was reluctant to open my door of hope, only to have it slammed shut once again.

My enormous frustration with the Washington bureaucracy was matched by the anger that was beginning to churn up inside me about Dr. Stiehm. I had trusted Dick Stiehm with the life of my child. I relied on him day and night. I could not understand why he hadn't suggested that we try intravenous AZT on Ari. I felt that there was no answer that made sense. If he didn't know about it, he had failed as a doctor, and if he knew and didn't offer it to us, he had failed as our physician. I was growing to love Dick Stiehm and I couldn't understand what had happened. Over and over, I had told him that as long as there was hope, we would keep fighting. I thought we had tried everything there was to try.

The next day I stormed in to see him. I was trying to control my feelings until I heard his explanation, but it didn't work very well.

"Dr. Stiehm, why haven't you told me about intravenous AZT? Phil Pizzo at NIH said they've had success with it there. Ariel has a broviac so she's all set up. All we'd have to do is give it to her! I can't believe that you would let us down!"

His face was expressionless. He said evenly and without emotion, "Elizabeth, I have tried to get intravenous AZT for four other families and Burroughs Wellcome has turned me down every time. How could I offer you a drug that I knew I couldn't get for you?"

I was enraged. "I do not fucking believe this! You are telling me that there is something that may help her and the drug company won't let us use it?!"

"Do you want me to try and get the drug for Ariel?"

"No!" I said. "You've been turned down four times already and there is no reason why they won't turn you down again. I will get this drug."

The next morning I got on the phone and called Tim Westmoreland. I had only met Tim two days before but I didn't know where else to begin.

I said, "Tim, I have a problem and I need you to help solve it. I want to get intravenous AZT for Ariel and her doctor said he's been turned down every time he's tried to get it for other families. Dr. Pizzo says she should have it and he'll do everything he can to help me get it. What should I do?"

Tim was quick. He said, "Call this man, he is the government relations person for Burroughs Wellcome. No, better yet, have Dr. Stiehm call him. If he doesn't help you, call me back."

My fingers flew over the numbers on the telephone. When Dick came on the line I said, "I have the name of the man at the drug company that you should speak to. Here's his number. Call him and see what happens." I hadn't met with that many people at this point, but already I was learning how to make things happen and was speaking with a conviction I lacked even one week earlier.

Calm and steadfast to the core, Dick got on the phone with the man from Burroughs Wellcome. "We want intravenous AZT for this family," Dick demanded.

The man said no.

Slowly and directly, like a stern parent, Stiehm said, "I think you had better reconsider. If you say no to me, I promise you Henry Waxman is going to call. And if you say no to Henry Waxman, I promise you Alan Cranston is going to call. And if you say no to Senator Cranston, I promise you in the end, the President of the United States is going to call you to get intravenous AZT for this family. This mother is not going to take no for an answer and you are going to save yourself a lot of time and energy if you just approve it right now."

Twenty-four hours later, the drug arrived. If they have to, bureaucracies can move fast.

The reason intravenous AZT is not expected to have widespread use within the general population is that it must be administered through a surgically implanted catheter. To be effective, the AZT must be continually infused.

There was a reason why the man said no. I'm sure it made perfect sense to him and all the people at the drug companies and the FDA. They can't let a drug be used outside of trials because they need the people to enroll to get the necessary information. But to a mother who is losing her child it made no sense at all. There is hope and you can't have it. Something may help my child to live and they won't give it to me. Ari's quality of life could be improved, but rules and regulations stood in the way.

I sat in my den, relieved that we had succeeded and furious at the inhumanity of a system that cared more about rules than lives. Did I love my child any more than the mother in Harlem, Miami, or Newark loved her child? Absolutely not. Did Ari deserve a chance any more than their children? No. Every child with AIDS deserves a chance. Were threats of presidential calls what galvanized action rather than compassion?

It seemed that no one really cared about people with AIDS. Our lives were expendable. If AIDS had struck white middle-class and heterosexual Americans, I firmly believe the epidemic would have been handled differently. But gays and drug users, blacks and Chicanos and poor whites? Were they written off as people we would never miss? Whose decision was this?

There in my den I realized my country was failing me. The compassion as well as the moral and ethical foundations of our society were being tested, and from my point of view, America was failing.

I had been brought up to care about others. I was raised to be compassionate every day, not at photo ops every four years. As part of a family struggling with AIDS I learned that few wanted to help enough to change a system that had become strangled by red tape. The ones who tried were often ignored because AIDS was something the Reagan administration refused to deal with. Someone had to care enough to be willing to shake things up, but I didn't know who it would be.

We started Ari on the intravenous AZT the day we got it. Paul and I had to learn more nursing skills, but that was no longer hard. AZT is a toxic drug. It was dangerous to her white blood count and bone marrow so they both had to be monitored closely. We counted days, one at a time, not expecting immediate developments since Phil Pizzo had warned it would take between three and four weeks to see signs of improvement. We waited. Nothing happened. Ariel still looked like a wisp of life. She could open her eyes and was able to communicate by blinking. I would say, "Ari, I love you so much." She would look at me as if she wanted to speak and I told her, "You can just blink your eyes to let me know you love me, honey," and she would blink.

The pain was still monumental for her at times. The screams would move in silent contortions across her face and her body. It was as bad to see them as it had been to hear them.

Two weeks went by and still nothing had happened. I called Phil. He said, "Keep waiting. Don't give up."

Three weeks to the day after we started intravenous AZT I walked into Ariel's room in the morning and she looked up and said, "Good morning, Mom. I love you."

She hadn't talked in three months! I could hardly believe it. Ari was back! The sky had opened up. I couldn't contain my joy. I ran to her and almost shouted, "I love you too, Ari! I love hearing your voice!"

It was the miracle we had been waiting for. I was shaking as I unhooked her feeding tubes. I tried to stay calm so I wouldn't upset her. When I was done I said, "Ari, wait here a minute, I'll be right back." I had to find Paul. I felt like I was running as I went down the hall to our bedroom.

My eyes were moist and as full as the moon. My mouth started to quiver. "What's wrong?" Paul said.

"She just said, 'I love you, Mom!' Honey, she talked!" I sat on the bed settling down before I went back to see her, while Paul took off down the hall.

Paul walked in and she said, "Hi, Dad." He sat down on her bed and he looked into her blue eyes and lost himself briefly there. Maybe miracles did happen. Maybe one was going to happen in our house.

When Paul and I were finally alone together, we hugged each other and cried.

Every day she steadily improved, being able to do more and more without help. It was as if the intravenous AZT was restoring her brain and bringing her back to life. Ari's friends who had continued to visit all along were also overjoyed once the AZT started to take effect. We were all on Ari's team, cheering her on.

She continued to improve over the next six weeks. At first she didn't fall down as much when she sat up, and we didn't have to use so many pillows to prop her up. Then one day she was able to sit up by herself. We were going through years of developmental milestones in a few weeks. A few days later she asked to hold a marking pen.

These achievements were nothing less than miraculous. I remember how joyous she felt when she found she could hold a paintbrush and make a picture. She then wanted to try to write her name. She slowly made an A, followed by the rest of the letters. She asked to spell other words, and we began to practice.

One day she felt strong enough to try to stand up, and Paul and I coached her, saying, "Lift your leg now and put it down." The next day she could take several steps and said she could do it by herself. Ari even asked if she could go swimming. We unhooked her from all her machines and took her in the pool. She wanted to show Jake how she could go underwater, because that was something he was still unable to do.

To see Ariel feel so proud as she showed Jake something that she could do but he couldn't was a great gift, both for me and for Jake, who idolized his sister.

One day when her friend Amy came over, Ari walked by herself for the first time, from the kitchen all the way across the dining room to the hallway. What a thrill!

We were all screaming, "Ari, this is fantastic! You are so terrific!" The intravenous AZT was unwinding Ari's cocoon of paralysis, and her six-year-old self was still underneath. Ari was proud and so were we. None of us had given up.

The whole world had started spinning again. We were all coming back to life with Ari. Ariel could talk! I knew she would be the miracle the doctors wanted. In March we were told to prepare for a funeral, and by May we had a shot at second grade.

Ari was going to make it. If Ari could make it, we were all going to make it. She was improvir̥g so steadily that she might even be able to go back to schoo Phil Pizzo later told me he had seen children as compromised as Ari return to their classrooms. After six months of intravenous AZT, the IQs of healthy children in his study increased by an average of fifteen points.

Phil had seen such spectacular results in other children at the National Cancer Institute but he had no way of knowing if the intravenous AZT would have a similar impact on Ari so he hadn't told us what might happen.

Ariel was eager to read again and we got out her first-grade book about the bears and she read it, word by word. We were exuberantly happy.

We were all accustomed to living in the moment, and once Ari was able to talk again, we never discussed how hard the past had been. The focus was always on what we could do, and now, anything seemed possible.

Ari took great delight in being able to draw with Paul again. They would make a picture and then another and then another. She was eager to do math and practice the alphabet. She wanted to write her name over and over. She wanted to go to the market and we did. She wanted to go for a ride in the car so we went to Lynn's house.

When we went on our nature walks we still used the stroller because Ari couldn't walk very far. But now, she was able to say, "Get me that flower!" We picked a lot of wildflowers and came back and pressed them to make pictures.

We still had to feed Ari intravenously, but she was able to begin eating a few things on her own. I remember going back to UCLA for a test and Laurie Reyen, the nurse who had taught us the TPN procedure, came by to say hello. Ariel was sitting in a chair and munching and crunching her way through a bag of Cheetos. We were all excited. A Cheeto was giving us goose bumps.

CHAPTER
❧ 7 ❧

The excitement I felt about Ari's progress renewed my determination to meet with President Reagan. A few weeks into Ari's comeback, I met Doug Wick for lunch to discuss the Reagan meeting. Doug was in the midst of producing *Working Girl* and spending most of his time back East where the movie was to be filmed. Lucy had asked him about the Reagans and he had agreed to approach them. Now it was my turn to follow through.

Doug has known the Reagans since he was a child. The two families always spent Christmas Eve and Christmas together, a tradition that continued throughout the presidency.

When I first approached Doug he was probably a little irritated. I guess it seemed almost arrogant to think I could make a difference. But the stakes were so high, he couldn't say no.

After we ordered our lunch, Doug said, "Elizabeth, you know everyone wants to get in to see the President."

At that moment, the reality of what I was trying to do set in. I realized that even for Doug, it was a big deal to ask for the meeting.

"Think about it this way," I said. "I'm a white heterosexual woman from their socioeconomic class and from Hollywood. Many people still think of AIDS as God's punishment for homosexuals. Even if the President doesn't believe that, there are still many political people who are not paying any attention to the epidemic. Maybe, just maybe, I can help change their views."

"One of the nice things about my friendship with the Reagans," said Doug, "is that I have never asked them for anything." He then told me about how he had turned down other friends who tried to use him to approach the President.

But by the end of lunch, Doug agreed to at least try. He said he would talk to his parents and find out the best way to proceed.

The meeting was now in Doug's hands, but I was on edge for the next few days. Every time the phone rang I thought it might be the call from Doug. Finally, three days later, he got through to Nancy Reagan in Canada where the President was attending an economic summit. Doug told Mrs. Reagan the essence of my story and asked if he could bring me to Washington to meet with both her and the President. Mrs. Reagan said she would check the schedule when she returned home and get right back to him. Doug called me and relayed the information. I held my breath a little bit longer.

Doug didn't want to get too excited. He thought if we were lucky we'd get the "fifteen-minute, shake hands, snap your photo" meeting in the Oval Office, one of a steady stream of people presidents have to meet every day. It would have been hard to have any impact in that setting.

And then it happened. Mrs. Reagan called Doug on Tuesday, June 21, and said she and the President could meet with us that Saturday at two P.M. Doug phoned me.

It was set for Saturday. It would not be in the Oval Office, but rather in the "family quarters." There would be no real time limitation. The meeting would certainly be more than fifteen minutes. I could already sense possibilities far beyond those I had imagined. I would go in. I would talk to the President, and maybe I would make a difference.

I was incredulous. As hard as I thought about it, as much as I had dreamed about it, I don't think I ever *really* saw myself talking with the President. It was only a few weeks after Ariel's stunning reversal from the intravenous AZT. I felt like a comet streaking across the sky.

One of the first calls I made was to Admiral Watkins. "I've got the meeting with the President! How should I handle it?" As it turned out, I was meeting with the Reagans on Saturday and Admiral Watkins was going to present his commission's report to the President on Monday. The timing could not have been better.

The report pulled no punches. It said there had been a "distinct lack of leadership" from the federal government. With nearly six hundred specific suggestions, the report was a step-by-step battle plan for fighting the epidemic and improving the nation's health care system so it could cope with AIDS in the decades ahead. The commission's report lashed out at discrimination, calling it the "greatest single barrier" to overcome in fighting AIDS, and urged massive federal antidiscrimination legislation.

Admiral Watkins had done his job well; now it was time for me to do mine. I knew in my head that to save my child, I had to get President Reagan to take the aggressive leadership role that the AIDS epidemic demanded.

I didn't know if my story would move him, but I thought if I could personalize the epidemic for him in some way, as Rock Hudson's death had, it might make a difference. I didn't really care about what Reagan had or hadn't done in the past. I had a chance of changing tomorrow. He was the President. I was getting my shot.

I flew into Washington on Friday night. The adrenaline was racing inside me. I was going to see the Reagans the next afternoon, just twelve days after my daughter had spoken for the first time in three months.

I met Rita for dinner at Nathan's, a longtime Washington watering hole which is just down the street from the Georgetown Inn.

Rita and I were brainstorming about what I should say to the President. Then she said, "Wait a minute . . . CBS ran a spot tonight on the news that said the Reagan administration was not going to pay any attention to the Watkins report."

"Rita, you've got to be more specific. I have to know exactly what was said before I meet with the President! I don't want to look foolish and not know if he's already made some decisions about the report."

Rita excused herself for a moment. All of a sudden she came back and said, "Come with me." Bill Plante, the White House correspondent who had done the spot on the commission's report, was eating dinner at another table in the restaurant.

Rita took me over there and introduced me as Betsy Meyer, her old friend from college. We casually asked Bill about his spot in the show. He said that although nothing specific had happened, the general feeling around the White House was that the administration was not planning to pay any attention to the report after it was released on Monday.

I sighed. At that moment, the mountain I was climbing doubled in size. I knew the Reagan administration had been extremely irresponsible in dealing with the AIDS epidemic. Even if the President didn't want to listen to gays or drug users, I was certain he would pay attention to his own commission's report. After all, James Watkins was an admiral, an insider, and a military man with impeccable credentials. How could the administration spend all that money investigating the AIDS epidemic for a year and then ignore the report that stated what needed to be done? Maybe he would feel differently after our meeting.

As I walked out of the restaurant with Rita, I thought that if I had a normal, healthy life, there is nowhere else I would rather live than in Washington, D.C. I was talking to Rita about a piece on the news and there was the correspondent who had reported it.

Rita came back to the hotel with me and I tried to outline what I was going to say to the President the next day. I wasn't going to write anything down, but I wanted to practice enough so I didn't blow it.

As the morning progressed, I became increasingly anxious. In my mind, there was so much riding on this meeting. If President Reagan accepted the leadership role I would ask him to take on, many things could change. With just a few words from him, slow-moving government wheels could be oiled and speeded up. This, in turn, could bring more money, quicker answers, and hope for people like me and my children.

If the President actually said, "We can't discriminate against people with AIDS or with HIV," the world would be a better place. I felt that if I could get the Reagans to care about me and my family, the rest was possible. If not, we would sink even deeper.

Doug met me at the Georgetown Inn at noon. Over lunch we talked about Ronald Reagan. We knew we would have a limited amount of time and that we had to capture and hold his attention.

"Every group in the world tries to get the ear of the President. I know that much about Washington," Doug told me. "They all have good causes and amazing stories. It's tricky to be remembered when you are only lobbing it in for fifteen minutes. We need to focus on a way to be remembered."

Doug and I both knew that Reagan loves anecdotes and he really understands sports. I thought maybe there was a way to encapsulate part of my story in a sports metaphor. I thought of a baseball metaphor, and Doug and I worked it out together.

After lunch we went back up to my room as I tried to compose myself worrying about which of two blouses to wear. I was too anxious and everything seemed important.

Blond, handsome, and classy, Doug looks like a surfer who went to Princeton. We were downstairs when the small black government sedan pulled up in front of the hotel. The driver asked, "Mr. Wick?" We were off.

I was excited. I knew it was paradoxical. Here I was, for all the worst reasons in the world, going to the White House to meet the President. My cheeks were hot and the adrenaline was racing through me like a brush fire.

As we pulled up to the entrance, right under the Truman balcony, a butler opened the car door and once again it was "Mr. Wick?" We walked into a room with a very large Oriental rug, table, and straight-backed chairs. We sat down and waited. My heart was pounding in my ears.

We waited a few more minutes, but it felt like a week. Then the butler came again and said, "The President and First Lady are waiting for you. Come this way."

We walked down the hall, passed the presidential portraits and then through some doors. All of a sudden we were in the midst of a hallway in the working White House, as busy and noisy as a cafeteria. At the end of the hallway there was a small elevator operated by a man who said, "Oh, Mr. Wick, so glad to see you."

When the elevator door opened again, there were President and Mrs. Reagan. Their dog, Lucky, was yapping and scampering at our feet. Nancy said, "Hi, Doug," and gave him a hug. He said, "This is my friend, Elizabeth."

As we walked down a short hallway toward the living

room, I was with Mrs. Reagan and Lucky, who was a perfect distraction. He was jumping up and down like a pogo stick, which gave us something easy to talk about and diminished my tension.

I had seen the President so many times on television that he did not seem larger than life to me. He seemed genuine and straightforward, and I began to feel slightly more relaxed.

The President sat in an easy chair beside the sofa and Nancy sat me right next to him on the couch, with Doug next to me. Nancy sat down beside Doug. After a minute or two, Doug, in his inimitable way, said, "Let's cut to the chase. Elizabeth is here to talk to you about something really important. I want her to have as much time as possible, so why don't we begin?"

I took a deep breath—I always have to take that deep breath before I start. I began by saying, "My life is very complicated, and I am here because I am hoping that you can help . . ."

I told the story of the past seven years concisely, because Doug and I didn't expect to have more than fifteen minutes of the President's real attention. I ended by saying that for months, Ariel had been unable to talk or walk, but that twelve days before, when I walked into her bedroom, she opened her eyes and said, "Good morning, Mom. I love you."

Both of them had tears in their eyes. We all did. There was hope. We just had to grab it.

Nancy said softly that her mother always used to say that we all get dealt a hand of cards in our lives and we play them out as best we can. I told her that was an analogy I had used many times in my life, wanting her to know that sometimes I thought like she did. Then the President asked a few questions. I felt that the Reagans were comfortable with me, and later Doug would agree.

Doug and I had talked about whether I should mention the issue of children attending school, which was still quite controversial. But I had the President's attention and I wanted to make the biggest impact on him that I could, so I talked about how dreadful the discrimination has been for many children as well as adults. I also emphasized that you can't get AIDS from casual contact. Then as we sat and talked, Nancy Reagan said to me, "How is it for your husband?"

"It's horrible. It has been very difficult for Paul, but he has been remarkable. He is our hero and he has stood by us."

Then she said, "What is your relationship with him?"

I blinked and wondered, *Relationship? What does she mean? Is this woman asking me about my sex life?*

I thought, *This is an administration that won't use the word condom. If I answer this question inappropriately, I may throw away the whole meeting, but if I don't answer it, I may seem rude.*

So I leaned forward and rather quietly said, "I'm not exactly sure what you are asking me. Could you please be more specific?"

Mrs. Reagan said, "I'm asking about your relationship."

I made a judgment call. "Are you asking me about my sex life?"

"Yes," she said.

I thought intensely about my answer and then replied, "Well, my husband and I continue to have a sexual relationship but we take the precautions that our doctors recommend. My husband kisses me and touches me and he is really quite wonderful."

I think Mrs. Reagan asked that because she felt genuinely empathetic and involved and was wondering what it would be like to be me. How do you live? How do you have a marriage? My choice was to answer her honestly because I knew if the Reagans were going to take a more active role in the AIDS epidemic, then they needed to know that my husband was not afraid of me, my kisses, or my sexuality.

Because I came from a world the Reagans had been part of, I knew it was probably easier for Nancy Reagan to relate to me than to some other women with AIDS. So I had spoken candidly to her about sex and intimacy, not something I would normally do with someone I don't know well. I wanted to underscore to the Reagans that this was a disease that wasn't transmitted through intimacy if people were willing to use condoms, and that people with AIDS don't have to be ostracized. Scientists and doctors will wage war against the virus but it's up to all the rest of us to fight fear and discrimination.

As I was concluding, I said to the President, "Let me tell

you a story. It's like this. There is a baseball team, and the baseball team, our team, has the most incredible players in the world: doctors, scientists, thinkers, and ordinary people, too. But we are up against the toughest team we could ever be pitted against. Those of us on the team are fighting really, really hard.

"Jake could get up to bat and he could hit a good hit, Mr. President. He could get to second base. And Ari, I never thought Ari could even play on the team, but you know what, Mr. President? Ari could make a little hit and she would hobble, with all of her strength, to first base.

"Mr. President," I said, "we need someone to bring my kids home. I need you to hit that home run and bring my kids across the plate. We have the brightest doctors, we have the most powerful people, we can win this game, but we need a leader. We need a team captain. We need our government to commit its resources now."

As I told the story, the President's eyes were riveted on mine.

When I finished, he said, "Tell me what you want me to do."

"I want you to do two things. I want you to be a *leader* in the struggle against AIDS so that my children, and all children, can go to school and continue to live valuable lives, so that no one with AIDS need worry about discrimination.

"Secondly, you have commissioned a report on the epidemic that's been written by a phenomenal man. I ask you to pay attention to that report."

President Reagan looked at me and said, "I promise you that I will read that report with different eyes than I would have before."

As we were walking back to the elevator, the Reagans talked wistfully about how sad it was for them to be preparing to leave the White House. I was tempted to ask them if I could see the rest of the mansion, but I knew I could not suddenly turn into Elizabeth Glaser, tourist.

It was over. They hugged me and we said good-bye.

Doug and I had not been there for twenty minutes—we had been there for an hour. It had been very intense. The Reagans had paid close attention. I felt encouraged and proud.

We walked down Pennsylvania Avenue because we were

both too excited to take a cab. Doug said, "Elizabeth, this was amazing. I have known this man my whole life. He responded to you. He said things to you that weren't idle at all. He doesn't need to say he is going to view the Watkins Commission report with different eyes; that's not something I ever expected him to say. This was far better than I ever imagined. You could tell from the questions he was asking that this was something he thought someone should do something about."

We walked back to the Georgetown Inn. I could not stop talking about the meeting. We passed a photographer with life-size cutouts of Ronald and Nancy Reagan. I almost stopped to have my picture taken, but it seemed silly. I was glad the Reagans hadn't had a photographer there. That made it a more serious meeting. Now I wish I had taken the picture on the street so I could see the smile that had turned my face inside out.

When I got back to the hotel, I called Paul, but he was out, so I called Susan De Laurentis. My feet had curled up in an awful cramp, probably from walking in high heels rather than sneakers, so I talked to her from the edge of the tub, with cold water running over my toes, recounting every moment step by step.

I also called Rita. I told her it felt like a major breakthrough that the Reagans hugged me after the meeting. I had thought they might feel people with HIV were untouchables, so the hug was significant to me.

I also called Admiral Watkins. When I told him what I'd said about the report he said, "Elizabeth, you're the only person who could have done it. I am going in to present it to him Monday morning and I will call you immediately afterwards."

Then Doug and I got on a plane and flew home. When I got back, I asked Ari to make a picture for the President and included a thank-you note that said this was one of the first times she had been able to draw a picture and write her name in months.

Monday came and I was anxious. When Admiral Watkins finally called me it was already four o'clock in the East. I had been worrying all day.

I picked up the phone and I could hear the excitement in his voice. "You did it," he told me. "You did what no one else could have done. I walked into that meeting and the President spent the first ten minutes talking about you. He didn't use your name, of course, or do anything that would jeopardize your confidentiality, but he said he had met with a woman who had shared her story and her situation and that it had moved him greatly. I think you put us over the hump." Watkins was ecstatic. We were convinced that we were on the threshold of major and significant political change.

We were wrong. . . . Time went by and nothing happened. It was almost unimaginable, but the White House took the report and put it on the shelf. Hope for thousands of Americans and people around the world sat gathering dust in some forgotten corner of some forgotten room.

I was with President Reagan for an hour. I know his commitment was genuine and his intentions sincere, but the decision not to act wasted more precious time. Each step of the way when nothing was done, thousands more people became ill or died. I looked at my country, my government, and the only conclusion to draw was that they still just didn't care.

I don't know what happened. Something went wrong. I suspect it was the people around the President, his top aides, who decided the report was just too much to take on in the final months of the administration. Maybe someone felt that with the Republican National Convention just a few weeks away, AIDS was still too controversial an issue to tackle vigorously because it would be so alarming to the GOP's conservative constituency.

In their eyes, political positioning must have been more important than the lives of men, women, and children. It's a common priority in America today, but one that has lost touch with humanity. Many people's lives are compromised so that someone can either get to or stay in the White House. It's just fine when you're the strategist, but when it's your life on the line, it's unacceptable.

The bottom line is that *nothing* changed. But I didn't realize it right away and for those first few weeks back in Los Angeles, I felt radiantly and spectacularly alive.

I'm not a great intellect or a great beauty. My strength has always been in my *joie de vivre.* I love being alive. And briefly that spring it seemed like a feeling I could finally hold onto for a while.

And then something else extraordinary happened. There

was good news in a call from Maureen Byrnes. Senator Lowell Weicker had gotten committee support for an additional nine million dollars for pediatric AIDS into the 1989 budget. That meant there would be enough for eight new pediatric clinical trial units immediately.

I was elated. My first trip to Washington hadn't been a waste at all. Maybe my efforts *could* make a real difference.

Paul had been in Miami off and on for two months while working on "Blue Lightning." We were preparing to move there when the writers' strike began and the film was shut down. It was upsetting to Paul and to me, but in retrospect it was a blessing because we were all together at a time when we needed to be.

In the weeks after my trip to see the President, I sensed that there might be a role for a private foundation to play in raising money to fund basic biomedical pediatric AIDS research. Sixty thousand dollars is all it takes to fund a researcher for an entire year. Many people in L.A. spend more than that on their cars. So it seemed logical enough to assume that if a few million dollars were raised and spun around immediately into research, we might find answers faster and accomplish something while waiting for the influx of government monies.

In my Government 101 course on the way Washington works, I had learned that once money is appropriated, it still takes eighteen months to two years before it gets to where it's going. It only took a firm grasp of the obvious to know that the government was not capable of moving fast enough to make a difference for children who had AIDS now. Plus, from my point of view, there was no guarantee they'd do the right thing anyway. I asked Paul what he thought about the foundation concept, but by then he was just letting me run with my ideas. "Fine," he said.

I knew the idea would only work if I could find people to help me do it. The job was too big for one individual and I could never put my name on the letterhead of an AIDS organization. After working so hard to keep our secret, that would certainly have blown it.

I talked about the idea with two of my closest friends. First I approached Susan De Laurentis, Francesca's mom, and a friend for the last five years. Susan and I had met at the swingset on the first day of nursery school. Francesca had been Ari's first "best friend." I had always felt Susan was unique, bright, and highly motivated. Equally as important, she was fun. She had worked in retailing before her children were born. Everything we did together was a pleasure and I was sure working together would be equally as satisfying. She said she would think about my idea. I said I'd ask one other person to be part of the foundation so no one would carry too much responsibility.

I spoke next with Susie Zeegen. Susie had been a devoted friend and by my side during my complicated pregnancy with Ariel. She had made many trips to my house when I was in bed, and not a single day passed in which she didn't call. Throughout our struggle against AIDS, her loyalty had been unwavering, and her cheerfulness sustaining. Susie has a master's degree in child development and now that her children were older, she had more time to spare. Susie wanted to think about it, too. Although both were close friends of mine, Susie and Susan had never met each other.

I also spoke with Michael Gottlieb. I wanted to know what he thought it would take to fund a significant amount of pediatric AIDS research. He came up with a figure of $250,000, and said that if we raised it, he thought AMFAR could distribute it. That way we wouldn't have to reinvent the wheel.

Washington had proved to me that people were moved by my story. I was hoping that I might be able to use it to fundraise as well. The downside was that I'd have to tell an even larger number of people. Paul and I still both felt it was vitally important to keep our identity private.

We weren't really frightened for ourselves. As adults, Paul and I could handle whatever came our way, and the truth was most people weren't afraid of me or Paul. The fear was the school and social realities for Jake. Even though a school has a policy on HIV in place, it doesn't mean the parents will welcome you with open arms. After the struggle we had had with Ari's friends, the last thing I wanted was to have to go through all that again with Jake's peers.

The parents of Jake's best friend, Tommy, knew, as did the parents of Louie, his other close friend. That was it. Our friends and the school administrators thought the community would respond well, but there were no guarantees as Paul and I knew all too well. So in order to protect Jake's childhood, we continued to guard our secret like Fort Knox.

I couldn't raise money publicly. I knew I would have to do it quietly behind the scenes, which meant I would have to get a few big donations rather than dozens of small ones. I remembered Josh's advice to think big.

Susan and Susie turned out to be the best friends I could have wished for. They met each other, talked it over with their husbands, and we all decided to move ahead whole-heartedly. None of us knew exactly what we were getting into. We knew it was work that was both essential and mean-ingful, and we thought that with three of us we'd be able to do it part-time. Without any further deliberation, we got going.

CHAPTER
❧ 8 ❧

It was early July during the summer of 1988. Ari had started to read again from the book that Joanie Green, the elementary director at Crossroads, had used to tutor her. Joanie stopped tutoring Ari when she became too sick, but never stopped coming over to visit. I got on the phone and called her. "Ari's reading!" She came right over.

It was one of those miraculous Los Angeles days when the sun, air, sky, and sea all seem perfect. It was a day that demanded that you be outside so, on the spur of the moment, I asked Ari if she would like to go down to the Santa Monica pier which has rides and a honky-tonk amusement arcade with cotton candy and stuffed animals for prizes. Ari was doing so well and she loved the pier. We invited Joanie to come along, too.

Ari was still in a great deal of pain. The AZT was reclaiming her central nervous system, but it wasn't curing AIDS nor removing the painful stomach complications she suffered from. Getting Ari into the car was always difficult. That day, as every day, we gritted our teeth and plowed ahead. Joanie sat in the back seat, in obvious agony at just being able to observe and unable to help. But Ari and I were used to this. I would just pick her up, put her in the seat in the car, and keep moving. Neither of us spent too much time focusing on the hard parts.

That day, Francesca was also at the pier. There was a huge Ferris wheel that was set up in the parking lot by the ocean. Ari adored the Ferris wheel and wanted to go, but Francesca was too afraid.

For the first time in months, Ari was ready, willing, and able to do something that Francesca was afraid to do. It made Ari feel triumphant. Here was Ari, who had been so dreadfully sick, braver and stronger than even her best friend, Francesca. When Francesca saw that Ari was going to ride the Ferris wheel, she decided to go too. It was a great moment for them both.

So Ari and I went on the Ferris wheel together, around and around, waving wildly, queens of the sky and sea. For a moment, I was experiencing the thrilling, unadulterated joy of just being a mom. It was as if the whole world had been unveiled again as I came spinning over and around on the Ferris wheel.

Though I didn't know it at the time, that day on the pier was Ari's last hurrah. Maybe there was something about Ariel that knew this was the last day that she was really going to get to be a little girl. She was going to taste the potato chips and the french fries and ride high and around in the sun on the Ferris wheel and spin to the music of the carousel. I think she knew all this but bravely kept it buttoned up inside.

Two weeks later Ari was readmitted to UCLA hospital. Her white blood count had fallen too low and we had to take her off the intravenous AZT. She was having fevers that we couldn't break. But I never gave up hope and persistently believed that this was just another crisis that we would have to somehow survive.

I have never been able to accept endings that I don't like. I fight to make life the way I want it to be, and at times, that makes me a difficult person to be around. It is because of this, I think, that I never believed Ari was going to die. In my mind, she would make comeback after comeback. She had survived pneumonia in March when the doctors said she would die, and now, although she was still very frail, the intravenous AZT had made it possible for her to talk, sit up, and begin to walk. This latest setback was another crisis but we would find a way to survive it.

Ari was admitted to the hospital. We got another experimental drug, GM-CSF (granulocyte macrophage-colony stimulating factors), to try to raise her white blood count and bring her fever under control. I was sleeping there every night and Paul and I were trading off the daytime hours.

Dr. Stiehm was getting ready to take his month-long summer vacation about the time we checked back into UCLA. I was petrified. I had come to rely on him so much and felt enormous respect for both his competence and decency. He never complained if I called him in the wee hours of the morning. Because he lived close by, he would stop by our house if we needed him. In his own quiet way, he helped us gather the strength to face each day.

When he told me he was going on vacation, I felt scared, as if we were being cut off from our moorings and being cast adrift. I didn't want him to leave. Realistically I knew he needed time off; if anyone deserved a vacation, it was Dick Stiehm, but I was fighting back my tears. I was afraid to be without him.

I said to him, "But what's going to happen to us?" And then he quietly said, in his soft and gentle, matter-of-fact way, that he wasn't going out of town, he'd be at home. Then he gave me the greatest gift of all—he said he'd drop by to see Ari every day.

My relief was enormous. I started to cry. I stood up and said, "Oh, Dr. Stiehm, I have to give you a hug. I have to throw my arms around you."

"That's okay, Elizabeth," he said.

I smiled through my tears. "That's the first time you've called me Elizabeth."

"I'm a Midwestern WASP and we were taught that you don't get emotional with your patients."

"I'm sorry," I said. "I'm a Jewish girl from New York, and I have to cry and give you a hug."

We were Dick and Elizabeth after that.

We had Ari's seventh birthday party in the hospital and Dick Stiehm came and gave her a UCLA T-shirt and told her it was what she would wear on the day she went home. The T-shirt brought us faith and hope because it meant that Ari *was* going to go home.

But Ari had regressed greatly. In a few weeks, we had slid back down the mountain we had climbed since June. She had lost almost all the milestones she had gained. She was back on the intravenous AZT, but it didn't seem to make any difference at all. We felt trapped. We kept groping to find something that might bring some of the joy of the last few weeks back into Ari's fragile life.

We snuck Susan's daughter, Francesca, into the hospital to play "Old Maid" with Ariel. Francesca was the only one who always managed to coax a laugh or a smile out of Ariel, right up until the end. It was a great gift. I smiled with them but inside I was fighting to keep my optimism.

Ari was dreadfully sick and her care was intricate and complex. On an hour-to-hour basis, the nursing staff, headed up by Nancy Potash, did a superhuman job of caring for her.

But all I wanted was to take her home. I kept trying to figure out how we could do the nursing at our house. I was so focused on the goal of getting home that I didn't realize that the good-byes had begun. But apparently Ari knew and so did several of my friends.

Susan De Laurentis was at the hospital when I had to go and talk with one of the doctors, and Ari asked her to sit with her. Susan told me later that Ari held her hand as she talked about what Francesca was up to. The two of them had just looked into each other's eyes for a long time and Susan felt afterward that that was when they said good-bye, though it was completely unspoken.

Gene Seymour, Amanda and Josh's dad, would also tell me about a strong connection with Ari in the days before she died. "It wasn't wishful thinking. I felt she was saying, 'It's okay. I'll be okay, I understand, and thanks.' "

We were in the hospital for three weeks, trying desperately to stabilize Ari's condition. Our nephew, David, who had lived with us during the first terrible year after we were diagnosed, came out to help.

On August 11, Ari was not doing well, but we were fed up with the hospital's inability to improve how she felt and decided we could handle her medical care at home. That evening, Ari asked to see David. Though he had just arrived from New York, Paul brought him right over to the hospital. I remember so well Ari lying there holding her dear cousin David's hand. She even gave him a kiss which was something she rarely did with people.

Though she was not doing well, I tried to hang on to hope. Paul and I were getting ready to take her home. She was deteriorating and her fevers were not breaking, but the doctors knew how much we hated being in the hospital and agreed that we could care for her at home.

It was Friday, August 12, 1988. We were packing up and assembling things in her room. Ari was very compromised again. She had lost all of the progress she had made on the AZT. She was lying in her bed and I said to her, "We have to see if you can sit in your stroller, honey."

And Ari said, "No, Mom, I'm going to walk home."

She couldn't move her legs. She couldn't sit up. She couldn't do anything. I looked at her and said, "Give me a break."

Ari said simply, "No, Mom, I'm going to walk home."

"All right, Ari," I said. "Go for it."

Paul and I continued getting things together. It was not until the last ten minutes of her life that I knew she was dying. I wasn't ready for her death. How could I have ever been ready for her death?

I don't really know what happened, but Ari suddenly began coughing. No, it wasn't coughing, she just couldn't breathe. It became harder and harder for her to breathe. Paul was on one side and I was on the other.

We put an oxygen mask on her. Our eyes were riveted. "Are you all right?" I asked. Doctors were in and out, in and out, but we paid no atention to them.

She looked at me. Paul was on the other side of her.

I said, "You know it's going to be okay. Are you scared?"

She said, "No."

And then very quietly, but very quickly, she died as Paul and I lay beside her in her bed.

She was never supposed to die. It was too short a time to have had her. Paul wept and I cried, "Noooo!" which stretched out into a scream that filled the room and seemed to go on forever. It was a no to everything that had happened in our lives. It was a no that wanted to turn back time and start all over again. It was a no to a world that had failed me. Ari's death was so unacceptable that all I could do was scream "No!"

I wanted to hold her, and the doctors who had suddenly appeared said, "No, Elizabeth, just leave her. She's gone. She's dead."

"No, no," I said, "you don't understand! I have to hold my baby."

I made them let me pick her up. I sat in the chair and I held her on my lap as I had done so many times before. There were no tubes and the machines had been turned off. I sat there and rocked her and held her. I stroked her hair and kept kissing her cheek. I whispered, "I love you, Ari," a hundred times over and over in her ear.

I didn't want to leave. Ever. But they finally made me; otherwise I would have stayed. I would have sat there holding her forever. Paul helped me lay her back in bed, he took my arm, and through grief and shock we managed to walk out of the hospital, leaving our beautiful Ariel behind.

Maybe she knew that day she was going to die. Maybe she waited until both of us were right there beside her. Maybe she did walk home, freed from the body that held her back so much.

All I remember is holding Ariel in my arms, her head leaning on my cheek, clutching her as close to me as I could. I don't remember anything else. I know there were doctors and nurses in the room who tried to comfort us by saying that her struggle was over and she was now at peace.

To a mother holding her dead child in her arms, those words make no sense at all. Nothing that anyone can say makes any difference in a world gone black. All I knew was I wanted to have my daughter back and I could not. Not today, not tomorrow, not ever. Nothing will make her death acceptable to me. I live with it, but I will never accept it.

Jake was waiting for us at home, expecting us to bring his sister back. As Paul and I were walking across the parking lot we saw Graciela drive up. She had come to visit Ariel. Ari's beloved "Ga Ga" had been with her since she was two weeks old. Graciela had never left our sides. I just looked at her and said, "She died, Graciela. She died."

Graciela wanted to go up and see her, and she did. She held her and also gave her a kiss good-bye.

If Paul and I talked on the way home, I don't remember what we said. Everything has blurred, except the moment of Ariel's death which is branded on my heart. Paul and I parked the car in the driveway, and Jake came running to the door fast on his four-year-old feet. He had been waiting all day for his sister to come home.

"Where's Ari?" he asked.

We slowly walked him to the hall stairs and we all sat

down. I held him in my lap. "Jake," I said, "Ari's not coming home. She was very sick and she died. We will never have her with us in the house again, but we will always have her spirit in our hearts."

"But where is she?" he asked. "I want to know where she is!"

"Her body is in the hospital, but her spirit is in the sky." We all just sat there on the steps, not finding any more words.

Jake seemed so precious and so vulnerable. There we were in the same house on the same street in the same town but Ari was never coming home. I said all the right words for Jake, but they meant nothing to me. All I could think was *Ari's never coming home.* Her face, her step, her smile, her anger, her love had been ripped from me, and I couldn't imagine going on. From then on, there would only be three of us, never four. This was a house that was meant to celebrate children, not mourn them. Nothing made any sense.

Paul called my mom and dad, Connie and Billy, and his own mother in Boston. We called one or two friends. No one was home. It was a Friday night. We became terrified of spending the night alone. Paul left a message on Lynn's, Lucy's, and Susie's answering machines. Susan was back East, so we called her there. We were in shock. We were numb and raw simultaneously, but we knew we didn't want to be alone.

After a while, friends started arriving at the house. I'm sure for many it almost felt like a relief, but it certainly didn't seem so to Paul or me. There were so many emotions I had denied or ignored that I was suddenly forced to confront. I really thought Ari was getting better and hadn't gone through any of those stages you are supposed to go through. I had to start from the beginning. But I wasn't alone; our friends were there.

Suzanne Buhai, the first friend who hadn't been scared of our diagnosis, arrived and Joanie Green came soon after that. Joanie had believed as much as I had that Ari would never die. But now she was gone and the whole world felt empty. I hugged them both closely, shutting out the rest of the world. We were all crying. I tried to put into words what they meant to me and how grateful I was for their love. I thanked everyone, telling them I couldn't have survived this ordeal without my friends' support. We were all sitting around on the floor

in the dining room. The women were all in one group. I'm
sure we were chain-smoking cigarettes as it was the only
thing that could keep me somewhat calm. I cried, and then
someone would tell a funny story about Ari. We'd all laugh,
and then the emptiness would follow, and no one would talk.

Paul was crying. He would cry, gather himself in, cry, and
then gather himself together again. He was hanging up photographs of Ariel, as well as the pictures they had drawn together. He was creating an eloquent collage of his daughter's
life. As he hung each one up he would say a little something
about it. Paul was in the process of reliving her life and the
experiences those photographs captured.

We started planning the next few days. That's what happens immediately after a death: you are barraged with plans
to make and questions to answer. Where will the burial be?
When will the burial be? Who will do it? Who will come to
the burial? The same questions needed to be answered about
the memorial service—who, where, when. We had to decide
where Jake would be. Should he be included or not. You plan,
plan, plan, and in between the planning you cry. We decided
to have a memorial service at our home on Sunday afternoon
and fly to Boston Monday morning. Ari would be buried
there beside Paul's father on Tuesday.

I called Jonathan Omer-Man who was on vacation in
northern California. It was impossible for me to imagine anyone else leading the memorial service. Like so many others,
Jonathan changed his plans and flew home to be with us as
we said good-bye.

It wasn't until late into the night that our friends left.
Maria slept in Jake's room with him. We went in Ari's room
and lay down on her wonderful canopied bed and cried softly
so as not to wake Jake.

We finally made it to our bedroom, but we were not the
same people. Now we were parents who had lost a child. Now
the hope was gone. Now nothing Washington could do would
bring back our daughter. It was too late. She was dead.

Laurie Reyen, the nurse who taught us the TPN feeding
system, came over the next day to pack up the medical equipment and get it out of the house. I couldn't look at it. I
couldn't touch it. Paul was very calm. He was thinking Ari
had suffered so long and finally she wasn't suffering anymore.
But I was experiencing a devastating grief. Laurie remembers

hearing a primal cry that came from deep within me. I was crying and crying and crying.

When we first began planning the memorial service, we thought that only people who knew that Ari died of AIDS should be invited. Then Paul and I realized that anyone who knew Ariel would want to come and should be included.

Rabbi Omer-Man flew in from Lake Tahoe. He seemed to be struggling to hold back his tears, afraid that he would get too emotional to be able to say anything.

We played tapes of the chamber music Ari had listened to at home and in the hospital every night before she fell asleep. Several of our friends spoke. My parents stood beside us. The atrium was filled with friends who for almost a year had often put our needs before their own to be supportive. We all had to say good-bye together and try to find a way to make life acceptable again. There was no way to make death acceptable.

Sometimes people try to find a way to "explain" Ari's death, to make it comprehensible. I stop those conversations. Her death is a fact, devoid for me of any meaning or any way of being comprehended. I know it can't be changed and I have found a way to go on despite her loss. I have learned to live with a gaping hole in my heart that I know will cause me pain for the rest of my life.

Our friends and Rabbi Omer-Man saw strength, grief, and perhaps some peace on the day of the memorial service, but Paul and I were in shock. We didn't know it at the time. No one can even begin to sense the magnitude of grief until they have been hurled into it. But the real grief and the real strength come gradually, one tear at a time.

Joanie would tell me it was a beautiful memorial service. We had displayed Ari's paintings and drawings, which brought her creativity, joy, and wondrous love of nature all around us. But Paul and I were numb.

Rabbi Omer-Man began his eulogy by reading from the passage from the book of Ecclesiastes which begins, "To every thing there is a season, and a time to every purpose under the heaven: A time to be born, and a time to die . . ."

Then he continued by saying,

This is our time to grieve. This is our time of heart-rending sadness. This is our time of confusion and incomprehension. This is our time of tears. This is our time to part from Ari. Ariel Glaser has gone. She left us at seven o'clock on Friday evening, at the age of seven years and one week, after years of debilitating sickness and months of terrible pain and suffering. . .

This is one of the most difficult things in the world, to face the death of a child. It appears so senseless, so contrary to the natural order of the world. . .

Rabbi Omer-Man spoke for several more minutes and then I spoke. I hardly remember what I said. I didn't read it on paper, I read it from my heart. I talked about my daughter. About my love for her and my respect for her courage. I talked about the lesson her life taught me, because Ari never complained about what she couldn't do, she just focused on what she could. She faced so many compromises, but she never gave up. I said her life presented a challenge to all of us to do at least as well as Ari had. She would want us to do that. To think not of what we'd lost but of what we had. I said the words that day but it wasn't until two years later that I would really find them in my heart.

My mother, who has always been the woman I admired most, read a eulogy she had written for Ari.

Her eyes bluer than the ocean waves, her rosebud lips like a coral strand, she moved like sea foam at the water's edge, lightly flirting with the shifting sand.

We walked together and built a bond with each new delight we found, sorting and touching the wonderful gifts from the sea, exploring nature, Ari and me.

The beautiful shells shared their fragility and strength with that beautiful little girl. As the shells live on, so Ari lives on for me, a beauteous gift that nothing can take away.

My mother is a remarkable woman and she captured Ariel so beautifully that day. They had their own special bond. Ari was my mother's first grandchild. Now my mother had to find the strength to go on knowing she might lose her own child as well. For Mom and Dad it was a brutal day.

Dr. Stiehm talked about the patient he had come to know and love as a friend. He concluded his eulogy by saying, "One measure of a successful life might be the amount of love exchanged and received over a lifetime. By that measure, Ariel received a full quota in her seven years, especially from Paul and Elizabeth. We all have been touched by this precious child."

My friend Rena spoke about the friendship between Ariel and her daughter, Sara. "Ariel was Sara's first friend and they discovered the world together, and Elizabeth and I experienced that discovery with them. We went to the park and the zoo; Elizabeth and I learned how to be mothers together."

After the ceremony, after the eulogies, while people were eating and crying and talking, I took Jake outside and spent some time pushing him on the swing, back and forth, back and forth. Lesa Grovas saw me and told me she thought: *This is Elizabeth, she is going on. She still has Jake, she doesn't know what will happen to either of them, but he's her little boy and she has got to take care of him.*

And that's just what I did. Jake had missed out on so much because I was always so filled with Ari. Now the intimacy of the emptiness left room for Jake.

We took a flight early Monday morning to Boston. Connie and Billy picked us up at the airport and drove us back to their house where their children, the cousins Ari loved best, were all waiting. These were all Ari's favorite people, and it felt like we were where Ari would have wanted us to be.

There had been much discussion with my parents and friends as to whether burying Ari in Boston was a good idea. But Paul and I knew the grave site wasn't the place where we would visit our daughter. Imagining her under the ground was impossible. As we talked, both of us agreed that no part of the little girl we loved would remain in the soil, so it really didn't matter if she was buried far away.

Unfortunately and painfully, I also had to think about where I wanted to be buried in the event that I died. I knew I would want to be buried beside Ari. I rarely thought about my own death, but Ari's dying brought home the possibility. It was strange to stop thinking about my daughter's death so I could think about Jake's and my own. But I had to make choices. I knew if the worst were to occur, that Ari, Jake, and I should all be buried together in Boston.

The burial was at eleven the next morning. Ariel Glaser had been on the earth for seven years and eight days. She was buried in her favorite blue outfit, which had been a present from her father. Gray bunny, the stuffed animal that she had slept with every night of her life, was beside her in the white wooden coffin as was a pink blouse of mine that had been one of her favorites. At the last minute I balled it up and put it next to her. When we were alone at the funeral home, Paul and I covered her with the quilt that Connie and Alisa had made as a baby present.

The day was rainy. There was a steady drizzle as we drove silently to the cemetery. Paul held a small card in his hand and read the passage about Ariel from Shakespeare's *The Tempest*. Paul's voice trembled, but never broke as he read:

> Where the bee sucks, there suck I;
> In a cowslip's bell I lie;
> There I crouch when owls do cry.
> On the bat's back I do fly
> After summer merrily.
> Merrily, merrily, shall I live now
> Under the blossom that hangs on the bough.

My mother did the most beautiful and wondrous thing. She had brought many of the seashells she and Ari had so often played with and admired. We scattered seashells and wildflowers on her coffin before the dark dirt covered her for all time.

Car doors slammed, we went back to Connie's house briefly, picked up Jake, and left for Maine. Connie and Billy were in one car and we were in the next. The ragged remnants of rain streaked the windshield with fat drops and jagged rivulets of water. Sometimes the steady beating of the windshield wipers was the only sound in the car.

We were driving through the farmlands of southern Maine when we saw a spectacular rainbow towering over us, stretching clear across the sky. It was brighter than any we had ever seen. The colors were so strong it stunned us. It was glorious. High beyond Route 35 was every smile she ever smiled in every color she ever loved.

Me and Mom in 1949,
waiting for Daddy to
come home.

I was named Elizabeth
Ann Meyer, but
everyone had always
called me Betsy.

Me and my brother, Peter, waiting to crew for Dad. I was eight and he was five.

I visited my parents in Puerto Rico just before I met Paul in 1975. Mom always closes her eyes in photos.

Paul with David Soul in a
1975 *Starsky and Hutch*
publicity photo.

We attended as few formal evenings as we could, but
every now and then we'd have to go to a black-tie event.

Me and Lynn in 1976. Paul and I were renting a beach house in Malibu at the time.

Paul and me in 1976, during the early *Starsky and Hutch* years.

Paul taking Ariel for a stroll in Palm Springs in 1981. His parents, Dorothy and Sam Glaser, were spending the winter there.

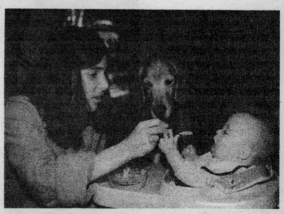

Our dog, Topaz, watching me feeding Ari. We were all learning.

My great friend Lucy Fisher with me and Ari at the beach. Ari had just turned one.

Since the paparazzi couldn't catch us at the typical Hollywood events, they had to find us at the airport.

Ari and me at a friend's birthday party in 1983. She was almost two.

Me and Ari taking Jake for a stroll. A very happy family.

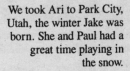

We took Ari to Park City, Utah, the winter Jake was born. She and Paul had a great time playing in the snow.

Graciela with Jake when he was ten months old.

Me and Paul on an airboat in the Everglades, scouting locations for *Band of the Hand,* the movie he was directing.

Christmas in Miami, 1985. Paul was directing, and Ari had just gotten out of the hospital. Her lips were still white.

Our family with Paul's sisters and their families—the Kantars and the Goldenbergs—including our special cousins David and Alisa Kantar, at Jonathan and Ruth's wedding. From left to right: Manuel, Eva, Penny (Paul's middle sister), Rachel Goldenberg, Jonathan and his new bride Ruth, Alisa, Connie (Paul's older sister), Deborah, David and Billy Kantar (Connie's husband).

Jake's second birthday party. All of Ari's friends were there.
From left to right: Ari, Taylor, Amy, Francesca, Sara.

Thanksgiving 1986. Shopping for pumpkins.

Ari's sixth birthday. Jake is almost three. Ari is just
starting to fail.

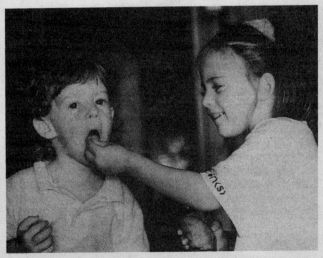

The summer of 1987. Ari and Jake in Maine, feeding each other
the blueberries we had picked.

Ari, Jake, and me taking a rainy walk in Maine.

Ari on the beach at Martha's Vineyard. She had started napping every day.

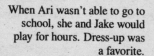

When Ari wasn't able to go to school, she and Jake would play for hours. Dress-up was a favorite.

Ari's last Halloween, when she dressed as a flapper and went back to Crossroads for the last time.

At UCLA during our first hospital stay, November and December 1987. We weren't doing well.

Jake with his big buddy, Josh Seymour.

Suzanne and me in Aspen in 1989. No matter what, I always smile when I'm skiing.

The Pediatric AIDS Foundation (PAF) is formed. From left to right: Susan De Laurentis, Susie Zeegen, and myself.

The *Immediate Family* premiere. This was the first night we appeared in public after the article was published. I think we both looked strained.

Me, President Reagan, Susan, and Susie at a PAF fund-raising event in 1990.

March 1990. Paul and I testify before Barbara Boxer
and the House Budget Committee in Washington.

On June 10, 1990, Elton John joined us at the
press conference for our million-dollar fund-
raiser, "A Time for Heroes." He certainly
deserves the hat he's wearing.

CHAPTER
❧ 9 ❧

Our plan was to not be alone. We would spend a week in Maine with the Kantars, and then visit Paul's cousins, Donna and Michael Moskow, on Martha's Vineyard. Being back in Maine without Ari felt like a bare echo of our former trips. Everything we did with Jake instantly reminded us of the last time we had done it with Ari. We were trying to be brave and strong, but it was hard.

We had told Jake we could camp out one night on the little island in the middle of the lake. We were desperately trying to find things to do with him that we hadn't done with Ariel. Alisa was going to join us. We put equipment and supplies in the canoe and of course the chocolate, marshmallows, and graham crackers for s'mores. It was dusk and the lake was like a mirror. Quietly we glided the boat toward the island. The only sound was the bow slicing through the water.

Suddenly, a loon surfaced right next to the canoe. It started making noises unlike any I'd ever heard a loon make. After a few sounds it stopped. We all sat there, mesmerized by the beautiful bird. Before I ever realized what I was doing, I found myself mimicking the loon's quiveringly melodic and haunting sounds. The loon answered back.

This exchange happened three times. When the loon left, I was shaking and crying. Paul's eyes were wide with wonder and amazement. Jake sat in silence. At that moment, we all believed the loon was Ari coming to say good-bye to us. For a brief few hours a peace fell over us on the island and we all slept well.

Most nights, uninterrupted sleep was impossible. Paul and I would climb into bed and usually we could barely look at each other. The pain was too great. I've read that eighty percent of all parents who lose children get divorced and I know why. Each time you see the other, the first thing you remember is what you've lost. Some nights we would be able to just hold each other and cry quietly so as not to disturb Jake or the Kantars.

We were suffering and mourning Ari's loss daily but her death only intensified my burning desire to save Jake's life. I had just lost a child. The last thing I was going to do was lose another.

For months and months it was the same. When I got into bed at night and closed my eyes, the only thing I could see was Ari dying. But when I woke up in the morning the first thing I saw was Jake who would soon be four years old.

Jake was furious with me. I think he blamed me for his sister's death, which was not surprising. So did I. I was the mom, wasn't I supposed to make everything okay? I was certainly the most logical person to be angry with. Jake didn't seem to love me at all, but I wasn't sure I deserved it. I knew it wasn't rational, but everything rational is buried in the sweeping flow of grief. It was difficult for me to distinguish between reasonable and emotional reactions.

Part of me felt it was my fault that Ari died. Even though I knew it was a virus and we fought it as best we could for as long as we could, part of me still felt like a failure because my love, courage, and determination had not been enough to keep my daughter alive. The doctors didn't have the answers. The answers that would save the life of my son and every other child with AIDS would only come from research. But no one was doing it. The government wasn't doing it. AMFAR wasn't doing enough. No one in decision-making positions seemed to know about or care about children with AIDS.

I couldn't wait six months or six years to recover from Ariel's loss because those six months might be the ones that could save Jake's life. The clock was ticking louder than ever before. If Ari had started AZT six months earlier, before she had been so severely compromised, it might have prolonged her life indefinitely.

I could not sit still in sadness. I didn't have that luxury. Every day that I wasted was a day that might mean life or death for my son. I knew that my family's journey was not over. I couldn't give up.

Up until this time, most pediatric cases were transfusion cases where a family had one infected child, often a hemophiliac, but the parents were healthy. If that child died, the parents were no longer in the midst of a battle against AIDS. Their struggle was now focused mainly on grief.

But Ari was dead and Jake's life hung in the balance. I had seen what could happen and I knew what I had to do. I couldn't stop fighting. I was determined to fight as hard for Jake as I had for Ari.

Since Jake was still healthy, normal, and strong, the fight would be, initially, a different fight. Though Jake was HIV-positive, he didn't have AIDS. I would have to enlighten Washington and get them to pay attention to the special problems AIDS presented in children, so that they would commit the money to deal with it. I would have to raise money now, for the research that would help the child I still had. I knew the goals, and I knew Susan and Susie would be by my side. I had no idea if we could do it, but we had to try. I was numb, but I had to be able to act and act fast. I had to combat Ari's loss with the belief that I could help Jake.

Paul's aunt, Vera List, is a wealthy woman. She came to Ari's funeral in Boston, but like many of the other family members, did not know the complete story of Ari's death. After we had been in Maine for a few days, I sat down with Paul and his sister Connie and asked them if they thought it would be appropriate for me to ask Aunt Vera for money for the about-to-be-formed foundation. They had no objections so I picked up the phone.

I barely knew Vera List. She was in her early eighties, recently widowed, and mother of four grown daughters. When I called her I said I was sorry we had not had a chance to speak with each other at the funeral. I told her that my life was horrible and that I might need her help. I asked if I could come and talk to her. She agreed.

From Maine we went to Martha's Vineyard to stay with

the Moskows, as we had every summer for the last three years. There is no way to explain the gratitude we felt as people opened their hearts and their homes to us. We were lucky to have a family like mine and Paul's.

A day or two after we got to Martha's Vineyard, I flew back to La Guardia and then took a bus to Connecticut where Aunt Vera lived in an expansive waterfront estate. I sat in the sun room of Vera's idyllic house and told her of my life.

Jake was the last Glaser. I said I wanted to do everything possible to save his life and as terrible as it sounded, very little was being done to help children with AIDS. With seed money from her, I would be able to start a foundation and raise money for pediatric AIDS research.

Aunt Vera said that much of her money had already been committed for the year, but that she thought she could give me $100,000. I was thrilled. We continued to talk and then she said to me, "Elizabeth, I am going to get you a half a million dollars."

I looked at her and tears formed in my eyes. I threw my arms around her. If one person was willing to help, maybe there would be more. Because of Aunt Vera we didn't have to waste one single minute. I'm not sure she still really understands how her generosity gave me the hope to go on. Maybe if Vera had said no, I would have lost the courage to move ahead. But she said yes, and a small ember began to glow where it had been all dark.

A half million dollars! As soon as I got back to the Vineyard, I called Susan and Susie. We were moving. We were on our way. It was the only hope I had to hold on to. Susie said she was trying to get a meeting with Merv Griffin. Lucy called and said she had arranged for a meeting with Steven Spielberg. Susan said we needed to call Michael Gottlieb right away. We now had twice the money Gottlieb said was necessary to fund a significant chunk of pediatric research. When I called him, I was delirious with excitement.

"Michael, Michael," I said, "I've gotten half a million dollars!"

"But I only talked to you two weeks ago!"

"I know, but would you please sit down right away and figure out how we are going to use this money?"

Susan, Susie, and I had asked Michael to figure out a way for AMFAR to distribute the money since the Foundation hadn't been started yet. We planned to get together as soon as I returned to Los Angeles. If the government hadn't paid attention to children with AIDS before, then we were going to work hard to change that.

In the early years of the epidemic, there were not a lot of pediatric AIDS cases so no one thought much about it. In 1986, the year Ari was diagnosed, the CDC only reported 410 cases of pediatric AIDS. But the CDC only counts children who have full-blown AIDS, like Ari had, and not kids like Jake who are HIV-positive and still healthy, so the numbers are always very misleading, way below the actual number of infected children. The number of pediatric AIDS cases jumped in 1987 to 737, and by 1988, the total reached 1,346. By June of 1990, according to the CDC, there were 2,380 children diagnosed as having AIDS in the United States, but it is estimated that at least another 20,000 children have contracted the HIV virus. They won't become an official statistic until they are diagnosed. Worldwide, there are more than 700,000 children infected. The World Health Organization has predicted that by the year 2000, ten million or more children will have been infected with the virus, and most will have died.

The number of pediatric cases began to increase when the AIDS epidemic spread rapidly among drug users who transmitted the virus sexually or through contaminated needles. Infected mothers gave birth to infected children. The families were poor and overwhelmingly black and Hispanic. On a political seismograph, these deaths register next to nothing.

Because the first wave of deaths in the AIDS epidemic were gays and drug users, people were able to distance themselves and say, "Can't happen to me, why should I care?" AIDS also clicked into a homophobic side of America which felt that these people somehow deserved whatever happened to them. AIDS was the price you paid for an "immoral" lifestyle.

Then gays got organized. A gay lobby was created and they were able to pressure Washington to start allocating money for AIDS. They made it an issue that could no longer be ignored.

So about four years into the epidemic, funding started. But even doctors were not aware that pediatrics was going to be a big problem. There were still few transfusion cases. The year we were diagnosed, the CDC was only aware of fifty similar cases, a number that would double, then quadruple, in the next two years. No one paid much attention to the fact that AIDS could be transmitted from mother to child.

Federal funding, when it finally came, was at least four years too late and pediatrics got what dribbled through the cracks.

Families didn't speak out because for the most part, like mine, they were often still in hiding. As time went on, if a child had AIDS, it often meant a parent did too, and they risked losing their jobs and medical coverage, if they were lucky enough to have it. The risks that come with exposure are enormous.

The other people who really knew the reality of pediatric AIDS were the doctors taking care of these children. But these people have little power. Most were on the front lines in the country's poorest urban areas. People like Dr. Jim Oleske, Dr. Margaret Haegarty, Dr. Dick Stiehm, Dr. Gwen Scott, and Mother Hale. They spoke out as had other mothers, like Helen Kushnick and Anna Belle Kaufman, but no one was really listening or if they were, as with the Watkins Commission report, "government" didn't care enough to respond in a significant way.

When you are in need, like my family was, you think someone will be there to help you, and that the world will care. But that was wrong. There was a handful of committed people, but most of the world? Most of the world didn't care and doesn't care now.

When I came back to Los Angeles, I sat down again with Susie and Susan and said, "The foundation is a reality now, are we still in?" They were. We agreed we would not take salaries and we still don't. We wanted every penny possible to go to the researchers.

We needed a name and after considerable debate settled on the Pediatric AIDS Foundation (PAF). We had no office, no telephones, and no board of directors. But we did have half a million dollars. We sat down with Michael Gottlieb and worked out an arrangement he'd present to AMFAR. We wanted AMFAR to set up a Children's Research Fund that would distribute whatever money we raised.

We then hoped to select four doctors to sit on a special pediatric advisory panel at AMFAR. These doctors would decide how the money would be spent. AMFAR would take no overhead out of our money since we were doing the work to raise it. Every penny we gave them would go to research.

Right away, we knew we wanted Dick Stiehm and Michael Gottlieb to be part of the panel. Michael suggested Art Ammann, a pediatrician in San Francisco who worked for Genentech now. Art identified the first transfusion case of pediatric AIDS. The last doctor selected was Warren Andiman, a pediatrician and researcher from Yale.

Susan and Susie and I would meet in Susan's kitchen or mine and brainstorm about moving ahead. Susie would be in charge of the fund-raising, and Susan would focus on the educational and medical issues, both here and in Washington. I would be involved in both areas and try to find big chunks of money fast. We knew there was no time to lose.

I felt as though I had no choice in what I was doing. I was following a mother's instinct to try and save her child. It was different for Susan and Susie. They didn't have to have their lives consumed with AIDS and me. But they chose to do it and nothing could have possibly meant more. I could not have done a thing without them.

The fall of 1988 was a terrible time. Dealing with Ari's death was becoming more and more difficult. Jake was in school, and without Ari I suddenly had too much free time to think and feel sorry for myself. So I focused my energy on the Foundation, but each day was still filled with unbearable sadness.

In fact, for the first six months after Ari's death, I appeared alive, but I was dead inside. Ari was dead and I was dead. I was not sure I wanted to go on living, because I didn't see how I could live without Ariel.

I never stopped loving Jake or Paul. I just wasn't sure I wanted to be alive. All I knew was I wanted to be with Ari. I continued to give love. The hard part was letting love in, letting their love touch my heart.

We felt Ariel's presence everywhere we went. Jake would see a pretty flower or a beautiful cloud and say, "Oh, Ari would have loved that." Anything pink or purple made him remember how much he missed his sister. We all missed Ari terribly. I would walk into her bedroom every day and throw myself on her bed and cry. The tears never seemed to run out.

Equally difficult were my interactions with Jake, which were often painful. I would say, "Jake, are you angry because Ari died?"

"Yes!" he would say fiercely.

"Jake, you know it is not my fault, and it's not your fault that Ari died. She was very sick and the doctors could not make her well, no matter how hard they tried."

But my words seemed to have no impact on him or on me.

I saw Rabbi Omer-Man a few more times. We would sit by the beach and watch the gulls and say the kaddish, the ancient Jewish prayer of mourning, which is a way of releasing the soul of the deceased to return to the divine source. But that didn't help either.

It might sound selfish, but despite all the pain she had been in, I would still have chosen to keep Ari by my side if I could. It was a loss so intensely penetrating that it seemed nothing would ever quiet the pain.

Paul and I became very isolated in our grief. We realized that in mid-September when we went to a fund-raiser for Dukakis at Norman Lear's house. It was our first time out since Ari died six weeks before.

It was hard to decide whether or not we felt strong enough to go. We almost didn't, but I wanted to hear Dukakis speak and get a sense of what he was like as a man. As we ventured into the outside world that night, Paul and I understood just how different we felt.

The world was flowing by like a river, and Paul and I were no longer a part of it. It was impossible, in those first months, to find any equilibrium. Our closest friends tried to share the sadness, but most people are intimidated by grief. They don't know what to say and so, fearful that they might say the wrong thing, they say nothing. I once again found myself wishing for the ordinary life I would never have.

When I heard Dukakis speak at the fund-raiser, I instantly decided to become active in his campaign. He said we have to do more for people who have less. His words touched me directly.

I now know what it feels like to live in a world that doesn't care. My psychological and emotional identification now is with the have-nots; with a group of people who on the surface are not like me. They are overwhelmingly poor, black, Hispanic, and ignored.

But my problems are their problems and their problems are my problems. We live with the same fear, pain, loss, and sadness every day. I know there are still huge differences. The mother in the South Bronx has to struggle with food and clothing and housing. I know I am fortunate not to have to face those issues. But Ari had food, clothes, and a house to live in, and it didn't save her life. What will save the life of Jake and every other child with AIDS is a world community that feels not only compassion, but responsibility for those who have less and those who need help.

Like most people with AIDS, I feel aligned with the powerless. Through the luck of the draw I have had access to offices most people don't. When I have met with people in power it's usually because they think I am one of them. In terms of color and economics, yes, I look the same, but I don't feel I have much in common with them. My goals are not their goals. They want to protect what is theirs. They want a kinder and gentler America for them, but not necessarily for others.

My family needs an America that is kinder and gentler to all. To poor people as well as rich. It seems America is kind and gentle to people who own savings and loans, to people who run insurance and drug companies, but certainly not to people who are sick from HIV. So I use my access to try and pry open doors and make people care. Jake might die if I don't.

I identify with the oppressed, but not as a victim. I was much more of a victim when I was just taking care of my family, trying to keep our lives normal without taking any risks. Becoming active in the fight against AIDS made me realize I'm not a victim. I have power and I can work for change.

I became active when I felt there was nothing left to lose. At first, when I was fighting to keep my family's privacy, I felt that I had something to lose. We would lose if we became ostracized, if people threw rocks at our windows, or if my child was barred from school. When I confronted Ari's death for the first time in March when she was hospitalized with pneumonia, I realized that what I was worried about losing wasn't really important because all that really mattered was life or death. Playdates and birthday parties don't matter when you're dead.

I made a choice that seemed like the only option. At least my life would have the potential of saving other lives. At least some good could come from it. If I die, I don't want it to be my death that has meaning. Death has no meaning.

Everyone dies. The choice and the challenge is in how we choose to live. And the more meaning you find in your life, the more reason you have to live. I want my life to change things, not my death.

Ari's life had meaning and there were lessons to be learned from it. She was a courageous little girl who gallantly accepted her life and lived it as thoroughly as she could. She never cried about not being able to go to school or being unable to see a friend. She never felt sorry for herself, nor did she ever give in or give up. Ariel had wisdom, strength, and courage. In my weaker moments, I try to be at least as strong as she was. I try to be a person she would be proud of.

But many of these revelations came later. During those first six months after Ari died, I knew things in my head that I couldn't translate into my heart or soul. It was horrible to feel dead but no matter how hard I tried, I could find no beauty in the world, not even in Jake or Paul.

I threw myself into the Dukakis campaign with a frenzy. He and the Pediatric AIDS Foundation became my hope. I had not dealt with my grief at all.

A lot of the energy that had gone into caring for Ari was shifted into the campaign. I was running hard to stay away from the sadness. The campaign made me feel as though all was not lost. I became a precinct worker. I got my friends involved. Jake and I put "Dukakis for President" signs up on our block.

But at night, I would close my eyes and see Ariel dying at UCLA. Several times a week I would have to take a sleeping pill because when I closed my eyes, all I could see were her last moments.

Sometimes I would dream. Dreams were sacred. They were the only way to get what I longed for most, the chance to see my child again. I didn't have many dreams that I remembered. But shortly after Ari's death I dreamed that I was in a car, and I was coming home. As I came to my house, I could see that it was glass. Ari and Jake were standing together in the house and Ari came outside. In the dream, she read me a poem. It was a poem that talked about thousands of years and thousands of people. The essence of the dream was that it wasn't just her, it wasn't just us; there was more to life than any of us understood. The dream was comforting because I was with my daughter again. Jake and Ari were happy together in the glass house, though I was afraid it meant Jake might die.

I could no longer feel happiness without feeling pain. When I was happy for Jake, I missed Ari. When Jake went zooming down the block on his bicycle, I would think that Ari never got her training wheels off. When I was skiing through powder, feeling the wind and sun and feeling immersed in the beauty of life, I would think that I might be dead before ski season came around again.

I am now living my life with an incredible intensity and consciousness because I never know if I will get a chance to do anything again next year, next month, or next week. Not knowing if I'm doing something for the last time makes me feel as though I'm doing it for the first time.

During the campaign, Paul was going through his own avoidance. "Blue Lightning" had been canceled because MGM was up for sale. Paul threw himself into golf. He would play four or five days a week. Golf was his escape. The concentration and focus it took to play the game kept his mind occupied and elsewhere. He didn't talk about his grief or sadness with the people he played with. He was still in shock.

After Ari's death, Jake began seeing a child psychologist. I told Jake the "talking doctor" was a place where he could play and talk about Ari. Jake was angry, aggressive, and extremely hostile for nearly a year. Susan Jay, the therapist he saw, specializes in dealing with loss and death in children. She said she had never seen a child Jake's age as bonded to his sibling as Jake was to Ari.

It was so hard for him. He had his sister's death to confront and then he had to grapple with his own mortality. He would say to me over and over in the car, "Ari died when she was young because she was very sick. I'm not very sick, so I'm not going to die when I'm young, right, Mom?"

I would say, "You're right." A child doesn't want to hear "I don't know." Even when Ari was ill, I kept telling her she was going to get better. Positive thinking was the only hope we had and although I could be brutally honest in my own life, it certainly never felt appropriate with my children.

Jake would also ask me if we could get another big sister. He'd say, "Mom, do you think some family has a sister they don't want that we could have?"

I did not try to hide all of my emotions from Jake. I never let him see me completely out of control, but he certainly saw me cry. Once when I was crying I told Jake it was because I missed Ari so much, and he said he didn't.

I asked him why. Jake said, "Because she is sitting in the tree outside my room." He told me that his sister came into his room a lot, and who knows? Maybe she did. Some people think children are much more attuned to spirits, and maybe he sensed her presence more strongly than the rest of us. Maybe it was Jake's own way of coping with her loss.

Ari died in August, and Jake turned four two months later. I remember taking him to the dentist he had seen before. I decided to call the dentist and tell him that we were HIV-positive and hope that he would still see us and also be trustworthy enough to protect our secret.

The dentist said he would see us and follow the guidelines set by the American Dental Association. He thought it might be easier if we came after regular office hours, and since he closed at noon on Fridays, we were able to come at one o'clock. I felt that was considerate, but basically I felt at his mercy.

When we got to his office, he put on two layers of gloves and one of those hideous blue masks that Jake hates because it reminds him of Ari and the hospital. I knew this was a good and kind man who was just following the textbook approach to dealing with an AIDS patient, albeit a four-year-old, but he wasn't drilling in Jake's mouth, and to me it all seemed excessive. However, I still felt too vulnerable to say anything and knew we were lucky the dentist was even willing to see us.

As September came to an end, there was one other important thing I wanted to do. We had not invited children to Ari's memorial service, but I knew that her closest friends needed some way to say good-bye and I needed a chance to see them. We had left town for all of August and school had started. Now it was time.

So, separately, I had her four closest friends, Francesca, Amy, Sara, and Taylor, come by the house.

We went up to Ari's bedroom and talked and looked at pictures. I told each girl that I thought she had been the best friend that anyone could have possibly been to Ari. I told them how much their visits had meant to Ari, even when she was too sick to play. I said it was important to be a good friend, and that it wasn't something everyone knew how to do. I told each girl that to know how to be a best friend at age six was remarkable.

I said that Ari would always love them and her spirit would stay close. I told them I would always love them, too.

Each girl chose a few special things from Ari's room. Amy chose a pink crystal rock and a stuffed animal. I think Francesca chose a geode and a stuffed cat, and Taylor took a little doll. Sara took some of Ari's nail polish along with a doll and a porcelain music box. I hope it meant as much to them as it did to me. The people we love are really all we have in life, and Ari and I will always have the most special love for those four girls. I wanted them to know how special they were.

Paul and I had talked of what we felt most comfortable doing with Ari's room. We didn't want to ignore it. We didn't want to pretend it just wasn't there. We both needed to be able to visit in her room.

Periodically, when Jake's friends come over to play, he takes them into Ari's room. We have left it just as it was when she was alive. We decided we couldn't imagine changing it. Jake will play with her dress-up clothes or wander in her bathroom. We each find our way into her room at different times and in different ways to tell her we love her. Her door is always open and Graciela always has a rose by her bed. It's not maudlin; it's just life. Ari's room remains though Ari is gone, and her spirit fills our hearts.

CHAPTER

❧ 10 ❧

The very inception of anything new is always extremely exciting. Even though I felt deadened by Ari's loss, the Foundation was my hope for Jake and it took on great meaning. The research would cost much more than half a million dollars. That money would only start things rolling. So we needed to raise a lot more money and *quickly.* To do that we needed an executive advisory board whose names would give us credibility. People who would be known across the country. We also needed a health advisory board of the most preeminent doctors fighting this battle. We would do it piece by piece, and as each one fell into place our dream became more of a reality. Each time someone offered to join the effort, our ranks felt stronger. And truthfully, each time someone said yes, it gave me hope for Jake. Somehow each success was directly related to his survival and each rejection as well.

It was still September when Rita Braver called me from Washington. She wondered how I was doing and I told her I was starting a nonprofit foundation to raise money for pediatric AIDS research.

She told me a friend of hers from college, Al Checchi, had recently moved to L.A. He was a very wealthy entrepreneur. Rita thought it might be useful for me to talk to him and agreed to call him on my behalf.

The meeting was set and Al wanted to include some guy

by the name of Bob Burkett. The name meant nothing to me. Al said he was someone who might be useful to know. In my life that can be anything from a shaman to a billionaire.

The meeting was the morning of September 28 in Bob's office. At this point, the only person I had met with for fundraising was Aunt Vera. Now I felt like I was playing in the major leagues. This was real. I was going to meet two people I didn't know at all and ask them for money. I was going to ask them to help me save lives, one of which might be my son's. I was very nervous. There was a lot on the line.

I told my story, keeping my focus on Al, since he was the one the meeting was really about. But Bob was the one who was asking the most questions. I said I had been to Washington and discovered that no one was doing much, certainly no one was doing enough, for children with AIDS. I described my meeting with the Reagans and what I thought should be done in pediatrics. I said we had started a foundation to raise money and turn it right over to research.

Suddenly Bob Burkett said, "I think you should meet with Mike Dukakis."

Mike Dukakis! For a month I had been thinking of a way to try and get to Dukakis. All I had heard was, "It's impossible. Dukakis is campaigning and has no time for anything else." And then, all of a sudden, here is Bob Burkett, whom I knew nothing about, and who really knew nothing about me, telling me that I *should* meet with him.

I grinned inside. "I like the way you think. How do I do it?"

Bob swiveled around in his leather chair, leaned back, and pushed a few buttons. It's terrific to see Bob tear into something. Boom, boom, boom, Christine, get me so-and-so, boom, boom, boom, let's keep talking, boom, boom, boom, Christine, could you also try this person, maybe he's on the phone right now.

I thought to myself, *This is the person I have been waiting for, someone with intelligence, commitment, and the power to make things happen.* I needed people who could punch numbers into the phone and get results. From the moment Bob made the first call, I knew that Susie, Susan, and I would have an important new friend.

I learned that Bob was a lawyer who worked as Ted Field's political advisor. Ted is a filmmaker, producer, businessman, and generous philanthropist. He'd been politically active for years and was a major fund-raiser for the Democratic party.

While I was still in the room, one of his calls was returned and I heard Bob saying, "I have someone here in the office who really needs to meet with Mike. We need to talk about this because it's important and I think Mike will really want to meet with this woman."

After the call, Bob said, "I know you are here for money." He asked me how much I would like Ted and Susie Field to contribute.

I said that I'd only received one donation so far and that it was for half a million dollars. It was a wonderful way to begin since it put me into a significant category right away. Susie Zeegen had been taking a fund-raising class and had learned that people donate money based on what others have given. If you say you've received checks for five and ten thousand dollars, that's what others will generally give.

Bob said he would speak to the Fields about contributing between fifty and a hundred thousand dollars. Within a few weeks, I had met with Susie Field and they had donated $150,000.

Al Checchi went on to become CEO of Northwest Airlines and, along with his wife, Kathi, has become one of our most reliable supporters. It had been an excellent meeting.

I knew I could teach children but now I was learning I could teach adults as well. I was learning to speak clearly, frankly, and decisively. I was learning to take risks. I was learning not to be afraid of failing. I was learning that the people I met with would respect me for trying.

Several days after the meeting with Bob Burkett, the meeting Lucy had arranged with Steven Spielberg took place. I sat down with Steven in his Amblin Entertainment office on the Universal lot.

Paul and I didn't know Steven well. We had met in Hawaii and had dinner together just before we found out our diagnosis. The most emotional meetings for me were with people who had known me before AIDS. It reminded me of where we had come from and the life I had lost.

We were in the middle of the meeting when Steven said, "How much money are you talking about?"

"I hope you will give me a few million dollars." I was amazed that those words had even come out of my mouth.

I think I said that if I had that kind of money I would donate it myself, but I didn't and he did and I needed his help.

Steven quietly gives away millions of dollars. He said he was impressed with me because I was doing this without any fanfare and was not seeking notoriety for myself. He said he had singlehandedly funded a children's research center the previous year at Cedars-Sinai Hospital, the hospital where Ari was born, and he wanted to find out if they were doing AIDS work there first before he made a commitment to me.

I was disappointed. Instinct told me that when people wanted to get back to me in a week, I hadn't hit home. Steven had given five million dollars to Cedars-Sinai and it was clear to me that it was unlikely he would come through with the amount of money I was seeking. But he did surprise me by volunteering to come on our executive advisory board. Since we were trying to put together a board that had national recognition, this was a breakthrough and one I hadn't even sought. Steven became our first executive advisory board member. It was a big piece of that puzzle.

A week later, Steven called and said that since they would be doing AIDS work at the Cedars-Sinai clinic he could only give me a donation for a hundred thousand dollars. I was grateful for both the money and his willingness to let us use his name on our masthead.

I was stunned and happy. In three at bats I had raised three quarters of a million dollars.

Meanwhile, Susan and Susie and I were looking for two important people. We needed a financial advisor and a legal advisor to complete our board of directors. We wanted the board to remain small with just four people. I would be the unofficial fifth participant.

Lloyd Zeiderman had been Paul's business manager since before I met Paul. He was Paul's good friend and as committed to our family as anyone could be. I knew a nonprofit organization was not Lloyd's type of thing, but I placed the call to him anyway. Lloyd never hesitated, he just said yes. Now we had our financial advisor and we needed a lawyer.

After striking out a number of times, I remembered that Maryly's husband, Peter Benzian, was a lawyer. Maryly had been my first new friend in L.A., and we had taught school together for three years. In fact, she gave me her apartment when she and Peter got married and that was where I was living when I met Paul. Maryly was the friend I called on our first date. Since Peter and Maryly had moved to San Diego I hardly ever saw them anymore. They knew nothing of my life but I finally decided to call.

It was a difficult call for Maryly to receive. She was so happy to hear from me. "Hi, how are you?"

"Well, not too good. Listen, Maryly, sit down. I didn't want to burden you with this, but I need Peter's help." It was a long phone call. Maryly put Peter on, and when I explained what I needed he never missed a beat. I think he actually said that it would be his honor, it would be a gift to let him help. Peter ran Latham and Watkins's offices in San Diego. We couldn't have had a better friend or lawyer. Now we had our board of directors.

Meanwhile, we were still trying to reach people in power. The chief of pediatrics at UCLA, Bill Friedman, told us his wife Denny was a good friend of Gayle Wilson, wife of Republican Senator Pete Wilson, and offered to introduce me to her. I took Denny up on the offer, met Gayle, and a month later, Gayle had arranged a meeting for me with Mrs. Bush. A year later, Gayle would join our executive advisory board as well.

Jake was in school at this time and seemed to be doing well. He missed Ari, but he was coping. Paul was still playing golf four days a week. It was his way of losing himself and coping at the same time. Two months after Ari died, Paul's back suddenly went out. It was extremely painful. Real, very real, pain. He'd do his yoga but nothing was working, and finally he was in bed resting and that lasted for months.

During those months my parents were very helpful but it was hard to really be together because the pain of the loss was so great. Everything was so tragic. My mother was worried about losing me, and I was mourning the loss of my daughter. It was hard for us to connect.

Our friends needed a break from the intensity of Ari's illness and death. Gradually and appropriately, the calls dwindled down from every day to once or twice a week. Many people who didn't know what Ari really died of just wondered why I didn't get pregnant and have another child. They could never realize how much more complicated our life was.

In the end, you mourn by yourself. Even Paul and I couldn't mourn together. Paul would cry on his morning walks when his back allowed him to get out of bed. He did most of his grieving alone and so did I.

I would take the same drive down San Vicente Boulevard, tears pouring from my eyes, screaming, "Ari, I miss you so much. I want you back. I don't know how to go on without you." I would cry intensely for five minutes and then a calm would come and I would continue with my day.

In mid-October, Barbara Bush arrived in Los Angeles accompanying her husband for the second of the presidential debates. Gayle Wilson had arranged for us to meet several hours before the debate at the Four Seasons Hotel.

In my mind this was a very important meeting. Whoever was going to succeed Reagan could potentially turn things around. Whether it be Bush or Dukakis, I felt it would certainly be easier to talk to the new president after the election if I had some contact before. Mrs. Bush was to be that contact.

I felt more nervous before meeting her than I was before going to the White House. I had complete privacy when I went to see the Reagans. My family's secret was not in jeopardy at 1600 Pennsylvania Avenue. But I was meeting Mrs. Bush in Los Angeles in a hotel crowded with reporters and campaign staff. I was afraid that someone would walk up to me and say, "Oh, Elizabeth, what are you doing here?" I always had an alibi in mind in case I needed it. That day I would have said I was meeting a friend from out of town.

The fear I felt was an outgrowth of the vulnerability one lives with when one is keeping a secret. When you are HIV-positive and hiding it, you often feel that everyone is looking at you, even when they are not. I often felt that way on the sidewalk or in supermarkets or department stores.

As I walked into the Four Seasons trying to be invisible, I lowered my eyes and walked over to a bank of phones and called upstairs to the Bush suite. I had given the security people my maiden name, Betsy Meyer.

A staff person came down and escorted me up to the top floor where the Bushes were staying. There were staff and security people standing outside every door and lots of cables running through the halls and telephones ringing and the kind of commotion that gives you the sense that something big is about to happen.

We spent about forty minutes together. I told her my story

and then she told me that she cared deeply about the AIDS issue and asked what I thought she could do. I said that if she and her husband got to the White House they could provide the kind of leadership that was needed to change the public's attitude toward the disease. I talked about the need for more funding and research.

Mrs. Bush was both gracious and maternal. It was comfortable to be in her presence, and yet I never really felt as though I made a connection with her. This surprised me, because she had lost a four-year-old daughter to cancer.

I told her that if they were elected, I hoped to have the opportunity to meet with them. She was noncommittal about that but supportive in every other way. When I walked away from the meeting, I did not have the sense of having accomplished anything significant, and I think I was right. I never have met with the President or his wife now that they are in the White House. Mrs. Bush, however, did recently tape the opening of a national parent education program we are developing.

Meanwhile, Bob Burkett had found out that it wasn't going to be possible for me to meet with Mike Dukakis, but he had been able to set up a meeting with his wife, Kitty. That happened just two days after the presidential debate.

Bob was now my ally and mentor. I called him after every meeting and gave him a rundown of what happened. I listened to his advice and came to rely on him for both guidance and support. Both of us had good political instincts. He knew that I liked to figure out the shortest distance between two points and that I'd want to find a way to work around anything that got in the way of my goals. Intuitively we understood each other well and that made working together easy and fun.

Even though I had campaigned for Dukakis, I firmly expected to like Mrs. Bush more than I liked Kitty Dukakis. Kitty always seemed like a wild card. I thought she had a very hard and tough veneer, which I didn't think I would be able to penetrate easily.

Dukakis was running so far behind in the polls it seemed preposterous to think that he could win, and that took some of the edge off my meeting with Kitty.

Our meeting was at nine-thirty in the morning in the Century Plaza Towers Hotel. Mike was campaigning elsewhere and security was far less daunting than it had been for Mrs. Bush. I was wearing my same suit and after an aide took me upstairs, the first thing a staff person said was, "I like your outfit."

Democrats! I thought. It was such a normal thing to say and the first time anyone had. The compliment meant a lot to me because I felt so alienated from the normal world. For someone to spontaneously say that I looked pretty or that they liked my dress reminded me that I was still like everyone else.

Mrs. Dukakis came out from her bedroom to the living room of her suite. We were introduced. She was dressed for a luncheon that day and looked very elegant. Her vibrant brown eyes captured my attention immediately.

At first I noticed her intensity. As she began to speak I realized how smart she is, and as I listened, how kind. At one point, as I was telling Kitty about our life, I saw her open her purse and then close it again. I knew what she was thinking. She wanted a cigarette. I wanted one too. I said to her, "Do you want to have a cigarette? It would be fine with me. In fact, I'll bum one from you."

From that moment on, Kitty and I sat there chain-smoking and talking like old friends. A short while later, her aide came in and told Kitty it was time to leave for Santa Barbara where she was expected at a luncheon.

Kitty was upset. "I feel so sorry. It's apparent that I have not left enough time to spend with you. I feel terrible about this. Is there any possibility that you could come back this afternoon after I get back to the hotel?"

She was the only person I had met with who wanted to spend more time with me. And she asked me in such a way that it sounded as if I would be doing her a favor. She could have so easily just apologized and said maybe we could get together in the future.

I told her that I'd be happy to come back later in the afternoon. When I returned, I had my same formal clothes on, but Kitty had been out jogging and came in with her Walkman. I wished I had worn jeans. We sat down and continued our intense conversation for another hour.

Kitty told me that regardless of what happened in the election, she would do whatever she could to help me with this mission. We talked at some length about the importance of my anonymity, and she agreed to be very circumspect about sharing what we'd discussed.

Kitty was very compassionate and spoke a lot about her own life and the rigors and pressures of the campaign trail. She talked about how hard it is to accept what comes your way sometimes. I remember her saying, "Here is what I want to do. I don't think we are going to be the people who get to the White House, but if we are, I want Mike to meet with you as soon as possible and make AIDS one of his top priorities. I will make sure that this happens. And even if we don't get to the White House, I want to help you. I'd like to serve on the board of your foundation."

I had not asked Kitty to come on our executive advisory board. Like Steven Spielberg, she volunteered. Now we had two.

The meeting had moved her as much as it had me. Kitty's kindness was mind-boggling to me. I could not believe the extent to which she reached out and tried to help. It was extremely emotional and dramatic.

Kitty was going to be speaking at a fund-raiser that night which Paul and I had been planning to attend. She said she hoped I would come forward to say hello and introduce her to Paul. I said I'd try, but we both knew there would be hundreds of people around and it might be impossible. I still felt such nonstop nervousness when we were out in public.

I saw Bob Burkett shortly after we arrived at the fund-raiser, and he said Kitty had told him how moved she was by our meeting. We sat through dinner with our friends, after which Bette Midler performed. Then Kitty got up to speak and I panicked.

Had I made it clear to her that she couldn't say anything about me? If she even alluded to our meeting, our secret would be jeopardized. My mind raced back and replayed our conversation. I wondered if I had stressed protecting the secret enough, especially in Hollywood where we knew so many people and rumors had been flitting about like fireflies. The day had been so intense and powerful for me; I knew if it had been the same for her she might accidentally say something that might give us away.

It was Sunday, October 16, just twenty-three days until the election. At one point in her speech, Kitty said something like "Twenty-three days is not a long time. But twenty-three days is too long for a person, who doesn't have a home, to wait for a home. Twenty-three days is too long if you are waiting for medical assistance. Twenty-three days is too long if you are a man . . . or a woman . . . or a child with AIDS waiting for help."

My heart was pounding. I was ready to explode. I had tears in my eyes and I tried to brush them away without being noticed. I knew she had added the phrase about women and children with AIDS because of our meeting. It was a small gesture but one that was deeply significant. It gave me both momentum and hope.

I still see Kitty to this day. In the last two years her life has gone through much upheaval and evaluation. I deeply respect her courage and determination and feel lucky that I get to call her a friend.

Then suddenly, it was all over.

November 8 gave the election to Bush in a landslide. Everything I had hoped we could achieve in a Dukakis administration had vanished.

The presidential campaign had been like a rip cord. I yanked it hard and it had carried me over the first few months after Ariel's death. It had given me focus and hope. Kitty and I had found such a deep and spontaneous rapport that I thought if they made it to the White House there might be a happy ending to our story. It wasn't a very rational thought but I held on to it. If Dukakis won, more money would be spent on AIDS, more research done, more answers found . . .

His defeat was a cataclysmic letdown. I felt devoid of almost any optimism. I began to believe that everything would end tragically and we would all die. I began to think I would feel dead until I died. I would still try to go out into the world and educate people about pediatric AIDS, but I knew I would feel cold and black inside.

Some books on death and loss say that grief comes in three-month segments. The first three months are a time of shock and denial and that's certainly what happened to me.

Now that the election was over, there was room inside for me to be engulfed by grief and sadness, and I was. On the outside, I still functioned normally. But I cried every day. I would go into Ari's room and lie on her canopy bed and sob.

It would often start in the morning when I woke up. I

would be scared and sad but try not to cry while Jake was still at home.

All I wished for was to have Ari back and slip into the habit of loving; to put my cheek beside hers, to brush her hair, to read *Make Way for Ducklings* just one more time before it was lights out. Wish is too simple a word for it. I *yearned* to have my child back. I yearned with a primal longing, and a raging instinct for something that I knew I would never have again. Grief has a gravity all its own.

Paul was probably the only one who knew just how wretched I felt inside. He watched me cry for days on end. He watched me fall asleep with tears on my cheek.

I knew I would have to find some way to cope with my life if I was going to go on living. After Ari died, I gradually stopped seeing the two people who had been so vitally important to me when she was sick—Jim Blechman, my holistic doctor, and Rabbi Omer-Man. It was too painful to be with them. They were both so linked in my mind to the time she was ill, being with them reminded me of how I was going on without Ari and I couldn't bear it.

I started to see a woman named Marianne Williamson three days after the election. She started a foundation in Hollywood called "The Center for Healing." Marianne also teaches something called "The Course in Miracles." I went to see her on the suggestion of a woman named Anna Belle Kaufman.

Anna Belle's son, Zack, had been infected with the AIDS virus after a blood transfusion at birth. He died when he was five years old. Anna Belle was the only other mother I knew who had lost a child to AIDS. We had too much in common. We knew about secrets and hiding. We knew about doctors and nursing. We knew about a society that didn't care. We knew about death. We knew about losing the most precious person you have ever loved.

Anna Belle had been both helped and impressed with Marianne and had been urging me for months to see her. I didn't really want to participate in a group because we were still desperately trying to keep our story a secret. But Marianne agreed to meet and work with me privately, which is something she doesn't often do. I cried my heart out with Marianne. She helped guide me through that awful time as

I tried to figure out if I was going to be able to start living again.

Marianne helped me think about love again. She encouraged me to trust my instincts and to look at how I was growing and learning. The anger, pain, frustration, anguish, grief, were all things I had to experience. The only way over the pain was through it.

She encouraged me to bring my highest self into the meetings I was having in Washington and to trust in my own honesty because there were no hidden agendas or complicated goals. She stressed to me that if you go before a group of individuals and talk from your heart, speaking from your essence which is really just love, everything will turn out fine and people will be moved. She was right. If you are caring, then most often others will be, too.

Then I spoke with Marianne about not being able to find beauty in the world. I knew that if I could find beauty, then I was not dead. I knew if I could touch my love again, then I was not dead. Beauty and love became linked. They were the things I wished I could find but wasn't sure whether or not I would.

My birthday was three days after the November election and I had said to Paul over and over again that I wanted to skip the whole thing. Ever since the diagnosis we had really been making an effort to celebrate my birthdays. When I turned thirty-nine, we had a big party because I genuinely feared not making it to forty. At forty, my mother had a luncheon for me with my closest women friends. But forty-one was one I wanted to ignore. I remember saying to Paul, "Nothing will make me smile on this birthday." We decided that we would have a quiet dinner with Lynn and her husband, Frank.

When I awoke on November 11, Paul said, "Wait a minute," went and got Jake, and the next thing I knew they walked into the bedroom singing "Happy Birthday." They were followed by a woman in a tuxedo who served me breakfast in bed for the first time in my life.

I was flabbergasted.

In the old days, Paul would be out running around at six P.M. on my birthday, trying to find a gift before the stores closed. I couldn't believe that he would have planned *any-*

thing in advance. Despite everything, he still cared for me a great deal—and that was priceless.

After breakfast I said I was going to take a shower. I had plans to see a few women friends for lunch. But Paul said, "When you're finished, get dressed for lunch."

"But it's only nine o'clock in the morning."

"Elizabeth, just listen to what I am saying and don't be bossy. Get dressed, don't ask questions, and come downstairs."

I did.

He walked me to our front door, opened it, and there a limousine was waiting. I didn't even have my purse!

Paul said, "Good-bye, honey, I love you."

As I got into the car, I said to myself, "Elizabeth, relax—you might as well enjoy this."

The limo took me into Beverly Hills and stopped in front of a beauty parlor. When I went inside someone said, "Oh, Elizabeth Glaser, happy birthday!" I had a massage, a facial, my hair was washed. Clearly, I was getting the works. A note said that Rena would be picking me up for lunch.

The nicest part of all was that Paul had made it happen. This came at a time when we weren't able to give very much to each other. Overcome by our own grief, there wasn't much room for love to be shared. But in the midst of everything else I felt lucky that day—lucky for having Paul.

I had lunch with Lucy, Lynn, Susan, Claudia, Jody, and Rena and then, happy and exhausted, I wanted to go home and collapse. Susan drove me back and when we pulled up in front of the house, there was the best surprise of all.

Sitting in our driveway was an old white Jeep—no top, no doors. Years ago in Tahoe I had a Jeep like that and Paul knew how much I missed it. Giving me that Jeep was Paul's way of saying to me, "You can still have fun." I didn't know that yet, but Paul did. He had listened to all my admonitions, "No birthday," and then gone right ahead and planned the best one of my life.

It was all too much. I said to Paul that I wanted to stay home. Going out to dinner was no longer necessary. Paul was still having bad back pain and we usually had supper in the den where he could eat lying down. But Paul said Lynn and Frank were counting on it, so we kept our plans. No one would tell me where we were going.

We were walking toward a steak house and I said I wanted to stop and get cigarettes. There was a diner right next to us. It was brightly lit and as I walked in looking for the cigarette machine, I noticed that there were a lot of balloons. I thought, "What a cute restaurant. Why haven't I been here before?"

Then, as my eyes focused, I saw my friend Carol Herman. What was she doing there? As my eyes widened, I realized all the people standing beside her were my friends. My heart did cartwheels inside. Paul had ended the day with a "surprise" party for me. He had given me gifts from morning to night. It was a fantastic party. My parents were there and so was my brother, Peter, and his wife, Janet. Even Donna and Michael Moskow had come in from the East Coast.

We had hamburgers and onion rings and then we danced like crazy to great songs from the sixties and seventies. I had never had a surprise party in my entire life and this was certainly the most incredible party I could ever have.

All of us had shared such anguish for so long. Now it was time to let loose. We had so much sadness to release. I danced with wild abandon. Paul's back was still terrible and so my girlfriends and I were partners. It was wonderful to feel momentarily alive and be able to have fun. Paul was the prince who made it all possible. For an evening we were AWOL from our tragedy. It was an invigorating diversion, but one that could not last more than a day.

On November 12, I settled back into my routine. Work was what I did on the outside while I grieved on the inside. Even when I felt so devastated, I still tried to keep functioning. Susan De Laurentis and I were meeting with doctors in Los Angeles who were working in pediatric AIDS. Since we had the money to fund our first grants, we were trying to determine what research was under way and what still needed to be done.

In order to do this, we were also coordinating a "think tank" in pediatric AIDS. We wanted to bring together a small group of doctors from around the country to meet at the National Institutes of Health (NIH) in Bethesda in mid-December and talk about where things stood and what direction the priority research should take.

Susan and I were preparing for our first trip to Washington

together. We decided to canvass the various NIH agencies involved with pediatric AIDS research and see where the basic biomedical work was being done. We didn't want the Foundation to duplicate what anyone else was doing. We knew that biomedical research is the kind of scientific detective work that would answer some of the most crucial questions facing children with HIV.

One of the key questions was why only about a third of all infected mothers passed the AIDS virus on to their children. What mysteries of the disease would be unlocked if we knew why the other two thirds didn't? If research could tell us when and how the virus was transmitted during pregnancy from mother to child, maybe there would be a way to block it. If a pregnant woman took AZT during her pregnancy, could it prevent her baby from being infected?

We also wanted to examine the opportunistic infections that impact children and look for potential therapies. Because a child's immune system is just developing, so much was different in the way the virus impacted children. I knew this from watching Ari. We had to examine all the differences that pediatric AIDS presented and figure out how to move ahead as quickly as possible.

We felt like detectives. Surely, once we followed up every lead we would find the hospitals or labs where the essential research was being done. But as Susan and I dove in, we were stunned to discover that the only research that was going on at the NIH was clinical and epidemiological. There *was* no basic biomedical pediatric AIDS research under way at any institute. We kept saying, this can't be true. It isn't possible. But it was. Children had been ignored. Money had gone everywhere except pediatrics. I raged inside.

Of course the clinical trials were important. They would test new drugs and therapies as they came along. The epidemiological studies are like radar systems that track where the disease is spreading and how fast. They're also important, but where was the science that was going to answer the questions specific to children? Where was the scientific research that would lead the way to understanding how and why this virus killed kids so rapidly? Most children died by the time they were two years old. Where were the studies that would save my child?

Susan was doing this investigative research. She was appalled. She showed me what she had found and I was furious. Once we broke it down, we saw a gaping hole. We had known there were problems. But we were convinced that something was being done somewhere.

We had already decided the Pediatric AIDS Foundation would concentrate its efforts in the area of research, but we wanted to work in tandem with the government. We had assumed it wasn't doing enough, but we never expected to find out that the government wasn't doing anything in this area at all. Neither Susan nor I nor the doctors we were working with ever expected to discover that *nothing* was under way. *No one* was doing any basic fundamental research in pediatric AIDS. *No one* was paying attention to the children. We felt like hounds who had found the scent. Our determination multiplied as we learned more and more about what wasn't happening. Meanwhile, the virus was infecting and killing children all over the world.

No one had yet commissioned a study on maternal transmission of AIDS by the end of 1987. Millions and millions of dollars had been spent putting together information about how the epidemic spreads, which kids were getting it, and where they lived. Facts like that were abundant. But no one had taken it the next step and said, "Okay, enough of that, let's find out how these kids get the virus from their mothers in the first place."

Part of what was lacking was any overall coordination in pediatric AIDS. There was an astounding lack of communication among agencies. You would think these people would talk to each other, but they don't.

Another part of the problem was that initially people didn't really understand that AIDS affects children differently from adults. Ninety percent of all children who are HIV-positive have central nervous system complications. This is, in fact, rare in adults. It was Ari's central nervous system complications that made her so debilitated and made her lose the ability to walk, talk, and write.

What was so amazing about Phil Pizzo's work at NIH with intravenous AZT was that he was able to reverse much of the central nervous system damage in children. Reverse. AZT doesn't do that in adults. Drugs impact children differently from grown-ups; children had to be studied separately!

AIDS in children impacts their growth and development.

Almost all children with AIDS fall off the growth chart and many babies just fall off the developmental chart as well.

The opportunistic infections that children get are much more varied because they do not yet have a fully developed immune system and they fail to develop antibodies. Jake could get chicken pox over and over and over again. We were finding that there were many questions that only applied to children. Why weren't they being addressed?

We came to discover the answer was frighteningly simple. Pediatrics is not considered "hot science." Pediatricians don't win Nobel Prizes. Pediatrics gets what's left over, if it gets anything at all. There is an Academy of Pediatrics separate from the American Medical Association because the needs of kids get lost in the bigger picture. Historically, this has been true and it has happened again with AIDS. No one took the time or found the commitment to set aside money from what became a large AIDS research budget to ensure that the necessary pediatric issues would be studied separately.

It is unthinkable and grotesque that we make the same mistake over and over again. There should be an uproar of children shouting, "What about me?" But they often can't speak and so their plight goes unnoticed until an outraged parent decides to speak out.

Susan had been working closely with three of the smartest doctors around, Phil Pizzo at NCI, Art Ammann at Genentech, and Dick Stiehm at UCLA. They were organizing the agenda for the think-tank meeting. She was excited. Our money now had become even more important in light of what our government wasn't doing. I was going to go to New York City first and then we would meet in Washington. I was looking for the right people to go on our health advisory board. I got to New York and stayed with Aunt Vera, whom I hardly ever got to see, now that I was so busy.

On that trip, my first meeting was with Dr. Jim Oleske at Newark Children's Hospital. I was trying to understand more about the evolution of pediatric AIDS as an issue, and Jim has been on the front lines ever since the epidemic began. He is the founder and director of the pediatric AIDS program at Children's Hospital. Oleske was one of the first to speak out on behalf of children with AIDS in 1981 but no one listened.

My first impression of Jim Oleske was that he looked so tired. It's been a lonely struggle for him. He has been watching children die from AIDS for a decade, and for much of that time no one seemed to care because they were poor and mostly black. He told me how he initially became involved.

"The first case of pediatric AIDS I saw was in 1976. She was a little girl whose mother was a prostitute. But of course I didn't realize it was AIDS then. I didn't know what AIDS was. No one did.

"By '78 when the little girl died, we thought we had an unusual case of a child with recurrent salmonella infections, LIP [lymphoid interstitial pneumonitis] on lung biopsy, high antibodies, and poor T-cell functions. If she walked in the door today the most inexperienced of medical students could make a diagnosis of AIDS, but then it was a mystery disease. It was baffling. We had no idea what was really wrong with her. However, we saved some serum and years later when we tested it we found out she was HIV-positive. She died when she was about six."

Oleske could not sense the magnitude of the epidemic that was looming. In the late seventies, the cases were still sporadic.

"By 1981–82, it was clear that something was happening in Newark. We were seeing more and more children with immune deficiencies and unusual infections that we couldn't pin down. The breakthrough for me came at the end of 1981. My lab did immunological studies. We were asked to study this new syndrome, which was then called GRID, for Gay Related Immune Deficiency, that was occurring mostly in gay men and drug users."

Oleske was asked to get a blood sample from a patient who was a drug user. Since he's a pediatrician, Oleske is an expert at drawing blood from difficult veins. When Oleske walked into the man's room, he recognized him. "His little girl had died six months before. A light bulb went on. She had been one of my mysterious pediatric cases. It suddenly dawned on us that this must be an infectious disease—maybe one that acted like a sexually transmitted disease.

"But this was not a popular thing to say back then. There was a lot of resistance to accepting the fact that children could get this disease. It was a disease of gay men and drug users—why should kids get it? I am not sure why there was such hostility. It was difficult to convince people that this disease was real and happening in children. Just as it was difficult to make people focus on adults because it was impacting gays and IV drug users."

If no one would listen, Oleske knew the best he could do was make sure that specimens were sent to the most advanced laboratories for study. His own lab—which had few machines and consisted of Oleske, a part-time technician, and a resident fellow—was not equipped to do state-of-the-art investigations.

So when one of his AIDS patients would die, even if it was in the middle of the night, Oleske would drive to the hospital to make sure the blood specimens and tissue were taken immediately and then sent either to the CDC or to NIH. If it meant driving the samples to the airport himself, he did it.

By 1985, Oleske had established, with his nurse practitioner, Mary Boland, the Children's Hospital AIDS Program. Its first funding came from the lifers at a nearby prison who raised a thousand dollars. Oleske had cared for one of the inmates' children. The big scientific establishment people didn't want to fund a nobody from Newark. Oleske had five grants turned down by NIH until 1987.

"Approved but not funded," Oleske explained. "That's like saying this is a good idea, but we are not going to give you any money. The biggest complaint was that we couldn't get good compliance. They thought that since these were all drug users, we'd be unable to get them to come back regularly enough to do a comprehensive scientific study.

"But we had already proven that if you have a social worker and give good care, people come back. We have about a ninety-percent compliance rate. Yes, some of the parents are drug users, but they care about their children."

I've learned that Congress often pays more attention to parents and families than to doctors and scientists, who are often seen as self-serving, and sometimes are.

In 1986, Oleske was asked to present data at a conference sponsored by the Surgeon General on women and children with AIDS. He sat down and tried to project where the numbers would lead. The CDC had been making projections, but they counted only cases of full-blown AIDS, people who were already sick, not the number of people infected with the HIV virus who were still healthy.

This distorted the reality of the epidemic. For example, the CDC would say there were twelve cases in the state of New Jersey when Oleske knew he was treating seventy kids at his hospital as outpatients.

So for the Surgeon General's conference, Oleske concluded that by 1991, there would be between ten and twenty thousand cases of pediatric AIDS nationwide, and that one in every ten pediatric hospital beds would be occupied by a child with HIV infection. People accused him of crying wolf and trying to exaggerate the problem. No one thought the numbers could ever be that high, but in fact, his high end turned out to be correct.

It's the same for Jim Oleske as it is for me. There isn't time to get angry. People continually ask me if I'm angry at the person who gave the blood. What good would it do? Is it going to help Jake Glaser fight AIDS? Is it going to help me fight AIDS?

I asked Jim to be part of our health advisory board and he agreed. I also asked his nurse practitioner, Mary Boland. Jim was glad that I was being listened to in Washington, but his feelings were understandably bittersweet.

He's been watching people die for ten years. It's embittering for him to know that it took a white woman, the wife of a television star, to bring attention to pediatric AIDS. "Why couldn't we care about the kids in Newark, too?" he asks. "It smarts."

He's right. It smarts. I'll be the first to admit that I'm a fine example of what's right and also what's wrong with our system. What can be more American than one person who tries to make a difference? But isn't it an outrage that no one listened before?

After finishing my meeting in Newark I felt bleak and overwhelmed. I wanted to go back to Vera's and lie down, but I couldn't. I had a very important meeting next. It was with one of Ari's favorite people, and it was about money.

After Ari died, Lucy and I talked about asking James Taylor to record a lullaby album, with the proceeds going to the Foundation.

So I went to meet with James Taylor and Kathryn Walker in their apartment in New York City. I was thinking of it as a business meeting and never expected the powerful emotions that I felt when I walked in their front door.

It was a world I had lived in with Ari, but never seen. There were the birds, the dog, the view of the Hudson River—everything James had described to her on the tape, which we had listened to over and over, was there. It was as though we had walked these halls together. I had to blink back the tears, but I was crying very hard inside.

We had lunch together and James said he was enthusiastic about participating on the lullaby album. His commitment in those early stages was vital. Another piece was falling into place. He said he'd call his manager, Peter Asher, and we'd get things under way.

Before flying down to Washington, I took a cab to Harlem Hospital, to meet with Dr. Margaret Haegarty, who is the director of pediatrics there. She also agreed to come on our health advisory board.

I arrived in Washington a day before Susan, who joined me the next afternoon. There were two critical goals: to participate in the Foundation's first "think tank" and figure out how to get the Food and Drug Administration (FDA) to speed up drug testing for children. Detectives Glaser and De Laurentis were back on the beat.

As I had so painfully witnessed in my own home, AZT was available for adults two years before it was ready for children. That was the way the system always worked. After the tragedy with thalidomide in the sixties, the drug companies and the FDA were very cautious about approving drugs for children, which is fine until there is a life-threatening epidemic.

My fear then, in late 1988, was that what happened with AZT would be repeated with each subsequent drug that became available for the treatment of AIDS. I worried about drugs not being approved in time to help Jake. It was imperative to work with the FDA and show the agency that following their rules could have awful consequences.

Bob Burkett had suggested that when I got to Washington, I meet with someone in Senator Howard Metzenbaum's office, because he is on the committee that oversees the FDA. So I met with Joel Johnson, Metzenbaum's young legislative director. Joel looked like the perennial class president, the clean-cut honor student.

We met in the senator's office with its high windows and

eclectic collection of art, everything from Red Grooms to old Chinese tea bins.

Joel gave me excellent advice. Despite his well-scrubbed appearance, Joel turned out to be a brilliant, cunning political strategist. Within a pragmatic, cynical exterior, he has a classic liberal heart. He said, "All the Democrats that you meet with will say that they want to help and they will mean it. But you aren't going to get anywhere unless you have *bipartisan* support. You can't just meet with Democrats. You have to sell your ideas to Republicans as well."

He said he would help and suggested I meet with Nancy Taylor, who was the staff person in charge of health for Senator Orrin Hatch, a conservative Republican from Utah. Metzenbaum and Hatch had worked together on legislation to help the "boarder babies," infants born infected with the AIDS virus and left in hospitals by parents who were unable or unwilling to care for them.

Like just about everyone else on Capitol Hill at that time, Joel thought that boarder babies were the extent of the pediatric AIDS problem. As he said to me, "People just don't think this is a problem of epidemic proportions. This is the first I've heard that pediatric AIDS isn't just an issue of a few drug-addicted mothers who were giving birth to babies with AIDS and abandoning them." By now I was no longer surprised to find out people didn't know much about what I was telling them.

I went back over to the Hart Building to meet Nancy Taylor. I will never forget our first encounter. It taught me as much as any one meeting I have had in Washington.

I spent over an hour with Nancy. She was bright, aggressive, and totally committed to her point of view. When I left I understood more clearly than ever before why it's so hard to implement change. It's because on every issue there are such good people with such totally divergent points of view. Each believes his or her viewpoint is correct. I felt scared because getting the system to change at all seemed formidable. What I didn't know was that Nancy Taylor would become not only a good friend but instrumental in helping us with significant legislation down the road.

I felt Joel Johnson had not adequately prepared me for the meeting, but he was one-hundred-percent right—it was a meeting I had to have. Without eliciting conservative support, I wasn't going to accomplish much at all.

Susan arrived in the afternoon and had arranged a meeting with Sandy Mitchell Brock, an old friend of her family who now was married to Reagan's Labor Secretary, William E. Brock. Our hope was that Sandy would serve on the Pediatric AIDS Foundation's executive advisory board. We wanted to be sure our board was balanced both geographically and politically.

We met Sandy for a drink. We needn't have worried. Sandy agreed to serve on our board even before we finished our pitch. She told us we could count on her to help.

We were excited about having Sandy come on board, but we really had no idea just how significant she was going to be.

The next day was the "think tank." Susan, Phil Pizzo, Art Ammann, and Dick Stiehm had done a magnificent job and the day ran smoothly. For an entire day, twelve bright and creative researchers focused all their attention on children with AIDS. At this point, we had raised nearly a million dollars for research. The purpose of the "think tank" was to figure out how that money should be spent and to discuss the Foundation's direction in the year ahead.

There were one or two moments when the doctors' conversation about dying children struck too close to home and I had to put my head down and hide my tears. I worked hard to keep my perspective. I was doing what I needed to do. At the same time that I had lost a child, in many ways, I felt I was giving birth to a new sort of child—a foundation that would hopefully save lives. The "think tank" was the first step.

CHAPTER
❧11❧

When I came home from Washington I was devastated for two days. Everything that I had shut off while I was going from meeting to meeting overwhelmed me. I became engulfed in depression and cried almost constantly. To sit in those Washington meetings and not cry, I had to be able to talk about my life but not really feel it. Upon returning to L.A., all the feelings poured out. I would look at Jake and think of how slowly things were moving in Washington and feel so frightened and helpless. I was also exhausted. I forgot that just day-to-day coping with my life is tiring.

Sometimes I get back from Washington and just cry when I finally get into bed. It isn't fair to Paul. He gets frustrated and says, "Look, you've been gone for four days, I've done all the parenting, and now you're back and you're crying!"

Sometimes Paul just throws up his hands and says it's too much. But after a number of trips to Washington, we both learned about this reaction to my work, and now we remind each other that it's always like this when I come home, and it will pass. In time, the trips to Washington have exacted less and less of an emotional toll, but initially they were extremely depressing.

This time when I returned, it was Christmas. For months I had been dreading Christmas and Hanukkah. I wanted to avoid being in Los Angeles. I could not imagine seeing all these happy families, knowing that Ari wasn't there. I knew I would resent my friends for having normal, happy, wonderful lives and they would avoid me, not wanting to be reminded during their holiday how horrible life could be.

The thought of lighting a Hanukkah candle without Ari was intolerable. The thought of staying home made me so despondent that we had made reservations to go skiing for a week in Canada with the Seymours and then fly to Hawaii for ten days, where we would be joined by our niece, Alisa Kantar. We would be away for the entire Christmas holiday. It was an extravagant idea but it was my plan for emotional survival.

We had been in Hawaii with Ari two years before. Jake was only two years old then and although we didn't know it, he remembered it vividly. We arrived on Maui on December 25. Jake's room at our condominium had two beds in it. When we told him his cousin Alisa would be sleeping in the other bed, he became furious. "That's Ari's bed," he insisted. "It's not for Alisa."

Hawaii became very traumatic for Jake. He cried every night about Ari. This was the first time he had cried so hard, and Paul and I felt awful. We didn't know how to help him. Jake fell apart completely and would not leave my side.

Hawaii was dreadful. It seemed that once the Seymours were gone and we were on our own, we just couldn't handle it. The vacation was filled with tension. Paul's back continued to be painful. He had back problems for eight or nine months after Ari died. There we were in paradise, and all we could do was cry.

One day we drove over to the Hana side of the island and climbed to the seven sacred pools of water that are linked together on the side of a mountain. As we reached the top, there was a double rainbow over the seven pools. Jake looked at me and we both sighed. We knew Ari was part of that rainbow.

I said to Jake, "Do you want to say something to her?"

He just looked up and ever so quietly said, "I miss you, Ari. I love you. I love your rainbow."

I had talked to Jake about Ari's spirit being alive and he would tell the people we met, "My sister's dead, but her spirit is still alive." But being able to say the words and really feeling her spirit are two different things.

When we came home Jake had four terrible months of emotional trauma. He had been going to nursery school by himself the entire year, but now he wouldn't go without me. Separation petrified him. I went with him every day for almost six weeks. When he didn't see me, he would panic.

I brought a book to nursery school, the biggest one I could find: *The Mists of Avalon*. It was one thousand pages. I sat in a little room that was adjacent to Jake's class. The door was open and he could see me. As long as I was there, he was fine. But if I even went to the bathroom, he would be crying by the time I returned.

Mary Hartzell, the nursery school director, and Joanne Mandakas, Jake's teacher, pulled me through. They never made me feel like I was a bad mother because my boy was having such a hard time. We were a team and it felt like we were all trying to help Jake.

They reminded me that while giving Jake love and support was important, I had to keep setting limits as well. Sometimes I would feel like I should just let Jake do and have whatever he wanted because who knew how long he would be alive. But that thinking went against everything I ever learned in early childhood education and I knew that ultimately it would not be good for Jake. Finding the balance sometimes seemed impossible. My fear and my intellect were constantly battling. In the end, I hoped for wisdom.

Thank goodness for the support of Susan Jay, Jake's "talking doctor." She was the psychologist who was seeing him once a week. She reassured me that because of Jake's powerful bonding to Ari, what he was experiencing now was not unusual, and that it would get better in time.

Paul and I had seen a therapist together a handful of times after Ari died. I think many people believe that the loss of a child brings couples closer together. But that's a Doris Day, happily-ever-after fantasy. Sharing a powerful and horrible loss creates enormous stress and outsiders only see the tip of the iceberg. Stress did not bring Paul and me closer together. Most of the time, it pushed us apart. For us, grief was very polarizing. It was sometimes impossible to either communicate or share our grief because it was so intimate.

Paul and I have always been a bit like an emotional seesaw. When one is strong, the other is weak, balancing each other out. But when I plummeted after the election, he plummeted too. Both of us felt weak and depressed.

I felt if I shared my sadness with Paul, it would be oppressive, and I think the same was true for him. So I ended up doing most of my grieving alone. But sometimes there is great comfort in just having the other one's presence in bed at night to hold you and silently say, "I'm here."

.I can't imagine a marriage being tested more than ours has been. Once you realize that the stress is not going to bring you together and has the power to dissolve everything that you have, then you begin to think of ways to prevent it. Sometimes you can find them and other times you can't. Our secret required us to put on a strong, brave front to the outside world. It takes a lot of energy to be gallant. When we came home, we were raw. We would be brittle and irritable with each other.

Our marriage is unusual in that, somewhere deep down inside, Paul and I don't feel we have the choice to leave each other. Other men might have walked away from a wife and two children who were HIV-positive, but not Paul. Neither one of us has ever really considered divorce as an option. What we have had to work toward is the understanding that we do have a choice and that we exercise that choice every day. We choose to stay together. Until we realized that, and sometimes we still forget it, our life often seemed like a prison with no way out. When we remember that we have a choice, then we are no longer victims, and that feels much better.

I was working to understand many things at that time but there was one I couldn't change. No matter how hard I tried, no matter how clearly I understood it, I couldn't change the feeling of being dead inside. I was angry at myself for wasting precious time. It was the first time in my life I wasn't living fully. But I couldn't make the spark begin to glow again. I could no longer find beauty in the world after Ari died. There was no joy. How could I find beauty in a world that had been so cruel? How could I really love? Without joy or beauty or love I felt dead. The world appeared to me in black and white.

I was grappling with these questions for months after Ari died. I was pretty scared about feeling dead inside for so long. The fear was intensified by my realization that my yearly ski trip was coming up.

Each year in January, my friend Suzanne and I go off for

a few days to Aspen with several other married women friends. We ski hard, we dance, we party, and we drink tequila. For me, it's also complicated because I never know if I will be back the following year. The first year I went to Aspen, I knew our diagnosis, but none of us was sick. The second year, Ari was compromised. This was the third year, and she was dead.

Now I felt dead too, and going off to Aspen that winter in 1989 seemed stupid. But it was also a test. Could I go and still be able to enjoy it? I wondered. Aspen would probably confirm that I would never again be able to be myself. I kept my feelings inside, but I knew the trip was somehow going to be decisive for me.

One Sunday afternoon, shortly before I went to Colorado, we had friends over whom we hadn't seen in years. I had spent all morning talking to them about Ari. I went into the kitchen to make tea. I put the water on and was walking to the cabinet when suddenly, I heard this strange noise beside me. It sounded like the humming buzz from a giant bumblebee. But it wasn't frightening. I turned very, very slowly and looked, but nothing was there.

The vibration continued and moved closer and closer to me, then passed through me, and as it did, I could feel my head reverberate with its force. Then it left my body and went on past the sink. The cats were sitting in front and as it passed, they both jerked their heads in unison to follow the vibration. But amazingly, neither ran away or even moved. Then it was gone.

I knew it had happened, but I didn't know what it meant. At another time in my life, I might have felt more disconcerted, but after going through such catastrophic events, small odd moments simply seemed curiously inexplicable. In my heart I hoped it had been Ari.

About ten days later as I was getting ready for Aspen, I realized that I hadn't been mourning Ari in the same way. That made me think. In the past three days, I hadn't felt that drenching sadness. I tried to remember when my feelings changed and my mind went back until it stopped at that vibration. Without any kind of epiphany or any conscious realization on my part, something had changed almost imperceptibly. I packed my bags and flew to Aspen.

We have such good fun in Aspen. I love skiing. I feel free,

fast, and powerful. I feel almost normal when I am racing down a slope. The wind is blowing through my hair and the cold dances on my cheeks. There is no time to think about anything but my rhythm and the quiet of the world.

Suzanne and I have learned how to really enjoy ourselves and each other despite whatever pains exist in both of our lives. I only wish sometimes my other friends and family could see me as happy as I am there.

One night, after skiing all day, we went out dancing. Usually we dance with each other, Suzanne, Sandy, and I being good dance partners, but this night a very handsome man started dancing with me. The other women wanted to go home, but I was having too much fun. So they left and I stayed.

This handsome man who knew nothing, absolutely nothing, about my life, was dancing with me, and I was having a great time. We danced for hours and when we stopped, much to my surprise, he gave me a long lingering kiss goodbye.

I'm sure I remained standing, but my knees felt weak. I had been dead to the world for months. But that night a spark glowed. I knew the struggle ahead was difficult and my future uncertain. But there in the Paragon Bar in Aspen, I realized that part of me could still feel. Like Sleeping Beauty, I was awakening after a kiss.

We said good night, and I went back to my room, and went to bed. The story ended there.

But I changed. I think the vibration in my kitchen was something that passed through me to help me live again. Maybe it was from Ari. Maybe it wasn't, but it comforts me to think that she could have sent it my way. In one of my silent conversations with her, I said, "Ari, I know how much you love Dad, and I know this has nothing to do with him. Thank you. You sent that kiss to me for all the right reasons."

I came home and I could feel myself coming alive again with Paul and with Jake. I started to love them again. If I could love, then I could live. It seemed possible that I could find reasons to hope. I had been like a flower encased in a shell of clay. The clay had hardened and I could no longer see or touch anything. The vibration had cracked the shell and the trip to Aspen had widened it. Air and light came in;

the flower hadn't withered. I felt invigorated and slightly re-
born; returning to work was more fun.

Susie and I plunged back into fund-raising. Susan was
working on the research grants. Without enough money, all
the work would be wasted. One of the things I had to do was
nail down the money from Steven Spielberg. He had said he
would give us $100,000, but we had not received a check. I
called and explained to someone in his office that we were
getting ready to fund our grants and we were wondering
when we might expect Steven's check.

A short while later, I got a call from Gerry Breslauer, who
was Steven's business manager. He asked to meet with me.
I thought, *Oh, swell, before I get the check, I have to sit down
and prove that I am not a flake and that the Pediatric AIDS
Foundation is real.* I was scared. There was a lot of money
at stake.

Breslauer's office was in a very tall building on the Avenue
of the Stars in Century City. We sat down together around
a circular table and I spread out some of the literature I had
brought about the Foundation. I was nervous but I jumped
right in.

"Well, I guess I'm here to convince you that it's okay to
give me the $100,000 that Steven has committed, so since I
don't know how much you know about me, let me tell you
a little bit about my life." When I finished, I told him about
the Foundation and explained that we had no office and no
overhead. Every donated dime went into research. We had
almost raised our first million dollars, without stationery,
business cards, or a telephone. We were using Susan's address
and telephone number at the time, and so far, all of our operating expenses came from our own pockets. Long-distance
phone calls went on our home bills, plane tickets went on
credit cards, and we planned strategies around kitchen tables
when our children were in school and while our husbands
were at work.

I talked in a very serious and businesslike way with Gerry
Breslauer for about forty-five minutes. Then he said he
thought he had a surprise for me. I looked quizzical.

"Well, I have a note here from Steven," he said, putting
it down as he kept talking. I strained my eyes to read upside
down. I could see the figure *$500,000.*

Breslauer continued. "The note here from Steven says he's giving you half a million dollars."

Sobbing and shaking, I got up and threw my arms around this man that I had known for all of forty-five minutes. I finally blurted out, "Will you hate me if I have a cigarette?"

"It's not good for you to smoke."

"I know," I said, "but when I'm excited like this, it's the only thing that will calm me down."

So I lit a cigarette and said, "I can't believe this. You must be Santa Claus. Even if you're Jewish, you still must be Santa Claus."

He laughed. As I got ready to leave he said how impressed he was with me and the work we were trying to do and wished me all the best.

I got in the car and I called both Susan and Susie and told them about what had just happened. We were all elated. I picked up Jake, and by two o'clock or so, we were home.

The phone rang.

"Elizabeth Glaser? Please hold for Gerry Breslauer."

"Oh, my God," I thought, bracing myself for the bad news. "There's been a mistake. It wasn't supposed to be $500,000, maybe it was $50,000, or $5,000 . . ."

Gerry came on, "Elizabeth, do you have any cigarettes handy?"

"Yes, why?"

"Well, light one up right now."

"Okay. Done."

"I just had lunch with Sidney Sheldon, the novelist. He is giving you $100,000."

It was too much to believe. "Gerry, you're telling me you got us $100,000 over lunch? This is unbelievable. You are truly my hero!"

In one day, we had raised $600,000. Each dollar translated into more questions we could answer. Money equaled hope.

Medically, I was still very stable. I would go to Gottlieb's office every six weeks and have my blood work done. This consisted of several tests. One was a complete blood count, called a CBC, which measured my hemoglobin, hematocrit, my white blood cells, and the differentials in my white blood cells. Another test was called a Chem Screen, or a multiorgan screen, which checked, among other things, my electrolytes, liver functions, and kidney functions.

The CBC was important because it allowed the doctors to monitor whether or not the AZT was making me anemic, one of the most common side effects of the drug. Likewise, the Chem Screen would tell us whether the toxicity of AZT was affecting my liver function, since this is the organ that metabolizes the drug.

Finally, there would be the T-cell test, which gave them a count of exactly how many T-cells I had. The lower they dropped, the more susceptible I was to infections. I felt vulnerable if I had a cold or cough, because I never knew if it was just a cold or the first flicker of something more serious.

As with Ari and Jake, waiting for the results of my blood tests was always nerve-wracking. What if the AZT was eating away at my liver? What if I had started to become anemic, and had to go off the drug? I tried to suppress my anxieties and rarely, if ever, talked about them to other people, but they are always there, silently lurking, like the virus itself. Over time, I've learned to block a lot of them out, but there are moments when it gets very, very hard.

My relationship with Michael Gottlieb changed over the course of Ariel's illness. During the first year, I would cry hysterically. During the second year, we were dealing with Ari's worsening condition, and since I had such complete confidence in Dick Stiehm, my visits with Michael became more routine. After Ari died, and the Foundation began to take shape, Michael and I would talk business. It was exciting to problem-solve together.

Susie, Susan, and I had goals for the Foundation right from the start. The first goal was to raise between two and three million dollars in a year. We thought that would fund a significant amount of research and fill in the gap until more government monies were appropriated.

When I approached people for money, I told them we weren't pursuing that strategy. I would say, "Could you please give the Pediatric AIDS Foundation everything you're ever going to give? We need to get the research going immediately. Three years from now is too late. I need as much money as you can possibly spare and then if you never want to see me again, tell me and that will be fine."

There were people who turned us down and people I could never get to see. I had hoped to meet with Merv Griffin, but that never happened. I was very eager to talk with Bill Cosby and Michael Jackson, but those meetings never took place either. We thought Elton John would be a wonderful person to see as he was already involved with the issue, but we didn't know how to contact him. There was no way for us to know that just a year and a half later Elton would approach us and offer to join our effort.

There were surprises as well. Our friends Jay and Linda Sandrich surprised us with a large contribution. My friend from camp, Jill Werner, and her husband, Tom, gave us a significant amount of money. Jane Fonda helped. It all added up to another $100,000.

The one CEO we did align ourselves with successfully was Michael Eisner, the head of Disney. I had taught his children at the Center for Early Childhood Education when I first moved to Los Angeles. Michael had been at ABC during the "Starsky" years so we'd known each other for a long time.

I spoke with Michael and his wife, Jane, for nearly three hours. It was very emotional, as it always is when I go back to the people who were part of the most enchanted years of my life.

After I was finished, he said, "Well, there are a number of things I would like to do for you. One is, I'd like to come on your executive advisory board."

It was amazing to me that the Foundation was assembling a remarkable executive advisory board without our even asking. People had said to me, "Don't even ask Michael Eisner to come on your board. It will never happen." But it did. The puzzle was taking shape.

By now our executive advisory board consisted of Sandy Brock, Bob Burkett, Michael Eisner, Susie Field, Steven Spielberg, Kitty Dukakis, and Senator Paula Hawkins, the ex-senator from Florida, who was Sandy's good friend and, as we were to learn, extremely dynamic. We were rolling and it felt good.

In March, Susan and I planned to make another trip to the capital. We were becoming wise to the ways of Washington. But wisdom only gets you so far. It was time to make things happen. It was time to confront the FDA head-on.

After the last trip, Susan and I, following the suggestion of Nancy Taylor, had sent a list of about twenty probing questions to Dr. Frank Young, head of the Food and Drug Administration. The questions were assembled by some doctors on our health advisory board, which at that time included Dick Stiehm, Art Ammann, Margaret Haegerty, Phil Pizzo, Jim Oleske, Yvonne Bryson, and Michael Gottlieb.

We carbon-copied the questions to Senators Hatch and Metzenbaum, though we had not yet met them, so Frank Young would know we had support, and power, behind us. We were bringing up the issues relevant to drug testing in pediatric AIDS. Why couldn't we start testing drugs in children almost simultaneously with adults? Lives were at stake. The FDA had to pay attention to the kids as well. They couldn't just continue to do things the way they had been. AIDS demanded new rules. Now we needed to follow up and meet Dr. Young in person. He had to know we weren't going to go away.

We also had to meet senators and congressmen on this trip and explain to them our concerns and our plan for making things better. We had put together an educational packet detailing two important things that needed to be done federally. Number one was basic research. Phil Pizzo had outlined twenty million dollars' worth of research that could be initiated *immediately* at NIH if the funds were available. We wanted a commitment for those funds. That was one priority.

Number two was the pediatric clinical drug trials. We explained what we had discovered to be a vital and urgent need: providing ancillary support for families once their children were enrolled in these trials. People who don't have phones, cars, or child care can't just pick up and enroll their child in a drug trial. Running protocols in children is more complicated and therefore more expensive than in adults. So more money was needed. What we envisioned was a clinic system where people could come and get their AIDS care in one place—a center that would have the necessary research facilities as well as social workers and home intervention support. This would help to ensure that protocols would be successful in getting answers.

There were thirteen pediatric clinical trials under way in March of 1989, and our doctors, who had their fingers on the pulse of the epidemic, thought that should be expanded to twenty-seven. That meant that we were really in town to urge that an additional sixty million dollars be allocated for pediatric AIDS.

Our first meeting was with Senator Tom Harkin, a Democrat from Iowa, and his chief staff person, Mike Hall. Harkin was chair of the Senate Appropriations Subcommittee on Health. In the end, his committee would decide who gets how much money. He was critically important. Susan and I spoke with him. He had no idea that the situation was as desperate as it was in pediatric AIDS.

"This is an inexcusable situation," he said. "Let's do what we can to fix it." His evaluation was correct and we were relieved to hear him say it. Tom Harkin's support would mean a great deal over the next year, as would the essential help Mike Hall would offer.

We had spoken with Joel Johnson on the telephone a number of times. He felt we should meet with Senator Metzenbaum when we were in town.

Susan, Joel, and I sat with Howard Metzenbaum around the little table in his office. He is a handsome man with a stately but gentle demeanor and a head of pure white hair.

Metzenbaum was so moved that at one point he began to cry. "This is so terrible," he said. "You don't know how much I love children." His tears startled me. I started to cry, and so did Susan, and then so did Joel. Washington was always full of surprises.

"You know," Howard said, "the person you really just have to meet is Ted Kennedy. He's the one who handles all of these health issues." And then, just like in the movies, he picked up the phone and said, "Sarah, get me Ted Kennedy right now." When she tracked down the senator, Howard said, "Ted, listen, I have a woman sitting in my office that you absolutely must meet. She has a story that you have to hear."

I couldn't believe it. One minute we're all weeping, the next minute Kennedy was on the phone. But he couldn't see us on that trip. In fact, we could not meet with him until almost a year later which was very disappointing.

Now, you have to understand that this was only our second trip to Washington. I had gone alone twice, but that was in anticipation of meeting the President. I had nothing down on paper then, but now Susan and I had come with recommendations. We were presenting ourselves as authorities. But we were still in a state of wonder much of the time. While we came off as very professional and serious in the meetings, as soon as we were alone outside we'd laugh and look at each other in amazement. Part of us still had a hard time believing we were really doing this successfully. As draining as it was, it was unbelievably exciting each step of the way. We knew we had our facts down, we just had to get people to listen and then care or to care and then listen.

The day went on. The tears kept us constantly reminded of the life and death struggle we were in. We stayed on our toes with adrenaline pumping. We went to meet with Senator Hatch for the first time.

Orrin Hatch looks as clean-cut as an FBI agent, but he has a smile that is as charming as it is captivating. I went through my story and told Senator Hatch and Kevin McGuiness, his bearded, good-looking administrative assistant, about our meeting the next day with Frank Young, the head of the FDA. I told Senator Hatch that we really had to find a way to speed up the FDA system and make drugs like AZT available to children a lot more quickly.

I ended each meeting the same way—saying they could not tell anyone they had met with us. The quality of our lives depended on everyone keeping the secret which protected our privacy.

As we were leaving, Nancy Taylor said, "Orrin, you know Susan and Elizabeth have started something called the Pediatric AIDS Foundation." That caught us completely off guard. We hadn't mentioned the Foundation to anyone because it really had nothing to do with educating Washington. We never planned to do any private fund-raising in Washington.

But after Orrin heard about the Foundation and what we hoped to accomplish with it, he said, "Well, let me know if there is ever anything I can do, because I would love to help."

After we left, Kevin talked to Orrin, whose position ever since the first AIDS bill was that AIDS was a health issue, and not—as some of his colleagues frame it—a homosexual issue. He also talked with Joel Johnson and Nancy Taylor. Even if more money got appropriated for pediatric AIDS right away, they knew that with the lag time it would still be a year to eighteen months until it went anywhere. One of them had the idea that maybe Orrin and Howard could sponsor a reception on the Hill. They were thinking about a low-budget, $25-a-ticket affair, where people milled around with drinks. They thought we might be able to raise a few thousand dollars and increase awareness of the issue. But we knew nothing about these talks.

The day over, Susan and I were stunned and excited. We were beginning to feel that maybe it was possible to make a difference. Though we weren't professionals and we lived on the other side of the country, we were quickly in the thick of things. We had this tingling sense that we would be a part of changing attitudes and saving lives. We had to store up those powerful feelings for the aggravating times when everything seemed to be standing still.

The next day the big meeting we had was at noon with Dr. Frank Young. This was crucial because he was the man with the power to speed up the approval of AIDS drugs for children. Both Metzenbaum and Hatch had told us to tell Frank Young that we had met with them. We knew he would pay more attention because of that.

We had done the preliminary groundwork with Ellen Cooper, the woman who coordinates AIDS issues at the FDA. She always told us that they were doing everything they could and were really committed. There was nothing adversarial in her attitude. It's just that the wheels of bureaucracy turn so slowly. But give me a break, that attitude wasn't going to save any lives. Pediatric AIDS needed to be moving forward like a race car at Le Mans. We knew that Frank Young was one of the people who could turn up the juice. But we had no idea whether he would be willing to.

We had begun our meeting with Ellen Cooper and Frank Young when his secretary buzzed. "You know, I hate to do this," he said, "but the Prime Minister of Chile is waiting in the next room." We were in the middle of the Chilean grape crisis. "Would you ladies mind? It will only take me ten or fifteen minutes, and then I will be right back to you."

God only knows where we got our gumption, but Susan and I, without a moment's hesitation, said, "We're sorry, Dr. Young, but we are on a really tight schedule and we're not going to be able to wait."

He seemed startled but he buzzed his secretary and said, "Tell the Prime Minister I'll be out in a few minutes. He is going to have to wait to see me."

Susan and I looked at each other in amazement. We weren't trying to be rude, we were just saying, in effect, pediatric AIDS is as important as Chilean grapes, and if you don't understand that, we're not waiting. We don't have the time and we have a lot of other important people to meet with. Frank Young was probably as startled as we were.

We walked out of that meeting having identified the crucial issues. How soon would AZT be licensed for children? How rapidly would the next drug that became available move through the process? Doctors like Phil Pizzo at NIH and Art Ammann at Genentech have argued that, once a drug starts its Phase I (or toxicity) testing in adults and it is not harming them, testing should be started in children two months later. That way, a drug would be available for children only sixty days after it is ready for adults.

As it turned out, there was still another year of waiting before AZT would be widely available for children. To this day that remains a disgrace.

After lunch we had a meeting lined up with Jesse Helms. Helms is probably the most conservative senator on the Hill with probably the worst voting record on AIDS. He seems to believe AIDS is a curse from God and has urged that those who have it be quarantined. The hope had been that maybe I could have swayed Helms with my story.

I was very scared. We braced ourselves and went to the Dirksen Building. But the meeting never happened. Helms had to go to a vote on the floor and didn't show up. We talked with his staff people, who were cordial, but not surprisingly, nothing productive was accomplished. I didn't have the chance to change his attitudes and he continued to make what I saw as unnecessary and uneducated trouble on the Hill, trouble that had direct impact on the lives of many people with AIDS.

It was more than a year later, in 1990, when I met Jesse Helms face-to-face. He was attaching terrible amendments to the Kennedy–Hatch Emergency Care Bill for AIDS (which later became the Ryan White Bill). I was standing in the Senate reception room when he walked in. I went right up to him and reached out my hand to shake his. Only then did I introduce myself and ask him to please let the bill pass. Senator Helms looked horrified, as though he had been turned to stone. Maybe he'd never touched anyone who was HIV-positive before.

As we were talking in Helms's office, someone came in to say Nancy Taylor was waiting for us outside. She seemed excited and insisted we come back with her to meet with Kevin McGuiness. "He must see you right away."

So we went into Kevin's office and he said to us, "I've got an offer that you can't refuse. But let me call Joel and see if I can get him in here, too."

Joel and Kevin are the opposite of what you would expect. Joel, the clean-cut class president type, works for Metzenbaum, the Democratic senator. Kevin, who works for Hatch, the Republican, looks like a cross between a logger and a leftist. Kevin worked as a labor lawyer before coming to Capitol Hill. He is gentle and sincere, which struck me as unusual for someone who had made it to the top in the cutthroat environment of Hill politics. Most of the time Joel and Kevin are fighting each other. Orrin and Howard agree on about one out of a thousand bills.

Hatch's and Metzenbaum's offices are directly across the hall from each other in the Russell Building so Joel came over and sat down. "Listen to this," Kevin said. "What would you think if Orrin and Howard hosted a fund-raising event for the Pediatric AIDS Foundation here in Washington in June? We think it would be a way of sending a message to all the Appropriations people that this is an important issue and one that both Democrats and Republicans should support."

Susan and I were dumbstruck. Our goal all along had been to be the first foundation *never* to have a benefit. Benefits usually aren't worth the time and energy. Their expenses are so high that it is hard to ever clear much profit. What went through our minds immediately was, "We live in California! We can't possibly do a fund-raiser in Washington!"

Even though we didn't see how we could ever say yes, we also were smart enough to realize that there are some things that you can't refuse. Kevin and Joel wanted to know how much money we would need to raise to make it worthwhile. They didn't tell me they'd been thinking $25 a ticket. We tossed numbers around. Even if we didn't raise that much money, the possibility was there to influence and educate powerful people who appropriate millions of dollars each year.

Susan said, "Well, if this were Hollywood, we would shoot for a million dollars, but in Washington, if we could raise $250,000 with the educational benefits added in, it would certainly be worthwhile."

Susan and I said we wanted to discuss it with Susie and take a little more time to think it over but our hearts were racing. Politically it was huge to have two divergent senators co-host an event for children with HIV. The pluses could be enormous.

Joel said he thought Howard would go for it and Kevin was sure that Orrin would too. They were right. The two senators did jump on board and they have changed the course of many decisions due to their strong resolve and commitment.

Later in the afternoon, Susan and I went to Congressman Natcher's office to meet with his chief staff person, Mike Stephens. You had to talk to people on both sides of the Hill. Natcher was Harkin's counterpart in the House on the Appropriations Subcommittee on Health so his support was crucial if we were going to get any money for pediatric AIDS on the Congressional side.

It's a lot easier to get what you want in a bill if the committee chairman is enthusiastic about it. The best way to get the chairman on your side is to convince his legislative aide, someone like Mike Stephens or Mike Hall, that your proposal is worthwhile.

We brought Mike Stephens our packet of material about pediatric AIDS funding needs. Our pitch was this: Not only did more money have to be allocated for children with AIDS, but the funds had to be earmarked for fundamental pediatric research, not just clinical and epidemiological studies.

It had to be spelled out just where this new money would go. We needed Mike Stephens to be specific.

We thought the money should be targeted toward the National Cancer Institute (NCI) and the National Institute of Allergy and Infectious Diseases (NIAID).

Though people don't like to be told how to do things, Susan and I knew that unless we were adamant, there was a real danger of the money being spent in the same areas once again. Mike Stephens was friendly but he didn't commit. He has been in politics for a long time, and it was hard to tell what he was really thinking. At the end of 1989 it would be Mike Hall, on the Senate side, who would put in the "report language" we had suggested.

Susan and I were exhausted by the time we finally got to the airport and were on our way home. It is always a joy for me to be with her in Washington. We're the kind of friends who are so in sync that we talk in shorthand and can finish each other's thoughts. Neither one of us alone could have accomplished as much as we did together in that first year.

Together we mastered the intricacies of the Hill. Susan's political judgment was usually unfailing, but equally important, when I started to feel sad, vulnerable, and overwhelmed, she was always right by my side.

The two days had been full of the "right" meetings, but it would not be until the fall that the money decisions would finally be made. Brick by brick, meeting by meeting, we were working to change attitudes that in the end would fill the holes in the pediatric AIDS picture. The mortar was filled with tears but we were now workers and determined not to fail.

CHAPTER
⊰12⊱

March came and we celebrated Paul's birthday in Sun Valley. We skied and took Jake on a sleigh ride. It felt almost normal and Jake had a wonderful time.

Meanwhile, at our suggestion, Kevin and Joel met with Sandy Brock. She had masterminded numerous GOP fundraisers, and we thought she'd have insight and expertise to share. We had decided the Hatch-Metzenbaum event would be an evening reception in June.

Sandy thought we should set our sights higher. "Let's just go for it," she said to us. "We have the uniqueness of these two senators who've never done anything together before. Let's try to get President and Mrs. Bush to come."

Suddenly it seemed foolish to have a chip and dip fundraiser if the President was going to come. Sandy Brock was now talking about holding a black-tie dinner at $1,500 a seat and raising a million dollars for the Pediatric AIDS Foundation! We were in shock but said, "Let's fly."

Sandy knew from experience that it usually takes a year to plan a gala of this magnitude. We were trying to do one in three months, but Sandy was up for the challenge.

We held off on setting a date because we kept waiting to hear back from the White House. But by the time the Bushes turned us down, although we were very disappointed, a big benefit was already in the works.

Susan, Susie, and I decided it was time to start looking for office space for the Foundation. We had done everything, so far, from our own homes. Rena Kramer's husband, Jerry, had just moved his office into a building in Santa Monica that wasn't filled, and he asked the owner, Peter Lomenzo, if we could use an empty room until they found a paying tenant. They agreed and we had our first official space. We were able to fit three desks in it if two of them were back to back.

We bought an Apple computer, which was the Foundation's first official expenditure. Up until then, everything had come out of our own pockets or been donated, begged, or scrounged. We had phones installed and we could finally answer the phone, "Pediatric AIDS Foundation." Now that was exciting.

We also now had an excellent board of directors, an impressive executive advisory board, as well as a national health advisory board. We hired our first employee, Beth Freeman. She came on board to answer phones, run the computer, do errands, and earn money for graduate school. Her natural ebullience charmed us from the moment we met her, and her competence turned out to be indispensable.

We moved into our office in May, six weeks before the event in Washington, now entitled, "A Night to Unite." It was a perfect name because the goal of the evening was to make people put politics aside in support of pediatric AIDS, as Howard Metzenbaum and Orrin Hatch had. The date was finally set for June 21.

We threw ourselves into the event with everything we had. It was six weeks of hard work, but on the other end was a million dollars. The Foundation had turned into more work than any of us had bargained for.

Susie put in long hours driving in from the San Fernando Valley day after day. But she was the coordinating point in L.A. There was a lot of work to do and it was all important: invitations, printing, programs, lining up and arranging travel plans for celebrities.

Susan was helping Susie with these chores even though it wasn't her area. Her main job was making sure our research grant procedure was in place because we planned to distribute the million dollars we raised in June within thirty days of the event, which was when our first research funding cycle would be ready for money.

Tables at "A Night to Unite" would sell for $15,000 apiece, and there would be $25,000 and $50,000 sponsors. It would be a black-tie event and we would have celebrities for entertainment. Ted and Susie Field had miraculously agreed to underwrite the cost of the dinner, about $200,000, which meant the million dollars we raised would all go to research. Ted and Susie are incredible friends to have.

But we also wanted to educate the eight hundred people sitting in the room about pediatric AIDS. We didn't want them to forget why they were there. Susan, Susie, and I had been talking for months about producing a documentary film. This felt like the time to do it. I wanted to be able to tell a story similar to my own, the story of a family with AIDS, through a film that I wouldn't have to be in. We had forty-two days to make it happen.

Sandy Brock put us in touch with Bob Johnson, one of the men who produced the Inaugural for President Bush. He agreed to produce the documentary and brought in Scott Iverson to write it. Michael Eisner got Disney to underwrite the $60,000 we estimated it would cost to make the film.

Now we got on the phone to UCLA and NIH to find families who would be willing to appear on film. It's not easy when you are dealing with children and AIDS, but we persisted until we found people who would participate. For each family it was a difficult choice, as I well know since I wouldn't have done it. It showed courage that I still lacked. We had to tell a story that would open people's hearts and also offer hope. I knew the story—it was my life, but could we successfully get it on film?

We also had to put a show together for the benefit. We needed twenty celebrities, one to sit at each corporate table. We needed stars to do the show and we needed an MC to bring it all together. It was the beginning of May, the only person we had a commitment from was Jane Fonda.

Then we had to retract Jane's invitation. The conservative Republicans did not want Jane there. The fear was that if people knew she was coming, some corporate sponsors would not contribute. Jane still wields a lot of political clout. Mortified, I had to call Jane, more apologetic, I think, than I have ever been in my life, and say, "I'm sorry, but having you come creates too many problems for us." I was amazed that people still held on to such emotional baggage about her. But she was very gracious and handled it like a real trooper.

Ironically, Sandy Brock had found herself a bipartisan co-chair. Sandy, a lifelong Republican who'd campaigned tirelessly for George Bush, had sat next to Kitty Dukakis at a Washington meeting. She and Kitty felt like long-lost friends. Like Senators Hatch and Metzenbaum, they were the perfect political odd couple. It made a strong statement.

We were able to assemble our supporting cast of celebrities quite quickly: Ali MacGraw said yes, as did Bess Armstrong, Dana Delany, Meredith Baxter Birney, Carol Kane, and Olivia Newton-John. They were the first to "sign on."

The ongoing tension revolved around the entertainment. We were getting calls every day: "We can't sell tickets to the event until we have a show!" Without a big star we were told that everyone would leave after the dinner and skip the documentary film about pediatric AIDS. We had to have someone to make the wait worthwhile. The film would be the critical part of the evening. We wanted to have someone with a little pizzazz, someone out of the Washington mold. I thought of Bette Midler. She knew how to be outrageous without being distasteful. But she was unavailable. We also asked Barbra Streisand but she couldn't do it either.

Someone suggested that Alan Alda might be a good choice for master of ceremonies. His gentle sense of humor puts people at ease. Paul and I had been friends with Alan and his wife, Arlene, years earlier through our friends Shirley and Sol Turtletaub. But since AIDS, we had cut ourselves off from them completely. In order to ask Alan, I had to tell Shirley what had happened to us. They were immediately supportive and tracked down the Aldas, who were in town. I met with Alan the next day.

Although I was nervous, I was equally determined not to let Alan know how desperate I actually was. I didn't want him to feel emotionally coerced into doing something he didn't really want to do. Even for the best of reasons it is always hard to ask people for favors.

No one wants to be a master of ceremonies at a charity event. These are celebrity chores. Alan was completely honest. "I hate doing these things, Elizabeth. I really do."

I said I understood, but that without him, there was no hope. So much for not sounding desperate. He called the next day, said to count him in, and never made me feel bad for asking. We had the first big piece of the puzzle in place, an MC. Now all we needed was the star.

I knew the time had come for me to do what I had been dreading—ask Cher to perform. It was extremely emotional for me because I had taught Cher's daughter, Chastity, when I first came to Los Angeles. Cher is forever linked to that time in my life.

Chastity, one of the youngest children in my homeroom group, was a sweet and wonderful child and I had felt especially attached to her. Being younger made it difficult for her at times. Chas had never read, and I was trying to teach her. I was her teacher for two years, and in that time we became very close.

After Ari died, when I missed her so much I would pretend she was like Chastity, a child who grew up but I never saw again. I was trying to find some way to adjust to the loss of my child and linking her to Chas helped.

So going to see Cher was complicated. If she said no, I would have lost hope. I left a message with her agent, and her secretary called me back. I said I couldn't explain why I needed to speak with Cher, but it was vitally important that I did. But nothing happened. On May 23, with the benefit less than a month away, I called again and said it was an emergency.

The next night at nine o'clock, the phone rang. "Betsy?"

"Oh, Cher," I said. "Thank God you called."

"What's up? I heard there was some sort of emergency. What's going on?"

"Cher, my life is so complicated. I can't even talk to you about it on the phone. When can I see you?"

"Are you tired?"

"Well, not really." (Actually, I usually go to bed about nine o'clock.)

"I'm at my house in Malibu. Can you drive out now?"

"I'll be there in forty minutes."

I got out of bed, got dressed, and jumped into the car. It felt good to drive fast up Pacific Coast Highway. The sky and the sea were dark and peaceful, but I was jittery and tense. The fate of our million-dollar fund-raiser was riding on this meeting.

Cher's house was right on the ocean. Her sister, Georgianne, was there and the three of us sat down on Cher's king-sized bed. They had a big glass canister filled with M&Ms which I dipped into as I began to talk.

I had not seen Cher in a long time. She did not know about my marriage to Paul or the births of Ari and Jake. I explained what had happened to my family and told her how Ari died. It was very sad to be telling her all of this. After describing the Foundation, I said that we were planning to raise a million dollars for pediatric AIDS research at a fund-raiser in Washington, D.C.

Cher looked at me and said, "I've been trying to figure out how you needed my help. Now I get it. You want me to perform at this event."

I said, "Cher, I *need* you to perform at this event. I don't know who else to turn to."

"Then I'll do it," she said simply. Cher looked at her sister and said, "Let's get Billy on the phone right away." Bill Samath is her manager.

By now it was 2:30 A.M. in New York.

"Bill, are you sitting down?"

"Cher," he said, "I'm asleep."

"I just want you to know that I am performing at an event in Washington on June 21. We'll go over it more tomorrow but I just wanted you to know. Bye-bye."

"Cher, are you nuts? That's only four weeks away. What are you talking about?"

"Billy, don't ask questions. I'm not going to tell you any more about it. This is something I am going to do. The people from the Pediatric AIDS Foundation will be in touch with you in the morning."

Cher was amazing. The minute she called Billy I knew she wasn't going to change her mind. She asked me a lot of questions about my family and she wanted to know how many songs she'd have to sing at the benefit. "Not many," I said.

Susan and Susie were jubilant. Cher hadn't performed in years and she had a new album coming out. By Washington standards, she was also risqué. The Republicans had been in office for eight years and people like Cher weren't coming into town very often.

The next morning I called Washington and said, "We've got Cher." At first everyone was thrilled. Alan Alda and Cher were more than anyone had counted on. The next ques-

tion everyone asked was, "What is she going to wear?" The
same people who were opposed to having Jane Fonda at the
benefit kept calling to ask if Cher had decided on her outfit.
I hadn't the slightest idea what Cher was going to wear, but
I assured everyone it would be fine. I trusted her.

That May, I took Jake in for his first developmental workup
at UCLA. The doctors would look at Jake's intellectual and
motor abilities to see if his coordination and learning were
appropriate for his age. I knew from Ariel's decline how rapidly this disease impacts the central nervous system once it
starts. The doctors wanted to have a baseline exam on Jake.

I was frightened because it might show that there had already been some erosion in Jake's physical development. Jake
did tests with blocks and puzzles and drew letters and threw
balls. It took nearly three hours, but the results were normal.
Paul and I breathed a sigh of relief.

Jake was also going in regularly to have his blood checked.
At first, it was every three months; now it's every six weeks.
This is another time of inescapable anguish. If and when his
T-cell level suddenly plummets then we have to contemplate
putting him on an anti-viral, either AZT or DDI, dangerous
and toxic drugs—but the only medical hope available now.

The hard part about that would be explaining to Jake why
he needs to take pills four times a day. In anticipation of that
possibility, I once told him that he and I have funny blood
which the doctors have to keep checking to make sure that
everything is okay. "I know that," he said, in his typically
savvy four-year-old style.

Then he asked me if Ari died because she had funny blood.
I paused. I felt I had to be as honest as I could. I said yes,
Ari had died because of her funny blood, but that we didn't
know she had it until after she was already very sick. I said
that since we knew about mine and Jake's much earlier, we
would keep checking it and we would be fine.

So far, that's been a satisfactory explanation. I only wish
I could really believe what I tell him.

That same May, I had to start aerosol pentamidine treatments. My T-cell count was hovering around 210, and since
the recommendation is to start the treatments when the count
is 200, Michael Gottlieb decided it was time. Pentamidine
isn't a painful treatment, but it is unpleasant. For half an

hour I sit alone in a small room and breathe in disgusting and distasteful air, a strong reminder of the vulnerable position I am in. I've finally adjusted to it and look forward to the hard candy that I suck when it's over to get the awful taste out of my mouth. I also look forward to the freedom I feel when I leave the office to join the world again.

Like Jake, I was going in for my blood work every six weeks. I had started taking AZT the previous March, around the time when Ari had pneumonia. Gottlieb hoped it would slow down the progression of the disease. The goal was to keep me stable.

I was still taking AZT, which meant two pills five times a day. So I was always looking at my watch; life was constantly interrupted by reminders of AIDS. I hid the AZT pills in a bottle of iron tablets. I didn't want to take one in public sometime and have someone recognize that little white pill with the blue ring around it. I was always scrupulously careful about guarding our secret. I didn't even write Michael Gottlieb's name in my week-at-a-glance book. It was always only "MG."

That spring of 1989 was busy, but it was also very difficult. There was never a day when I didn't miss my daughter. There wasn't a day when I didn't feel incredible sadness about her death. I walk by her bedroom and know she is not in it. Her pictures are still all over our house and although they keep her joy and beauty with us, they also remind us of how much we have lost. I let the sadness sweep through me and then I let it out, because I know that if I keep the sadness inside me, it will destroy me.

Paul and I were having a very hard time communicating that spring. We were at a real emotional standstill and had lost touch with the love that is the foundation of everything we are. Sometimes our lives are just too complicated and our private and independent grieving has put distance between us.

Paul's back was still very painful, and he had to spend a lot of time lying on the couch in pain. I was working hard and had almost all the responsibility for Jake. I resented Paul for not helping more.

Paul felt his own resentment. At times he hated how involved I had become with the Foundation. He thought I was using it as an escape to avoid facing my emotions. We were not connecting with each other at all, so we finally started to see a therapist together to get our marriage back on track.

We saw Dr. Friedman about ten times. I think most of the time all we did was scream and get very angry at each other. I don't even remember what we were angry about. It was just that our lives made us so angry. Maybe we needed a safe place in which to let out all the resentment. All I know is that in time things got better again. Paul and I started caring again and that felt wonderful.

Bob Johnson, who was producing the documentary, came into town early in June with a rough cut of the film, entitled *A Gift of Time*. While Scott and Bob had been off writing and filming, Susan's husband Robert De Laurentis, who is a writer, and I were working on the structure of the film here. Robert has a great sense of story, and it was very challenging to work with him. He even came up with the title. But when the footage arrived Susan, Robert, and Susie were all out of town. I screened the film and didn't like it. It was twenty-four minutes long and not to the point. They had done a good job, but no one knew the story as well as I did. So I became an editor, and started working with Bob and Scott to recut the film.

I had sat with Paul in many editing rooms and watched lots of dailies and knew I had an eye that I could trust. But this was the first time I'd ever used those instincts. We worked for twelve hours a day for three days straight, and Paul came in to help, which was great because he is a fine director with a flawless sense of picture and timing.

The film was about families struggling with AIDS. But because all of our lives are so similar, their story was my story. I knew what the most critical parts were. The film had to be perfect. "A Night to Unite" was only ten days away.

In the midst of all this, I got a call from a friend of mine who told me that a woman I knew peripherally was onto our story and talking about it. Panic swept over me. This was what we'd been fearing all along.

She had approached at least two of my friends and asked them if it was true that Ariel Glaser had died of AIDS. They gave her the brush-off. But the third person said, "You're not supposed to know and you're not supposed to tell!" which immediately gave the woman the corroboration she was after.

I picked up the phone and confronted her. My breath was

short. Appealing to her sense of compassion, I said, "Now that you have this information, you need to treat it the same way as my best friends are treating it, with total privacy. If I had wanted you to know, I would have told you. Now that you know, the only important thing to me is how you're going to handle this." She apologized, denied any wrongdoing, and said she would say nothing about it to anyone else. I was so scared to confront her directly, but I had to and it worked. She never said another word.

It is somehow inhuman to imagine that, with all the horrible things families battling AIDS have to face, they have to worry about isolation and rejection as well. When you have a child who may die, or after your child has died, what you need is love and support. People with AIDS still feel like lepers because our society treats us that way. We live in secrecy. It is debilitating and degrading. It is unfair, unjust, and uneducated. But it is real, we are living with it, and there is very little we can do about it. We are dependent on others to make it all right.

Around that same time, Bess Armstrong, a friend of mine, mentioned at a party that she was doing volunteer work at the Foundation and Jeremy Dreyfuss said, "Oh, isn't that the foundation that Elizabeth Glaser is involved with?"

Bess was shocked. She knew I was guarding our secret. She called me. Once again, it was time for damage control. I called Jeremy who is a lovely, lovely woman and told her we needed to have lunch. As we sat at the table, I told her that she couldn't ever mention anything about me again to anyone! She told me who had told her, and I tried to figure out the source of that leak.

I backtracked mentally until I could deduce who the most likely source was and then I called her. "I just discovered that so-and-so has been talking about our story and I know you are a friend of hers. I'm so frightened by this, and it puts us in real jeopardy. Could you please call her right away and ask her to keep quiet?"

So I constantly felt like I was plugging holes in a leaky dike. It was exhausting. We expended so much energy keeping "the secret." Even if nothing was happening, part of me was always on the alert for the next weak spot.

The benefit had forced me to confide in many more people and it was taking its toll. That compounded my acute sense of anxiety. I never knew if one day I would walk into the supermarket and see our story spread all across the *National Enquirer* or some other cheap tabloid.

If that happened, what impact would it have on Jake? Would his friends' parents be educated enough to know that they didn't have to be afraid? Would they understand that Jake posed no danger to them or their children? Would some child come up to him and say, "You have AIDS and you are going to die"? These were the constant fears that kept me working hard to protect Jake from what had happened to Ari and her friends.

Protecting the secret throughout the actual event was another real concern. It had turned into a major, major affair, and it was natural for people to wonder how and why it had all happened. Susan and Susie would be the only representatives of the Pediatrics AIDS Foundation in Washington. What were they going to say when asked why they had started the Foundation? It had to be believable, but it couldn't be the truth. No one was to know about my participation.

With the help of my friend Jody Uttal, who is a media trainer, Susie and Susan finally decided, after much debate, to say that they had created the Foundation because they'd known and loved a child who had died of AIDS. This wasn't a lie, but it wasn't the whole story. Jody coached them on how to avoid any more probing questions from the press.

By the time we got to Washington a few days before the event, we already knew it was sold out. We had raised a million dollars and eight hundred people were expected to attend. Amazingly, the benefit had been pulled together in three months instead of twelve. There were a lot of last-minute preparations on June 20. We had to thrash out the seating arrangements with Kevin and Joel, like who would sit next to whom and which table would get what celebrity. We stayed up until midnight. It was exhausting and scary, because we all wanted it to be perfect. But it was also so much fun. We had all become good friends and now we had a million more dollars for research to show for it.

Even if I had to be there anonymously, I knew this would be the biggest night of my life. Paul's back was still too painful to make the long flight, and we also thought that his presence might attract too much attention. But my parents were coming. I had decided that if anyone asked me why I was there, I would say Susan and Susie were my friends.

Susan was staying with her parents, and Susie and I were staying with Sandy Brock. The night before the event, I got back to her house at one A.M. I was almost ready to turn out the light when she knocked on the door.

"Elizabeth, I really think you should take care of yourself tomorrow and try to relax. I think you need to distance yourself from the benefit."

I said I was fine, but Sandy became even more insistent about my taking the day off to rest. I've been around long enough to recognize that polite mumbo jumbo for what it was. A ruse. Something must be going on and I asked Sandy what it was.

She finally said, "A friend who is a television reporter called to say that her TV station knows that something is happening behind the scenes of the benefit and they want to break the story." Sandy was trying to coax me into lying low.

It was one in the morning and I was exhausted. But I am never too tired to be afraid. I couldn't go to sleep. At four in the morning I was still tossing about. I had visions of walking into a phalanx of cameras the next night and having our secret blown to bits. Everything felt vulnerable. I felt alone and I was scared. I finally slept for three hours.

I told Kevin and Joel how afraid I was when I went up to Capitol Hill the next morning. They got very upset and said if the station tried to go with the story they would find ways to pressure them into killing it. They were so protective and certain that I believed them and felt somewhat reassured.

Susie, Susan, and I decided I would skip the opening VIP cocktail reception from six to seven, and arrive that night as people were being seated at their tables. I was going to sit with my parents and Rita Braver, who was my "date" for the evening, as well as Peter Benzian, the Foundation's lawyer; Paul's agent, Andrea Eastman, and her husband, Richard Wilsker; Lloyd Zeiderman, the Foundation's financial consultant; and our friends from New York, Richard and Sheila Lukins.

By the time I arrived with my parents, everyone had gone inside, including most of the paparazzi. But as we were walking in under the canopy, someone called out, "Elizabeth!"

I choked in panic and turned around. It was Jim Hill, one

of the doctors from NIAID. He said, "You remember Dr. Tony Fauci," and my heart skipped a beat. Then in somewhat of a stage whisper, I said to them, "But I'm not supposed to be here and you are not supposed to know me."

Jim Hill looked at me and said, "But it's your foundation, isn't it?"

I said, "Yes, yes, it is, but no one here tonight knows I am a part of it so please don't say anything."

I felt stupid explaining to these two important doctors that they had to help me be invisible, but I had no choice.

Susan De Laurentis and Susie Zeegen opened the evening. I was so proud. They looked radiantly beautiful in their long dresses. I had goose bumps. I was like a mom at a piano recital who is so nervous for her child that she can barely even breathe.

After Susie introduced and thanked Howard and Orrin, they joked about their political differences, then quickly became serious. "Never have I been involved in a project that is so moving, so tragic, and so very urgent," said Metzenbaum. He went on to talk emotionally about mothers and families with AIDS, and how much the audience would learn that evening.

Orrin then came forward and said, "We in Congress have focused on adult AIDS. Unfortunately, we overlooked an important fact. We missed one of the most horrible and tragic aspects of this terrible disease: babies are born with AIDS; small children get AIDS; AIDS is not bound by age. Thank God for some special friends from California who've helped educate us." As Orrin said these words, many of his wealthy and powerful colleagues were probably learning about pediatric AIDS for the first time.

If anyone had tried to tell Susan, Susie, or me ten months before, when we started the Pediatric AIDS Foundation, that this would be happening, we would have either laughed or felt too intimidated to continue. But here we were in Washington, and it felt both important and right.

During one of the speeches I stealthily slipped backstage to find Cher and thank her. She looked like a mermaid in a long, slinky, strapless black dress with tiers of fringe.

Cher threw her arms around me and said, "You know what I remember? I remember when the director of the school called me in for a conference about Chas. She thought

Chastity should be in therapy and you disagreed. We were both so upset that when we walked out of that meeting you and I threw our arms around each other and cried." I knew at that moment we both wished we could go back and recapture those simpler times. As my eyes started to moisten I gave Cher a big hug and told her the truth: we could never have done it without her.

I snuck back to my seat just as Alan Alda began the show by making a few jokes about Washington politics. A children's choir then sang a beautiful song called "I'll Be Your Candle on the Water." They lit candles as the room went dark. In the flickering candlelight, *A Gift of Time* began. We had been warned that people would chatter, nibble, and gossip during the film. I was advised not to get upset. The film begins with the loud staccato ticking of a clock. The room was dark and still. No one talked and no one moved.

The brave families in the film began to tell their stories:

"Zack taught me that when you love the world it loves you back . . ."

"I had to learn to find strength in myself that I never knew I had . . ."

"I would do whatever it took to keep him as happy and as full of love as possible until the end . . ."

"We went to a military hospital, and they didn't want to touch him. They wouldn't weigh him. They shut us up in a room and wouldn't let us sit with other people . . ."

"It's probably the most invasive thing that can ever happen to you. It rapes every aspect of your life. It's an insult to you, your children, your family, and friends. Nothing is ever the same afterwards . . ." Not a sound could be heard.

I sat in the back of the huge room and held my mom's hand and cried.

These people were me and I was them.

When the film ended, many in the room wiped tears from their eyes. No one even murmured. Alan Alda came back onstage and spoke movingly about the parents from the film whom he'd met with that morning at NIH.

"It was an extraordinary experience," he said. "I don't think those of us who haven't been attacked by AIDS can understand how courageous these families are to get up on the screen and be public. It is not like any other disease. . . . These families lost their friends; in many cases, they just turned away. They lost their jobs in some instances. They had to sell their homes and move out of the neighborhood. . . .

"Today I felt I was in the company of people who were stronger than I was, more resilient than I was, and I didn't walk away from that meeting feeling low. I walked away from that meeting feeling like I now had the strength to do things in my life that I didn't think I could do before because of what I saw they were able to do."

For me it was an extraordinary moment to hear Alan speak so eloquently about families with AIDS. The families who appeared in the film were all seated at a table in the center of the room. The spotlight focused on their table, and as they stood, so did everyone else in the room to give them a standing ovation.

I stood and clapped and cried. It was unbelievable to me that eight hundred people were applauding families like mine, that we weren't being rejected.

When the emotion subsided, Alan Alda introduced Cher.

Cher. With her wild mane of hair and her slinky dress, she looked like a goddess and sang her heart out. After the first number, she paused and said, "Okay. That was for the Republicans." She walked offstage and returned a split second later and said, "This is for the Democrats."

Swoosh! The bottom half of her dress was gone, leaving Cher in a fringed mini with high black boots. It was as brilliant as it was bawdy. Everyone in the room loved it.

Cher knew where I was sitting in the back and just before she sang "If I Could Turn Back Time," she pointed at me and threw a dramatic stage kiss in my direction.

I started to panic, but no one really noticed. But just before she made her exit, she said, "I want to thank you all. I'm here tonight because of a teacher my daughter had in school. . . ."

But fortunately, the sound system was weak and many people didn't catch it. A few reporters in the press box were asking each other what she said, but no one heard enough to realize its significance.

The evening concluded with the song "Tomorrow," from the show *Annie*. Cher was joined onstage by Senators Hatch and Metzenbaum, Alan Alda, Kitty Dukakis, and Sandy Brock.

I knew this would be the hardest moment of the night for

me and it was. "Tomorrow" was one of Ari's favorite songs. We had watched *Annie* endlessly at UCLA: from the very beginning, before she was diagnosed when she was getting gamma globulin infusions right up until the end. Cher began by singing "Tomorrow" in such a languorous way that it sounded almost tragically sad. Then, as everyone joined in, my mom took my hand and squeezed it as hard as she could. Somehow, we made it through.

Back at the hotel where most of the California contingent was staying, a small group of us gathered in the bar. We decided it was not only "A Night to Unite," but a night to celebrate and Susie, Susan, and I started making tequila toasts. I was exhausted. I'd had almost no sleep the night before.

Just as I was ready to go up to my room, Susan said, "We've got to do one more."

"I can't, Susan, I'm too tired," I said.

"For friendship. We're doing one drink to us, Elizabeth, just you and me." When Susan said this I suddenly remembered all we'd been through together: the pressure of the event, the secret, the trips to Washington, Francesca and Ari, and the Ferris wheel. At that moment, Susan felt like the most important person in my life.

We downed the last shot of tequila and gave each other an immense hug.

CHAPTER

❧13❧

In coordinating the benefit, I had exposed myself to dozens and dozens of people and our secret remained secure. I felt I had pushed it right to the edge, but made it through without incident. I was confident that the people who knew would remain silent, and that I could continue to work quietly behind the scenes.

A few days later in Los Angeles, I went to a fund-raiser for Senator Tom Harkin, the chair of the Senate Appropriations Subcommittee on Health, who was up for reelection in Iowa. It was that afternoon that I realized we were really having an impact in Washington. In his speech, he actually talked about the need to allocate more money for pediatric AIDS! I had never heard anyone say that before.

Afterward, when I went up to say hello, he said he wanted to meet with me again in Washington. Another first. No one had ever asked to meet with me. It was always the other way around. At that moment I loved Tom Harkin. I told him we were heading back East on vacation in a few weeks and I would plan to stop in D.C. for a day and meet with him.

Paul and I knew this was going to be a difficult summer for us because a week after Ariel's birthday would be the first anniversary of her death. We knew we could not stay at home. We decided to make our annual trip to Maine for a week in July and then go to Martha's Vineyard for two weeks at the beginning of August. We hadn't been to Ari's grave since she was buried and we knew we had to do that too.

Paul and Jake flew to Washington with me. I planned to meet them two days later in Maine. I went right out to NIH and met with Tony Fauci. I wanted to go over some funding issues with him before I met with Senator Harkin the next morning.

When I checked into the hotel, I found a message from Michael Gottlieb. I was surprised. It wasn't like him to track me down. I was anxious about returning his call, because I'd had my blood tested just before leaving Los Angeles. I was afraid the news would be bad.

It was. My T-cell count had dropped by nearly a third, to 140. This was the biggest change in my numbers since I had become Michael's patient. I tried to stay calm on the phone. We talked about whether I should try to be retested in Washington, but decided against it. Michael's advice was to wait until I got back to L.A. and then be tested again.

I hung up the phone and cried alone in my hotel room. I felt tremendously vulnerable and alone. Paul and Jake were in Maine, and Susan wasn't with me. It was the first time that I had really agonized about my health since the very beginning when I was diagnosed.

I felt strong, but I had been battling this virus for eight years. Had my body now started to weaken? Fewer T-cells meant it would be harder to fight off the opportunistic infections that could seriously compromise or even kill me. I was afraid the process of physical deterioration had begun. Somehow, I had always hoped it wouldn't and I would just keep my 200 T-cells forever.

I sat on the bed and said to myself, "Elizabeth, get a grip." Maybe things would be bad, but maybe they wouldn't. No one could say for sure what was going to happen. While I might not be able to have an impact on the virus, I can certainly have an impact on my fear.

Through the turmoil and inner questioning I had gone through after Ari's death, I had decided that I really wanted to live. I wanted to live for Jake and for Paul, I wanted to live for the Foundation and for all the meaningful work that lay ahead. But most of all, I wanted to live for me. Despite all the sadness and pain I face every day, I've also found a way to see beauty again. My life, albeit horrible, is quite an adventure. I'm living each day fully, whether it be in tears, rage, or action. Even living in tears is better than not living at all. If Jake becomes sick, I don't know how I'll feel, but right now, I want to live.

As I sat by myself in my hotel room, I told myself over and over that Michael had said the numbers can jump around. Down a third one month, up a third the next. I told myself that if I felt fine, I was fine. So until I got back home to Los Angeles, I would just have to bite the bullet and power through. I told the fear it would have to go away. But I was afraid, and my numbers never did go back up.

The next morning I met again with Senator Tom Harkin and the head of the Appropriations Subcommittee staff, Mike Hall. The first time we met that winter, he had said he wanted to make sure that the Senate turned the situation around. Now, however, Harkin was dealing with a federal budget squeeze. Although he was still committed to the issue of pediatric AIDS, he had to juggle what he wanted with what he realistically thought he could appropriate.

Harkin had been over the budget figures repeatedly with Mike Hall and they thought they could direct ten million dollars of the 1990 budget toward basic pediatric research. That was terrific, but it was not "new" money. The money would be siphoned off from existing AIDS programs at the NIH. If appropriated, however, the ten million dollars would be the first government funds ever specified for basic biomedical pediatric research. I was proud, but it was only half of what we needed. Another ten million dollars' worth of research questions would have to wait to be answered.

It was important to make sure that the ten million dollars, when allocated, would be earmarked strictly for research and wouldn't be diverted into more epidemiological or clinical studies. In order to eliminate any ambiguity, we wanted the language in the bill to contain specific guidelines detailing how the money could be spent and to which institute it could be given.

That's what my meeting with Tony Fauci had been about. He helped me figure out what approach to use. Fauci is well respected on Capitol Hill and I knew that his imprint on this legislation would help ensure its support and subsequent passage.

Fauci and I had met in his office. He and I had developed

a good working relationship over the past year. When we first met, he seemed cool and polished, but now I felt I could trust him and rely on his judgment.

Susan and I agreed with Mike Hall's recommendation that sixty percent of the money go to NIAID and forty percent to NCI. Fauci agreed, believing that pediatric AIDS research needed to become a higher government priority.

Half a year later, when the money had been appropriated to NIAID and NCI and I called to get follow-up on how the funds were being used, I had a rude awakening. While Tony and I had discussed potential plans, NIAID in the end was unable to use the money as we had discussed, given the time frame allotted. I sat at my desk in the office and cried for an hour.

I called Tony Fauci, I called senators, congressmen, and staff to ask how this could have happened. I was on the verge of losing all hope. With all the work, six million dollars of hard-to-get money still had not been put into fundamental research. Tony understood my deep concerns and reassured me that next year, despite the fact there was no guarantee that NIAID would receive extra funds, they promised to move ahead with plans in basic research. I was glad Sam Broder and Phil Pizzo at the National Cancer Institute had been able to use their four million dollars in the manner it was directed through their intramural programs, to fund critical basic pediatric AIDS research. In the end with this knowledge I realized at least something positive had happened—but I vowed not to let NIAID off the hook and to find a way to ensure this didn't happen in the next fiscal year.

At the end of our meeting, I asked Fauci about the precipitous drop in my T-cell count. He agreed that numbers can fluctuate from one month to the next and that I should try to relax until I got home to Los Angeles.

After a day of nonstop meetings, I finally was on the flight to Maine. I missed Paul and Jake. Even though we had only been apart for a day, I felt lonely. I was scared about my health and needed my family near me. It was hard for me to be heading back to Maine as the first anniversary of Ari's death approached, yet I knew it would have been worse staying away. As the plane started skimming through the clouds on its descent, I knew I would feel the tug-of-war between joy and sadness more this summer than ever before. I was eager to see Jake rollicking through the woods and splashing in the lake. I wanted to rub suntan lotion on his back and wipe ice cream from his chin. With his freckles and spunk he could have been Huckleberry Finn. I knew, too, there would be some things I would simply be unable to do ever again, like picking blueberries on Pleasant Mountain.

Now, I am thrilled by the time I have with Jake but then my happiness with him deepened the desolation I felt about Ari's loss. I couldn't watch Jake run on the beach like a sandpiper without wishing that his sister were chasing him.

But as soon as I arrived in the Portland airport, I began to feel better. The mountains and woods of Maine have brought me contentment ever since I was a little girl at Camp Fernwood. As the car brought me closer and closer to the lake, I could feel the sadness receding.

My brother-in-law, Billy, jogs several miles to town every morning for the newspapers and I started going with him. I wasn't sure if I could do it. I didn't know if the drop in my T-cell count would prevent me from doing the things I loved best. But the running was invigorating and I proved to myself once again that numbers measure neither my stamina nor my enthusiasm.

Paul spent a few hours each day working to complete a screenplay he had been writing for several months, but he always made sure he spent time with Jake. One night he took Jake fishing after dark, which was a big thrill for Jake. They bought night crawlers in town that were twisted together in a small carton of wet dirt, baited their hooks, and sat side by side on the dock. Jake caught several small guppies and felt like a real fisherman.

It was a relief to feel comfortable as a family with nothing terrifying on the horizon. We knew the first anniversary of Ari's death was only a few weeks away, but that would be a pain we'd have to learn to live with from year to year. The sense of relief came from knowing that Jake's childhood world was stable and secure; he had friends and a school that he loved, and through therapy some of the intense grief and anger he experienced after Ari's death was being resolved. His health was good and we wanted to enjoy ourselves.

On our way from Maine to Martha's Vineyard we stopped in Boston for a few days. We wanted to see Paul's mom, my brother, Peter, and his wife, Janet. Kitty Dukakis had wanted me to meet Mike and the first night we arranged to go out to dinner with them and Paul's cousins, Michael and Donna Moskow, who had gone to high school with Michael Dukakis.

I wasn't sure what to expect, but I was very excited. Without knowing it, Mike Dukakis had pulled me through a critical time in my life. Dukakis was funny, relaxed, and fascinating to talk to about the campaign. He was open about discussing the mistakes he made and outlined the things he would have done differently.

I tried to tell him how much he meant to me. Without becoming too maudlin, I told him that the campaign had carried me through the months immediately after Ari's death. I had to have something to believe in and someone to fight for. I told him how Jake and I had hammered "Dukakis for President" signs into our neighbors' front yards and how we wept together when he was defeated.

Kitty said that we should stop by the State House in the morning so Jake could meet Mike. When we went into Mike's office, Jake was adorable, darting immediately into the cubbyhole beneath his desk. Mike let him sit in his chair and have his picture taken. As we were getting ready to leave, Jake said, "Wait a minute, I want to show you something!" and he started doing somersaults across the Governor's thick carpet. It was pure Jake.

Of course in many ways, the most important part of the journey East was to Ari's grave. Paul and I had talked about it a lot. We had decided to visit the grave site the second day because we needed some transition time to prepare and then if we wanted to go back we could. I didn't want to get to Boston and just think "Grave . . . grave . . . grave."

I didn't know what to do about Jake. He hadn't been to her funeral. I had talked to Jake's therapist about it, as well as to Jake's teacher. I finally decided that Paul and I would go alone but we would let Jake know where we had been after. If he was interested in seeing her grave we would bring him another day.

We went that afternoon to the small New England cemetery. We drove silently in the car holding hands. It was three P.M. The air was hot and humid. Everything felt heavy, oppressive, and final, as though it were reflecting our life.

As Paul and I reached the cemetery we barely knew what

to do. There were so many roads we hardly knew where to go. But the memory of the drive a year before was stronger than we realized and instinctively we drove right to where she and Paul's dad were buried. There are no tombstones, just plaques in the ground with trees and grass around. Paul got out first. I just sat in the car unable to move. Finally, I joined him—or I joined Ari—I don't know. I saw her name written on a little square. Paul was sitting on a stone bench, crying.

All I could do was lie down on top of the grass and weep. Ari and I had been beside each other in bed so many times when she was sick. I was in bed with her during the final months of my pregnancy hoping with my whole heart that everything would be okay.

Eight years later I was face down on top of her grave, wishing there was some way to get to her through all the earth. Warmed by the summer sun, the grass smelled sweet, but I couldn't find Ari that day. I knew her body was there, but my Ari was somewhere else, I just didn't know where. I couldn't feel close to Ari at her grave. I needed to find Ari in my heart.

Paul and I barely spoke. Most of the time our sadness is still too intimate to be shared in words. Tears are the vocabulary of our grief. We held each other tightly in the cemetery, standing beside our daughter. Then we got into the car and drove away.

By the time we got back to Connie's we had composed ourselves. Usually, we try to do that for Jake. We told him where we had been and without hesitation he asked if he could see where his sister was buried. We said yes.

And so the next day we drove once again to the cemetery. Before we had left we'd gone into Connie's back yard and Jake showed us the flowers he wanted to pick to bring to Ari. We found an old soda bottle and filled it with water and he carefully placed the lilac, the iris, and the rose in place.

We stayed at Ari's grave only a short time. Paul talked to Ari and then Jake did also. He said, "I love you. I miss you, Ari. I brought you these flowers and I learned to ride a two-wheeler." We stood together and gave a "family hug" and sent it to Ari as well. Then we got in the car and drove back to Connie's. Jake was his boisterous self, and that helped me and Paul find the strength we needed to leave.

The next day I was relieved when the ferry finally pulled away from Woods Hole for Martha's Vineyard with a blast of its horn. Sea gulls followed the chunky steamer on its seven-mile trip, diving and circling in huge loops to catch the bread and potato chips the passengers threw from the deck. Real daredevils let the birds snatch the crumbs directly from the fingertips of their outstretched arms, but on that day Jake and I didn't feel that impetuous.

When I got to the Vineyard, I felt like I was home. There was peace in my heart and I felt protected by the love of our family. Paul's cousins, the Moskows, have a house in Chilmark, just down the road from the ocean, and David Kantar, our nephew, had flown in from New York to join us, which was a great treat.

Ari and Jake loved it there because they have horses, a sheep, geese, and rabbits. It's a paradise for kids. In the morning we used to follow the deer tracks on the sandy road.

We arrived at the beginning of the month, just before Ari's birthday on August 4, when she would have been eight years old. Before leaving Los Angeles, we had thought about what we would do on that day.

Jake's teacher, Lisa, had lost a child and she told me that every year on his birthday, they release balloons. I thought about it and talked to Paul and we both decided it might be a nice thing to do. We asked Jake and he said he wanted to. I told a few friends about the idea and they said they'd like to participate. We agreed to all do it at the same time, at seven o'clock in the East and four in the West. What I didn't know was that friends called friends who called friends and many people were preparing to release balloons.

The day was traumatic for me. From the moment I woke up all I could think about was Ariel. Her life flashed before my eyes. I remembered the day she was born and the day she died and everything in between. I wanted to go back through the last 365 days and find Ari again in her bed at UCLA, alive, her eyes twinkling at the seven candles on her cake.

Jake had insisted on having a cake for his sister, and while it broke my heart, I couldn't say no. He picked out her favorite, chocolate cake and white icing with pink and purple flowers. We ordered it from a bakery in town. I was determined to take my cues from Jake and do whatever he felt he needed to do to remember his sister. But I had to grit my teeth when I gave the order to the college girl working at the counter.

"And what would you like on that?" she asked cheerfully.

"Happy Birthday, Ari," I said, choking back the tears.

At six-forty-five, Donna, her son Cliff, David, Paul, Jake, and I made our way to the top of the sand dunes. We had eight pink and purple helium balloons. At the end of each ribbon, we tied a feather, a seashell, or a flower. At precisely seven o'clock each of us let go of our balloons, as did friends all over the country. We put our arms around each other and sang "Happy Birthday." As the balloons drifted up over the ocean, we stared as they became smaller and smaller dots in the sky. It was as beautiful as it was sad. Paul held Jake and David held me.

When I woke up the next morning, I was so glad that we had made it to August 5. In the aftermath of Ari's birthday I felt empty, sad, and quiet. But it was over, and we made it through.

In seven more days it would be a year since she had died, but we had already decided not to commemorate it in any way. The day of Ari's death means nothing to me. Her birthday is what's difficult. I looked forward to a quiet week in the ocean, dunes, and meadows of the Vineyard, where I could find solace in the stillness of my soul and the beauty that was at my fingertips and beneath my toes.

Then the phone rang.

It was Susan. There was something funny going on at UCLA with our insurance company. She said Lloyd Zeiderman, our business manager, had become involved and we should call him.

Paul dialed Lloyd. The guillotine began to drop.

Dr. Stiehm's office had gotten a call from the insurance company needing some information. They wanted to verify a few facts about Ariel Glaser's death from AIDS. The nurse, who was accustomed to receiving inquiries on insurance claims, had unwittingly answered the questions.

She had taken the caller's name and number and had asked Lloyd to call him back. When Lloyd placed the call it was a nonworking number. Lloyd said based on the information the caller had received from Dr. Stiehm's office, he thought we might be in trouble. We didn't want to panic, but we'd better be careful. We called Josh Baran and our friends to warn them that somebody might be snooping.

For three years and three months, Paul and I had protected our family's privacy with our souls. We chose to keep AIDS a secret for only one reason: to protect our children.

Ultimately, we were powerless to control whether Ariel and Jake lived or died, but we were powerfully prepared to preserve their childhood at all costs. We did not want them to be ostracized, tormented, ridiculed, or stigmatized in any way because of AIDS.

Reports of strange calls started coming in for the next two days. Paul's sister, Connie, said someone had called her home in Massachusetts and said he was an old friend of Paul's from drama school at Boston University. He told Connie he was shocked and saddened to learn of Ari's death. He said his wife was a pediatric AIDS researcher at the Centers for Disease Control in Atlanta and that he and she were on their way to an AIDS conference in Paris. He told Connie he wanted to talk with Paul before he left for France because he thought there was something he might be able to look into for Paul at the convention.

Connie took down the man's number. Paul and I thought the story sounded preposterous. Immediately suspicious, we tried calling back. There was no such person at the number.

What would happen next? People were asking questions. Strangers. What had triggered this? Who had told them? How far were they willing to go? Who were they?

Now we were on the phone nonstop, warning all our friends back home and telling them to be exceedingly cautious and not to speak to anyone about us. UCLA immediately alerted all the nurses and doctors who had worked with us that someone was using aliases and lies to get information about our family and would apparently stop at nothing.

The hunt had begun. My family was the target.

I am no stranger to fear, grief, pain, death, loss, or tragedy. I think of myself as a strong woman. But nothing I have ever experienced prepared me for the savage terror that was unleashed on my family the day after my daughter's birthday.

While we were on vacation, Beth, our assistant at the Foundation, and her boyfriend, Adam, were house-sitting for us. Beth began noticing that there were a lot of hang-ups on our answering machine at home.

So the stranger now was using our unlisted home numbers to troll for information. Adam took a call one day from a man who claimed to be a friend of Paul's. He wanted to know where we were and when we would be back. Adam said we were away, but that we did call in for messages. He asked the man for his name and number, but the man declined to give it, saying he'd call back in a few days. He told Adam his wife had met me at Cedars-Sinai when Ari was born.

"What's happened to the Glasers is so sad," the man said. Adam pretended not to know what he was referring to. Then the caller said, "Well, Paul and I are going to go out fag-bashing." Shocked, Adam ended the conversation immediately because he knew that Paul would never tolerate a friend who spoke like that.

Beth was at the epicenter of the assault. They were calling our house. Then she started to get weird calls at work every day. The phone would ring and a man would ask to speak with Elizabeth Glaser. Now at that point, my involvement with the Foundation was still a secret. My name was not connected with it in any way. Even though the Foundation had an office, our address was not listed anywhere so someone asking to speak to me immediately made hearts stop.

Beth told the stranger that no one by the name of Elizabeth Glaser was affiliated with the Foundation. Then he would ask for "Betsy," implying that he was someone who knew me from before I met Paul. Beth still insisted that the man was mistaken and he hung up.

Joanie Green's assistant at Crossroads School received a call from a man who said he was the father of a child with AIDS. He said Elizabeth Glaser had referred him to the school and he would like to have information about enrolling his child there in the fall. She said nothing.

While all of this was happening in California, we no longer felt safe even on the Vineyard. I didn't know if a photographer would spring up from behind a dune. When I went for a long walk on the beach I would always be aware of what was ahead of me or if anyone was following too close behind. I was hypervigilant, always alert, on guard.

If I would walk into Menemsha with Jake to watch the fishing boats come in or to get a carton of fried clams, I would tense up when I'd see a car slow down or swerve ahead of us. There was no way of predicting when the next bombshell might explode.

Every time the phone rang at the Moskows', Paul and I would jump. It was always for us and always another piece of disturbing news. We could hardly sit down for a meal. One of us would say, "We haven't called so-and-so." The other would already be on the phone. We'd lie in bed at night talking about what would happen if our story came out. What would we do? We had imagined this for a long time but how bad things would really get we didn't know. The only thing we did know was that we had each other and we'd be going through it together.

The week after Ari's birthday would have been a hard week for me and Paul no matter what. But now we felt like we were being stalked. We had no idea who was after us, how long they would pursue us, or if they would try to confront us directly. The reports of inquiries being made by strangers began to pile up, one on top of another, slowly building to what we could then only imagine would be a horrible crescendo.

They had gotten one piece of information from the nurse at UCLA and now they were looking for corroboration. There was no depth this man would not sink to. He had a different line each time. He was good. He fooled people who had already been warned.

On about the fifth day, when we were all on the verge of exploding, Beth came back to our house and pulled up to the end of the driveway. When she got out of the car, a stranger suddenly appeared from around a corner in our yard wearing khaki slacks and a blue T-shirt.

Apologetically, he turned on the charm and said, "I don't mean to scare you. My name is Bill. I just moved in down the street, and when I met Elizabeth and Paul, they said they would give me the names of their gardener and pool man." The imposter was so smooth and believable that Beth was not immediately suspicious.

Beth said she was house-sitting and offered to take the man's telephone number so she could call him when she got the information from me. He brushed off that suggestion and said wouldn't it be easier if he just came into the house with her because the numbers were probably on the kitchen bulletin board. Beth refused. "Bill" said he'd stop by again in a few days. She called us on the Vineyard and we told her we had no new neighbors. Beth was scared and so were we. He had almost gotten into our house.

The doorbell rang on the day when Anna, our housekeeper, was cleaning. When she answered it, a man asked her, "Aren't you afraid to work here? Don't you know that this family has AIDS?" Terrified, Anna slammed the door in his face.

A few days later Adam was studying in the apartment he shares with Beth when the phone rang. The imposter, who even knew Adam's name, said he was a director friend of Paul's who was looking for a house-sitter. Adam said he needed to speak with Beth, and took the man's name and number. When they checked it out with us, it was all fake.

Beth was upset that someone now had her name and her telephone number. I was furious. How could any human being be doing this? It was unethical, immoral, a total outrage. Paul intelligently told Beth to start carrying a camera because if she could get a picture of this stranger he would undoubtedly disappear for good. He told her to be angry instead of scared. Paul can be so smart.

The next day Beth was alone in the Foundation's office. She was talking to Susan De Laurentis on the telephone about how frightened she felt. Suddenly, she had a strange feeling that she was not alone. She looked up and there was "Bill."

She gasped. He pretended that he had never seen Beth before and was an entirely different person. He said he had come to pick up some information he'd requested a few days before. Beth had been alone in the office all week and knew no one had requested information. Beth asked him how he found the office and he said he looked it up in the phone book.

"But we're not listed," she said. He ignored her remark.

Beth asked him to wait a minute and pretended to put Susan De Laurentis on hold. Susan had heard enough of Beth's end of the conversation to say, "That's him, that's him! Don't hang up, I want to stay on the line until I know you're okay."

Beth gave the stranger an empty informational packet and a brochure. Susan came into the office that afternoon and Beth left for the bank. As she was walking down the block she had a creepy feeling and when she looked up, she saw the man up ahead of her.

He had been following her, possibly for days. It was the only way he could have known where the Foundation was located. Beth walked up to him and stared. He turned and walked away and never bothered her again.

The last and most grotesque thing we found out was that the man turned up on the UCLA floor where Ari had been a patient. He lied to the nurse on duty at the nursing station by saying that his father was our rabbi who was planning a special memorial service for Ariel when her family returned from vacation to commemorate the first anniversary of her death. Even though the nursing staff had been warned, no one believed someone would stoop so low to lie like this. He asked the nurse if she might be able to share a few anecdotes about Ariel with him and she did.

Anger raged inside of me. This man was our enemy. Although we did not know for sure who was after us, Paul and I assumed it was one of the supermarket tabloids, one of those that has yet to see a tragedy it is unwilling to exploit.

It was all about money. No one cared about our life. No one cared about our privacy. They wanted to sell papers to get more and more money. It was the ultimate voyeuristic monster and nothing was sacred except the dollar bill.

The fact that someone might try to use our tragedy to sell their magazine was both revolting and obscene. It showed how weak and immoral America had become. We felt as though we were under a terrorist attack, and in a sense, we were. Nothing felt safe. We never knew where the next assault was coming from.

The dreaded phone call came on August 11, the day before the anniversary of Ari's death. Never more than a few feet from the telephone, I picked it up after one or two rings.

A man's voice said, "Hello, is Mrs. Glaser there?"

Shaking from the inside out, I said, "No, I'm sorry, she isn't here right now." I was clenched in a spasm of terror.

He said, "This is the *National Enquirer* calling. We have a story about the Glaser family. It's a very sad story, and we want the Glasers to have the opportunity to talk to us about it."

"I'll make sure she gets the message," I said. I was trembling so hard I felt like I was rattling inside. My mouth was dry and my heart was racing.

That was it. That was the call we never wanted to receive.

Now we knew exactly what we were up against. We immediately called our lawyer in Los Angeles, but we couldn't reach him. We called Peter Benzian, the Foundation's lawyer and our friend. He began drafting a letter to the *Enquirer,* threatening legal action if they ran the story.

We had been on the phone with Lloyd every day. Josh Baran, our publicist in L.A., was checking in every few hours. He was monitoring the situation as best he could, counting the dozens and dozens of phone calls from all over town.

When the *Enquirer* finally called Josh at his office, he played dumb, saying we were somewhere out of town. The caller said that we were on the Vineyard and gave Josh our number there. Josh wondered to himself whether they had people following us.

Josh did some digging of his own and found out when the *Enquirer* planned to run the story. We had about seven days to try to figure out a counterattack that might successfully block them.

Paul and I had been planning to return to Los Angeles that week. We canceled our plane reservations, which had been made in our own name, and rebooked them under an alias. Our fear was that the *Enquirer* would have a photographer at one of the airports to try to take a picture of our family. Josh felt it was very possible that the *Enquirer* might have offered as much as $25,000 for a picture of the three of us together.

We drove back to Boston, spent one night at Connie's, and then headed for our home. We were completely paranoid about what might happen at the airports. Logan went fine and we were relieved, but we still didn't know who might be stalking us at LAX. We felt we needed protection. Susan and Robert would meet us at the airport. Robert would get the luggage, and Susan would drive us quickly away if necessary. Cindy Wick was coming as well to run interference. Fortunately for Jake and us, no one was there.

As soon as we got back to L.A. we met with Josh and Jake Bloom, our lawyer, to map out our strategy. We decided to have Josh call the editor of the *National Enquirer.* The goal was to buy time, either by threat of legal action, or by having Josh enter into some sort of false negotiations.

When Josh called the *Enquirer,* the magazine said that if they could get one quote from us, they would not print the whole story about our family. They would run an "alternate" story instead, saying only that Ariel had died from AIDS after being infected from a blood transfusion. There would be no mention of me or of Jake.

Here is a magazine that pretends to be legitimate and yet unabashedly offers to run an "alternate" story just to get a quote!

I think the lawsuit had scared them. We were saying, and rightfully so, that while Paul was a public figure, Jake and I were not and information about us was not public domain. I believe they decided not to run the whole family story because of their own vulnerability, not because of anything else.

The *Enquirer* then decided to hold the story for a week. We don't know why—probably to rewrite it without me and Jake. The delay bought us vital time.

Josh stalled, telling the *Enquirer* that he would go over their offer with us and get back to them in a few days. We were convinced that no matter what we did, the story was going to run. Josh did not think that there was any way that we could get it killed. The only option was to beat them at their own game and break the story in another publication *on our terms.* If we couldn't kill the story, we could at least tell it our way first.

Josh knew a reporter at the *Los Angeles Times* named Janet Huck. Paul and I couldn't decide immediately what to do. We listened to Lloyd and Josh and Jake Bloom, but we were scared. What if we told our story and the *Enquirer* held theirs? But we didn't have the luxury of time in which to make up our minds. If we were going to go ahead and tell it, the *Los Angeles Times* needed days to get the piece together. I was hedging but Paul said, "Elizabeth, we have no choice. Sooner or later this will come out." He looked at Josh and said, "Call Janet Huck." The decision was made. We knew we weren't turning back.

Josh called Janet and explained what was happening in our lives. He said that we would like to give the *Los Angeles Times* the full story exclusively. All that we asked was that it run before the *Enquirer*'s article. Huck called her editors.

We waited to hear back. Twenty-four hours later, Huck got the go-ahead.

But before the *Los Angeles Times* story appeared, we knew we had to tell the parents at Jake's school. We had several emergency meetings with Josh or Mary Hartzell, the director at First Presbyterian, or Joanie Green, the director of Crossroads Elementary. Crossroads decided to send a letter to the parents in the lower school, explaining the school's involvement in our lives and telling them about the story that was about to break.

But we decided that the nursery school parents should be told in person by Paul and me since Jake was going to be returning to preschool at First Presbyterian in just a few weeks.

On Friday night, August 18, Mary called the families whose children Jake played with in class and said, "I need your help. Please come to school at ten o'clock tomorrow morning. It's important. It does concern the school, but this is not about your child."

All ten families were there the next morning. Paul and I walked into the room, and I felt so scared because these were the parents whose children had already been in school with Jake for a year. Their children had played at our house, and Jake had played at theirs. The only couple that knew was Annie and George Solomon, and they were in New York. If anyone was going to feel enraged about being left out of our secret, these families might be the ones.

Mary introduced us and I told our story. I explained that the *National Enquirer* had given us no choice except to go public. I talked about Ari's illness and death and my hope that Jake might be able to have a different outcome. Paul spoke of his hopes and fears as well.

One couple that we thought might be very angry was sitting close to me. I couldn't read their faces and the tension was escalating in me so rapidly that I finally stopped, turned to them, and said, "Please, I just need to know what you think about all of this right now."

"Oh," they said. "We found out about this three months ago, and we decided that it was fine for Eric and Jake to continue playing together as they always had." I was stunned. Was it possible that many people knew and had already decided it was okay?

The parents were all supportive and the meeting was better

than I ever anticipated. Mary Hartzell wasn't surprised. She felt all along that if we went public, the school community would embrace us.

On Monday morning, August 21, we sat down to be interviewed by Janet Huck. Paul and I were apprehensive and fearful. We were now telling the story that everyone would read and were obviously concerned about how the story would be received. We didn't want pity. We didn't want to seem like freaks. We wanted people to feel compassion and we prayed they would be educated. After the story was published, we wanted to be treated just like everybody else.

We thought carefully about what we said. It seemed everything was riding on how this reporter told our story. Would our community accept or reject us? Would they care enough to become educated if they were not? Could this help educate Washington about pediatric AIDS as well as raise money for research? There was a lot at stake, but nothing was more important to us than Jake's well-being.

The day after the interview, a photographer came to take our picture for the article. Paul and I stood together in the atrium. Here we were, having our picture taken not because we had done anything important, but because we had a tragic life. It seemed surreal. I started to smile. I almost started laughing. Nothing made any sense anyway, so why not smile and try to look pretty? The photographer was not happy. He had come to photograph a serious picture of a couple in pain. He told Paul and me to try not to smile. That made it almost impossible for me to look serious. I remember saying to him, "Look, in my life you either laugh or cry, there is nothing in between." But he got his "serious" shot and that was the one the *Times* used.

Other than the deaths of our children, this was our worst fear. We had demanded our friends keep secrets, we had directly called people we hardly knew and begged them to stop talking about us. We had lied so many times to so many people, all to protect Jake and Ari. Now we would know how far the world had come since they burned the Rays out of their home.

Would people throw rocks at our windows? Would they ostracize Jake? Would they gawk at us as we walked by? We had worked as hard to keep AIDS a secret as we had to keep Ari alive. Now that was about to be over and we were scared.

In a surprising yet natural way, the fear and the peace of being an army of two was unusually bonding for Paul and me. We had been dealing with our pain so privately. Now that we were under attack, we were alive again. We felt very close. For the first time in a year, we felt like a family. Paul and I were standing side by side, guiding each other through the minefield.

I remember loving Paul deeply at that time. It was so comforting not to feel alone.

The very next day was step two of Mary Hartzell's plan. We planned a meeting with *all* the parents from the nursery school. Mary, Paul, and I all agreed that this issue was too important for families to stumble across in their morning newspaper even when it did not affect their child directly.

Mary felt that leadership from the school was essential because AIDS was so frightening to so many people. She believed strong moral leadership would help prevent irrational fear from sweeping in and holding firm.

On Saturday, August 19, the school's "phone tree" had been activated and the parents had been telephoned. They were told that there was a child in school who was HIV-positive. It was Jake Glaser and the Glasers wanted them to know the full story before it appeared in the newspaper later that week.

Susan and Susie began working relentlessly to organize information to give to the parents at the meeting. Mary Hartzell gave them a list of all the pediatricians who saw children in the school. They hand-delivered invitations to all of the doctors, explaining why the meeting was being held and urging them to attend because we knew they would be getting plenty of questions the next day about it.

Susan also managed to get a draft of an upcoming report from the CDC on the spread of AIDS through household contact. The report concluded that there had never been a documented case of AIDS being transmitted from one household member to another through casual contact, even in homes where people were infected for several years before they found out their diagnosis. Lots of people were working overtime to prepare for Tuesday night.

All in all, about two hundred parents came to the meeting, almost the entire parent body, as well as twenty pediatricians. It was standing room only. We had an information table set up and each family got a packet of material on children and AIDS.

Dick Stiehm and Jay Gordon, Ari's doctors, came to help answer questions and many of our friends showed up in support. I didn't know what to expect, and I thought that if there were any problems, our friends could explain how they had been dealing with my family for the past three years.

The room was overcrowded and hot. I was numb and afraid. Saturday's meeting had gone well, but I took nothing for granted and was unable to relax. The *Enquirer* experience had so thoroughly traumatized me that I wasn't sure my world would ever feel safe again. I didn't know if I would ever again be able to let down my guard. For three years, the secret had been a fortress around our lives. Now it was overrun and I felt defenseless and faint.

Robert De Laurentis was standing by my side. I needed fresh air. I felt like I couldn't breathe. We walked to the window and I said, "Robert, if we don't start right now I'm going to pass out." He let Mary know and she got everyone seated.

Mary welcomed the parents and doctors, then introduced me. I started. I don't remember exactly what I said. Once I began talking I lost all sense of myself. Although I had told our story many times, I had never spoken to so many people who mattered so much.

When I began, I was sitting on a chair in the front of the room. Someone in the back asked me to stand up. I sloughed it off by saying, "I'm so short, it won't make any difference if I'm sitting or standing." Everyone laughed, which broke the tension in the room. I couldn't believe those words had come out of my mouth at that moment of sheer terror.

My breath was short, but I started talking. "We come to you not by our own choosing at this moment. We are here because we need your help. When I tell you about our lives, you will understand why." I then told the complete story, ending with the *National Enquirer.* Then Paul spoke about how important each person in the room was to our lives. How we needed each of them to help make our life feel normal. You could have heard a pin drop.

When we finished speaking, there was silence. Then everyone in the room stood up and began applauding. It was overwhelming. They weren't running out of the room. They were saying, "My God, your life is complicated and hard. You're here to tell us and we applaud you for that."

When people became quiet again, I became very emotional. I was thinking about something that I was afraid to share. I felt embarrassed but said to myself, "Elizabeth, you have little left to lose. Just follow your instincts and say what is in your heart."

"When we were first diagnosed," I said, "I had an ongoing nightmare about going into the supermarket and having everyone move away from me. I would walk down an aisle and people would walk the other way. I would be standing at the checkout counter and in slow motion everyone would disappear whispering and staring. I always awoke from that nightmare anxious and depressed.

"In my wildest dreams, I never imagined that anyone would ever applaud me or my family, but you just have and now part of that nightmare is over. I thank you." My eyes were watery. I felt weak but happy.

Then, to my surprise, Paul said, "I had a different supermarket fantasy. I thought when people found out about my family, I'd go into the supermarket and they would give me the groceries for free." I couldn't believe at such a serious moment my husband could have told that story, but he did. It was a typical Paul wisecrack—cynical, funny, and real. People laughed and the atmosphere became more comfortable and friendly.

Alan Miles, the father of Jake's good friend Skylar, raised his hand and stood up. "My wife and I have only one question," he said. I held my breath. "Can Jake come over and play tomorrow?" Tears began to well in my eyes. All the right attitudes and commiseration wouldn't guarantee Jake playdates. I knew that from Ari's experience. Now here in front of everyone, one family stood up to make a promise. It was more than we had wished for at that moment.

Several parents told us they were proud to have us at First Presbyterian and thanked us for giving the school a chance to unite as a community and do something they would all be proud of. All in all, about ten families stood up and said something positive about the overall situation. It was astounding.

We were stunned by the love and commitment of Jake's school. We realized we wouldn't have to fight this battle alone. We were part of a community that was willing to link arms and walk beside us, however long or steep the road might be.

Paul and I left a few minutes later. We wanted to give people a chance to ask Mary Hartzell, Dick Stiehm, or Jay Gordon any questions they might have hesitated to ask in our presence.

We got in the car and looked at each other. "It went well," I said.

Paul nodded. "I think it went very well," he said. "I can't believe it's over. Now comes the hard part for them. They have to look at this without us in the room and face their fears." We were both so tired. We had summoned all our emotional strength and now drove home to once again wait for the final word, hoping that it had all ended well.

Suzanne and Jeff Buhai came back with us to wait until we heard how it turned out. We were home by nine o'clock. By ten-thirty, no one had called and I started to panic, thinking that the tide had turned in the other direction after we left. I couldn't sit still. I'd get up, then sit down. I aimlessly walked to the kitchen. Paul finally said, "Relax, it's out of our hands now."

We learned later that, as we expected, the questions became more specific after we left. Biting was an issue of concern to some parents. But as one of the pediatricians explained, biting isn't a threat since saliva is not a means of transmitting the AIDS virus. Biting could only be a risk if someone has a mouthful of infected blood when they bite someone else.

One family did stand up and say they weren't happy about having Jake in school. Very calmly and compassionately, in her remarkable way, Mary told them that she heard what they were saying, but if they didn't like the policy they could leave. The rest of the room applauded and there were no further comments like that. It was the kind of stand every family with AIDS needs but many don't get.

Mary said that after the meeting, one couple, both of whom were doctors, said, "We can see what a child with HIV has to gain from the school's policy, but what does our child get from it?"

Mary said to them, "Your daughter has the benefit of going to a school where we have people who are open and confront issues head-on. Your daughter benefits by going to a school where teachers and parents are compassionate and value individuals as well as life."

Some of the other parents told Mary they appreciated being forced by the school to think about AIDS because it was an issue they would have tried to avoid on their own.

Lucy finally called to say the meeting had ended well, and we should relax. Susan stopped by about one A.M. Paul had gone to bed, and Susan and I had a beer. She filled me in on what happened after we left. We marveled that it was finally over and we had come through it. We sat and shared a common bond until some of the energy of the night dissipated.

Eventually, two families told Mary Hartzell that AIDS was too frightening and they were unprepared to deal with it. Mary acknowledged their fears but said the school's policy was decided and if they could not accept it they would have to leave. They did.

The meeting we had dreaded was over. To the credit of every family in that school, we were treated with dignity and respect. Many new hands began to reach out to us that night to offer help. It was a miracle we were happy to accept.

CHAPTER

⇻14⇺

Josh called the *Enquirer* that Tuesday, the day of the First Presbyterian meeting, and said Paul and I *would not* provide a comment for their story. We knew that meant they would run their piece the next week. It would probably hit the stands the following Monday or Tuesday.

On Wednesday, the day after the parents' meeting, the *Los Angeles Times* called the editor of the *Enquirer* and asked him to comment on reports that his magazine was hounding the Glaser family. He slammed the phone down.

Then the *Enquirer* had the gall to call Josh and say that they wanted to run the address of the Pediatric AIDS Foundation at the end of their story so people could send donations. We refused. We would never let them camouflage their scandalous behavior behind an appeal for funds.

Then on the morning of Friday, August 25, like countless other Los Angeles residents, I opened my front door and picked up the *Times* from the sidewalk. There, smack-dab on the cover of the "View" section, was a half-page color picture of Paul and me. We were flung across front lawns and driveways and doorsteps all across Los Angeles. I started reading the story immediately. Beneath a bold headline which read, "Breaking the Silence," it said, "Starsky Star, Wife, Share Their Family's Painful Battle Against AIDS."

When I walked into the house I spread the newspaper out

on our big kitchen table so we could both read it together. Paul and I had not seen an advance copy of the text. We were so anxious that we read the whole article standing up. When we finished, Paul looked at me and said, "Now we wait and see what happens."

We had no way of anticipating what the reaction would be to the article. We had hired a security guard to be at home in case something happened. The school meeting had gone well but we were still very scared of how the rest of the community would respond. We didn't know if there would be TV cameras and reporters staked out on our front lawn trying to get a comment, or if there would be a glint of paparazzi in the bushes waiting to snap our picture.

We were frightened enough that we had tentative plans for Jake to play at a friend's house for most of the day in case it got too frantic for him to be safely at home. Another friend had invited Jake to have dinner and spend the night if necessary.

Paul and I had talked about being out of town when the article appeared. We thought about going back to Martha's Vineyard and renting a house for a month. But we knew it was ludicrous to run away because we'd have to come home eventually. Now that the story was out, it was not the way we wanted to live our lives, running and hiding. So we decided to stay at home and face whatever came our way.

As it turned out, the day was remarkably uneventful. Our biggest fears, of turning into some macabre media event, never materialized. Our friends called nonstop to say they had read the article and to offer support. That evening, Ron and Carol Herman came over and brought dinner. When nothing happened the next day, we began to relax. We let the security guard go, and that night we ventured out in public. We were determined not to hide in our house. We were afraid, but knew we had to get right back on the horse. We thought if we waited to go out, the anxiety would just get bigger and bigger. So along with Lucy, Doug, Lynn, and Frank, we marched back out into the world.

We went to a Vietnamese restaurant on Wilshire Boulevard that we had been going to for years. No one said anything to us. The six of us were amazed. It seemed nothing had changed.

The *Enquirer* article came out but we never read it. I felt

that would somehow mean the tabloid had won. I did see the
pictures. I thought they had already done everything terrible
and atrocious that they possibly could but I was wrong.
There was a picture of Ari's grave site. It was the final assault
in a violent rape. Thinking that someone had walked into that
cemetery and stood over her grave to take a picture, I could
have killed without remorse or shame. We never found out
who the photographer was or how much he was paid to pil-
lage our lives. In this case, human dignity was no match
against the big green dollar.

I have learned a lot about forgiveness. I have forgiven the
donor of the infected blood, the government that didn't respond, the society that didn't care, but I will never forgive
the *National Enquirer* for invading the sanctity of my family
and my friends. Had it not been for the *Enquirer,* Paul and
I would have continued to keep our privacy. But those at the
Enquirer, fueled by a society willing to support them, decided
we had lost that right. And then they took it from us.

We knew keeping the secret was a tremendous pressure but
we didn't realize how great it had been until it ended. It felt
like a huge chunk of cement was lifted from our backs. Over
the years, I had become accustomed to its crushing weight
and didn't notice how debilitating it had been until I could
stand up straight again without it.

Gone was the fear of being found out. I was finally free
to be actively and publicly involved with the Pediatric AIDS
Foundation. I no longer feared being rejected by our community. I worried about someone saying something to Jake inadvertently, but I knew that he was not going to be ostracized
by any of his playmates.

The world in August 1989 knew much more about AIDS
than it had when we were first diagnosed in 1986. Most important was that the scientific community had said defini-
tively that AIDS wasn't spread by casual contact. Kissing,
hugging, sneezing, and coughing would not transmit the
virus.

Nationwide, there was still an epidemic of fear about AIDS
and hysterical incidents were still occurring. We were aware
of that at the Foundation. People called to request information, then pleaded with us to send it in a plain wrapper without a return address so no one would know it was coming
from an AIDS organization.

When we went public in 1989, and people within our community reached out for answers, the doctors were able to provide definite and reassuring facts that they did not have when we were first diagnosed three years before. Consequently, it was a lot easier to be our friend in 1989 than it had been in 1986.

President Reagan was now out of office and living in Los Angeles when he saw the article in the *Times*. He called Janet Huck and asked her for our phone number. The Reagans had not known about Ariel's death until they saw the story in the paper and they wanted to speak with us. Janet called Josh and he called me. "Be prepared for a call from the President. Plan what you will say. You will only have this one chance."

It was Sunday morning and Paul was stretched out on the couch in the living room reading the paper when the phone rang. He answered it and when I heard him say, "Oh, hello, Mr. President!" I looked up. "She's right here. Hold on." He smiled when he passed me the phone and whispered, "It's him."

President Reagan said he was so sorry to hear that Ariel had died. He said that even though he was out of office, he would be willing to do anything he could to help.

I thanked him for his kindness and said that I was sure there was a way for him to play a role in helping the Foundation achieve its goals. Maybe I could meet with one of his staff members to discuss different options. President Reagan thought that was a good idea and said he'd have someone get back to me in a day or two.

I thanked him and moments after I hung up, the phone rang again. It was the President, calling back. "Elizabeth, this is President Reagan again. I'm sorry to bother you, but Nancy didn't know I was on the phone with you. She was sorry that I hung up before she had a chance to talk. Could you please hold on a moment while I get her?"

Nancy was extremely compassionate and told me how saddened she was by Ari's death. She said she knew from her own experience with breast cancer how hard it was to go through an illness in public. But she said as difficult as it is, it can do a great deal of good. She was astounded by the number of women who wrote to say that they went in for mammograms after her mastectomy.

Mrs. Reagan said that she felt our being out in public

would help bring attention to the issue of pediatric AIDS and the problems families face. She also offered to be of any help that she could to the Foundation.

On Monday, one of the President's staffers called me and asked if I could drop by the following morning. I agreed, amazed that things were happening so quickly. I had asked for a meeting and it was set.

President Reagan's office is in Century City, a cluster of modern high rises between Santa Monica and Beverly Hills. From the moment you walk in the door you feel as if you have entered a vault. Secret Service agents with their stand-up-straight demeanor take you to a security desk where you are cleared to go upstairs to President Reagan's office on the top floor. The atmosphere is cool and hushed.

I sat down with Mark Weinberg, the President's director of public affairs. He was young, efficient, and very friendly. After a few minutes he said that President Reagan was in and wanted to say hello. Reagan and I traded pleasantries and had our pictures taken and then Mark and I got back to work. (Over the next nine months I ended up having more pictures with Reagan than I ever could have imagined when I first met him that day at the White House.)

Mark said that the only thing the President would not do was fund-raising. However, he said the President was eager to talk about pediatric AIDS in speeches he made around the country. I said that would be very beneficial. Mark added that the President was willing to do a public service announcement about children and AIDS if we thought that would be helpful. I eagerly accepted. He also said he and Mrs. Reagan might be willing to come on our executive advisory board—which they subsequently did.

In thinking of ways the President could help, Susan, Susie, and I had thought of the possibility of a public service announcement. We never expected it to be offered without having to ask. I called them as soon as the meeting ended and they were as thrilled as I was.

Our story was out—things were starting to happen. Dawn Steel, who was then the effervescent head of Columbia Pictures, called us immediately after she read the article. "We want to do a benefit, a film premiere for you, right away. How about *Immediate Family* with Glenn Close and James

Woods?" It was a wonderful idea because our friends were the producers. It would be like family.

The premiere was significant because it would be our first fund-raiser in Los Angeles and it would also be the first time that Paul and I faced the Hollywood community since our story had become public. The date was set for October 24, almost two months away.

Two days later, Marlene Canter, whose daughter had been in our "Mommy and Me" group with Ari and Francesca, called Susan. Marlene wanted to help. She and her husband have their own small office building in Santa Monica. Within three days the Pediatric AIDS Foundation had finally found a permanent home, for free.

Ironically, now that we were out in the open, our lives had improved tremendously. We received hundreds of letters from strangers and friends in an outpouring of love and support. Now when people asked me what I was doing, I was able to talk about the Foundation. It was a great relief.

Because of the complications of lying and the devastation of losing a child, I had gradually curtailed the time I spent in public. It was what I needed to do to survive and I adapted.

But now that I didn't have to lie about my life and almost everyone knew I had lost a child, seeing old acquaintances or meeting someone new was no longer threatening. I felt more like myself than I had since we were diagnosed.

The worst parts of our lives were still the same; Ari was dead and Jake and I were HIV-positive. But I realized that now we were at least going to be able to live with dignity.

Two weeks after the article came out, Paul's friend from Warner Bros., Allyn Stewart, invited us to spend a long weekend with her in Sun Valley. It was bliss. It was one of the happiest times we had spent as a family since Ari died. Because she had never been to Sun Valley, all the memories there belonged to Jake.

I felt lucky to be able to have adventures now with Jake. It was like putting down our footprints in fresh snow. We were doing things we had never been able to do with him before. He was almost five, and able to sit on his own horse and manage a trail ride. He and I put on backpacks one day and hiked up to a sparkling clear lake. It was three miles round-trip, and Jake had no trouble keeping up.

The Turtletaubs, our friends who had put me in touch with

Alan Alda, were there at the same time we were. We went hiking together one afternoon and Jake was getting tired and cranky. Sol, who was ahead of us on the trail, started dropping pennies. Jake was exuberant. "Mom!" he screamed. "I'm finding treasure." To Jake the world was becoming exciting again and maybe it was to us as well.

We could finally relax and begin to enjoy what we had. It was a spectacular few days and we felt grateful, if not triumphant, to be back in the mainstream again. In a month we had gone from the nightmare of the *Enquirer* hunt to a life that was hectic, happy, and significantly better.

We returned to L.A. filled with wonderful memories of a few days in the mountains. Labor Day was over and Jake was getting ready to start school. This felt like our last big hurdle. The parents had only had a few weeks to absorb the news. Maybe things wouldn't go as well for us as we had hoped. Maybe the publicity had affected people more than we anticipated.

In order to allay some of my mounting anxiety, we invited twenty kids from Jake's class over for a pool party a few days before school was starting. I thought, *If they all come to our home, then things will be okay at school.* It was my secret test.

The day was boisterous and chaotic. Everyone came and had a great time. I felt elated. The school anxiety was subsiding but there was something else.

From the day I first saw our house, I imagined it filled with children and now, for the first time since Ari died, my dream was coming true again. As I looked at the pool filled with wiggling five-year-old tadpoles, I remembered how Paul and I once thought we were growing AIDS in that pool. It seemed like a long time ago.

Three days later, at nine o'clock in the morning, Jake and I drove up to First Presbyterian. My instinct was to lower my head to avoid direct eye contact. I resisted. I held my head high, looked in people's eyes, and nodded or smiled when I could. No one avoided me. People's eyes sent silent messages of love and support.

I could have cried but I didn't. Ten months later, at the end-of-the-year lunch I tried to explain to these families how much they all meant to me. They can never really understand that it was their strength and moral commitment to helping a family in need that allowed us to stay afloat that September.

When you're battling AIDS like my family is, each person you meet can make a difference. It's as simple as that. If only the world could follow the example set by our little nursery school in Santa Monica, other families could have the help that we did. So at last, the school issue was finally over for us.

The *Los Angeles Times* article had prompted numerous inquiries from other media. One national magazine wanted to do a cover story on us, which could have potentially raised a lot of money for the Foundation, but at that point Paul and I didn't feel comfortable with the idea. We had inquiries from Diane Sawyer's staff and from Jane Pauley.

Paul and I were now faced with choices we never had to make when we were hiding. Should we do this interview because it would bring in money for the Foundation? Should we do that TV show because it will influence Washington? Or something else because it might have an impact on both?

On the one hand, Paul and I wanted the attention to be over. But now that we were out in public, we also felt an obligation to help focus attention on pediatric AIDS.

After Paul and I discussed our options and talked to a few friends, we decided we didn't want to do anything except "60 Minutes." With its fifty million viewers and reputation for serious journalism, it seemed like the best way to communicate our story to a national audience. The only problem was that "60 Minutes" hadn't called us.

So I called Rita Braver in Washington and she spoke to Don Hewitt, the executive producer of "60 Minutes." He said they would consider the story and arranged for me to meet Ed Bradley's producers, and in a few weeks, I did. I told them about our lives and why I thought this was an important story for "60 Minutes" to do.

I said I thought the piece should focus on how pediatric AIDS was different from adult AIDS and the difficulties we were having in Washington. It would not be a story about our family as much as a story about the issue. We didn't need people gawking at our life. We needed them to learn more and care more so things would change.

They seemed interested, but had to pitch the story to Hewitt and Bradley back in New York. Several weeks later we got the call that "60 Minutes" wanted to do a segment with us. It would start filming later that fall.

All right! In one fifteen-minute shot, fifty million people would learn that children were dying from AIDS and that almost nothing was being done. The Pediatric AIDS Foundation would become known nationally overnight. The office was excited.

Now that Jake was back in school, I started going to the office every day. It was very satisfying. Many people in L.A. were calling to offer help. Did we need someone to write copy? Did we need office volunteers? Could they help us raise money? Doug's sister, Cindy Wick, offered to help us find a way to get our printing done for free. Ted and Susie Field said they would underwrite a fund-raising event in L.A. in the spring. We wanted to raise another million dollars but this time at a Sunday afternoon family picnic. Ted also said we could use his Santa Barbara ranch for our next "think tank," which Susan was planning for February.

One of the pleasant parts about being out in public for me was the positive reinforcement I was now receiving for the work I was doing with the Foundation. While I was in hiding few people knew what I was doing. Our work in L.A. was extraordinarily low-key and we did not have much contact with local AIDS groups, and when we did, Susan and Susie were the people they knew.

Susan suggested that now I might want to participate in the National Pediatric AIDS Conference in Los Angeles. We decided I would join a small, informal session for parents and families.

It was the first time I had publicly said, "Yes, I am one of these families with AIDS." Even though I had been so involved behind the scenes, it was a different feeling entirely not to have to elicit pledges of secrecy afterward.

I sat in a room with people whose lives were much like mine. Some of the families had been in our documentary and I was glad to speak frankly with them. It felt good and it felt scary. There would no longer be a way to deny any part of our life now at any time. Listening to other families talk about their lives made mine feel poignantly real and immediate.

In the past, Paul and I would pretend to some people that our life was fine. It worked for brief moments—an hour here, thirty minutes there. Now that was gone. I felt raw and exposed.

When I left the meeting, I sat in the car with Susan and cried. We both felt maybe it had been too much, too soon. We decided to think more carefully about the opportunities that lay ahead. Not just to think about how something would help others or the Foundation, but what emotional impact it would have on me.

Because Susan and Susie had lived through so much with me, and because they also knew everything about the Foundation, they were able to help me make choices. It was so much easier for me not to have to sort it all out by myself.

When we started the Foundation the year before, we had no idea what we were getting into, how to proceed, or if we could be successful. We had motivation, commitment, determination, and good instincts, but we were not sure where it was going to lead or what we could achieve.

Now we knew and felt proud of what the three of us had managed to accomplish. We had worked hard, raised almost two million dollars so far, and we were now able to take credit for what we had done without lying about why we had done it. I felt we were really beginning to make people pay attention to pediatric AIDS. We were respected as a foundation and I felt we had earned it.

At home the immeasurable weight of worrying about keeping the secret was gone. Paul and I had come through this part of the battle together and there had been moments of great intimacy. The years before and after Ari's death had been very exhausting, demanding, and isolating. As we faced our grief we each found separate ways of dealing with it. Paul would play golf and exercise diligently when his back allowed. He focused on his career and developing projects at various studios. I had my Foundation work and my very close relationships with my women friends.

When I was sad, I would usually call one of my friends rather than go and find Paul. We were struggling to handle our own individual pain, and it just seemed like too much for him to handle mine or for me to help with his as well. The time we spent together was often at a movie or lying in bed watching TV or doing something with Jake. I think we unconsciously left very little time when we could actually talk. We just didn't have the strength to hold each other up.

But in many ways the *Enquirer* siege had brought us back together for those few weeks. We spoke at length every day.

We had to talk honestly about many things we usually avoided. We had to look at our fears, our losses, our future, and stand strong. It felt very good. I felt deep love for and trust in Paul during the end of August. But once the danger was past, we found ourselves slipping back into our old ways. We were talking and sharing less again, involved in our own separate worlds. We knew it was happening and afraid of how we would end up.

One night we felt particularly frustrated. We sat down and talked about what we should do. We decided to see our therapist again. It was hard, but we felt we had no choice.

In Dr. Friedman's office, we tried to say all the things that we usually kept inside. All the feelings that created the distance and isolation between us came out. These were not feelings of love, but of anger, hatred, resentment, and sorrow.

Sometimes Paul is consumed with anger and fear about our life and it makes it impossible for him to feel any love for me at all. He isn't HIV-positive and could be living a normal life if it weren't for me. At times, I know he resents it. How could he not?

In those sessions, we let out our worst thoughts and I remember thinking that the marriage might not make it. Even after all we had been through, there was so much still to overcome.

A month before, Paul and I had planned a three-day trip to Santa Fe. We knew things were shaky and thought if we had some time away and alone it might help. The trip came a day after one of our worst sessions with the therapist. We barely made it to the airport. We were fighting in the car, and I was sure Paul was going to say to hell with the whole trip. But he didn't. We both got on the plane. I cried through the entire flight. I felt tired behind my eyes and my throat felt like it was closing off. My head throbbed from crying so hard and I would have done anything to end the tension between us. Our marriage felt hopeless.

Why were we fighting? Why, when everything was finally better, were we suddenly so enraged with each other?

I think when life is terrible, when we are in a state of crisis, we block out everything to survive. Denial can be a powerful ally, and it is part of the armor we rely on when we are in an extreme situation. When the crisis is resolved, all of the feelings we've pushed aside overtake us.

Maybe Paul and I have to have one foot dangling over the abyss before we feel we can pull each other back in.

We landed in Albuquerque and Paul went to rent a car. When he came back to pick me up, I was seething. "Give me the keys," I said. "You fly back to L.A. I'm going to Santa Fe by myself and then come home. I can't spend three days with all this hatred."

Paul just looked at me and said, "Come on, let's go." He got into the car, slammed the door, and we left Albuquerque for Santa Fe. The trip took an hour.

We sat silently staring at the high desert scenery. Neither one of us dared to look at the other. I said to myself, *Elizabeth, do you want to say good-bye to this man? Do you want him out of your life?*

The answer was no. So I sat there thinking, *What can I do? How do I stop feeling so angry and sad?*

In one of the more important moments of my life, I reached out and put my hand on his. We sat like that for a while. Then Paul reached over and put his arm around me and pulled me closer. We sat quietly driving to Santa Fe, realizing that we didn't want to say good-bye. As the love slowly and softly drifted in, the anger just as gently floated away.

There is no one else in the world who can understand what Paul and I have been through except each other. We share the same trench, and like soldiers in combat, we've experienced a camaraderie no one else will ever understand. No one can offer us support like we can to each other. But when we are angry and hurt, there is no one who can make us feel more isolated than each of us to the other. When Paul and I feel estranged, it's like living on opposite sides of a wall.

All of the pain in our life can overwhelm everything else if we let it, and we certainly had by the time we got to New Mexico. Our love has had so much to overcome that sometimes we become completely severed from it. We can't find it at all.

What happened instinctively on that drive, and what I consciously realized later that weekend, was that there was no way to work back down through the pain to the love. I had to circumvent all the anger and resentment to connect with the part of me that loved Paul.

I think when Paul and I realized on that drive that we were on the verge of losing our relationship on top of everything else, we were able to defuse the tension and decide to let ourselves love.

The hotel was charming. Paul and I sat through dinner holding hands and enjoying the peace we both felt inside. The room was cozy and we kissed and made love for the first time in a long, long time.

The next day, we drove to Bandolier National Park which sits right below Los Alamos. The clay rocks are pink and very dramatic. Paul and I started walking along a path that led to the site of some ancient cliff dwellings. We climbed narrow trails worn away by centuries of travelers. The air was clean. There were no sounds but the wind quietly singing in our ears.

I imagined the people who had lived there hundreds, even thousands of years before, and I felt comforted by the connectedness of it all. Sometimes it feels safe to feel small, and to remember that I am part of all that has gone before and is yet to come.

Paul suggested walking barefoot like the Indians had. The path was soft and quiet and the dust felt warm and powdery between our toes. At one point the path was so narrow we could barely squeeze between the cliffs. As we reached to climb a rock wall our fingers would find the imprints made by the Indians as they climbed the same path over and over, day after day. Paul and I both finally felt alive and in love again, and what a joy that was.

I felt in the last twenty-four hours life had taught me possibly its most important lesson. I wanted to talk to Paul about love. It all seemed so simple. I didn't want to lose the essence of what I was coming to understand.

I'm sure there were other times in my life when a simple touch had great impact, but I don't remember it.

This is what I came to understand that day in Santa Fe: Our life has layers and layers of painful complications for me and Paul. This leads to anger, fear, frustration, resentment, sadness, every painful emotion you can think of.

While all of these emotions are understandable, they are not pleasant to live with. When Paul and I would start at the top and try to systematically work through all the problems, we would always get stuck. It was too thick, too dense, to ever work through.

The bottom line was that Paul and I loved each other

deeply but it meant little if we couldn't touch that love. When we were stuck in all the top layers, we needed to shake off the mud and move to the clean waters of caring. Each of the problems of anger, frustration, and sadness could be faced and were workable when we started at the bottom with the love.

Both parts of my life are equally real, the pain and the love. It just depends on where I choose to begin. If I start at the top with the pain, I usually stay there. But if I start at the bottom with the love, the weight of the pain usually eases.

Of course for me, the hardest part was to remember to go to the love when I felt so angry. The fear and anger for me created a maze in which I could be lost forever—a life in which I was never able to look beyond the next turn.

I guess we are all lost in our own mazes, making daily choices, confronting daily problems. Shall I turn right or left? Each choice feels so important and the maze often feels dark and gloomy and scary. What I realized that day, reaching for Paul's hand as we stood on the brink of divorce, was that I could choose not to spend my life in that maze. I could rise above it and view it from a completely different perspective. I had the power to change how I lived.

That weekend, Paul and I learned many things together. We flew home touched simultaneously by the complexity and simplicity of life. But we knew the struggle wasn't over. Wisdom is sometimes very hard to hold on to.

The plane touched down, and I had little time to reflect on the weekend. As soon as I got back home, the pressures of the Foundation were upon me. I learned that only one third of the tickets for the *Immediate Family* film premiere had been sold. The benefit, which we hoped would raise a quarter of a million dollars, was now only a week away. The pressure was on. Susie and I started calling up everyone we knew, asking them to help sell tickets.

By the end of the week, the benefit was sold out and we knew we had made our $250,000. I was relieved that we had met our goal, but extremely nervous as the evening drew near. As co-chairs of the event, Paul and I had to speak before the film began. The movie theater would be filled with fifteen hundred friends and colleagues from the Hollywood community. Public speaking has never come easily to me and I certainly had never spoken in front of so many people before.

On top of everything else, "60 Minutes" was there doing its first filming of us. Paul and I were miked for almost the entire evening. It was one of those moments when remembering the humor in life would have helped.

When we arrived, the photographers and crews from the local TV stations were lined along the entrance to the theater calling out like street hawkers, "Over here!" "Could we get a comment?"

Now that people knew our story, they could ask us any questions they wanted. But the cameras that were there that night weren't looking for hard news.

After Dawn's brief welcoming remarks, everyone in the theater grew still. The room was dark, except for the spotlight shining on Paul. He thanked Dawn and began speaking of the pain of being powerless in the face of death:

From the day when AIDS changed our lives, it seems that we have experienced the gamut of emotions—along with just about every kind of fear imaginable. However, the greatest fear, the most debilitating, was that of feeling impotent. Impotent in the act of life; powerless in the face of death. It's a common fear. Mine came from a perception that I had no choice—that this was my lot.

I struggled with this fear for a long time. Then I realized that I did indeed have a choice. I could run and hide, or I could stay and fight. And in having and making a choice, I was, in fact, empowering myself. It rendered me potent. In the face of all my fears, I had the power to choose. Then I had to act on that choice. That I couldn't do by myself. I couldn't have done it without you.

To those friends whom we see often, to those friends whom we see only occasionally, and to the industry that, I believe, always knew in part, sometimes only as a rumor, some version of our story and chose to honor our privacy and now has rallied around us, and as evidenced by tonight, chooses to continue to support the issue of pediatric AIDS, to all of you, my deepest thanks.

His voice cracked. Paul's pain and anguish that is usually so private, reverberated through the room. As I listened to

Paul's words I felt proud of his courage and blessed by his
love. Ari and Jake could have no finer dad.

When he regained his composure, he introduced me, saying: "I have learned more from her than any person I have
ever met."

Working to keep my composure and as the applause finally
quieted, I thanked Paul and Dawn and then said:

> Some causes are so easy to embrace—rain forests, our
> bay, clean air. And then, there are some that are
> harder—and we don't really care about them until we
> are directly affected.
> Until tonight, some of you may not have even known
> there was such a thing as pediatric AIDS. Well, there
> is, and Paul and I know too much about it. . . .
> Two years ago, when Ariel started to fail, there was
> no hope, no drugs, no therapies, only questions. Now,
> two years later, we are fighting to write a different story
> for our son and all the other children and families bat-
> tling AIDS. . . .

Everyone stood and applauded. The community we feared
at one time might reject us opened their hearts in an outpouring of love.

As the evening ended, we were flushed with the support
surrounding us. Susie was proud of pulling off her first successful event. Eight months later she would raise a million
dollars at a once-in-a-lifetime family picnic called "A Time
for Heroes."

While I worked very closely with both Susan and Susie in
the first year, Susan and I spent so much time together that
we became like one. In the second year, however, as Susan
needed to devote more time to her family, Susie and I grew
closer and closer. In time, our friendship grew deeper than
either of us ever imagined. She and I became like sisters.

CHAPTER

❧15❧

A few weeks after the benefit, I had to stop taking AZT. Over the summer and through the fall of 1989, I had been feeling increasingly tired. It never stopped me from doing everything I needed to do, but I was always aware of a nagging sense of exhaustion. Even when I opened my eyes in the morning I would feel tired.

I spoke to friends and doctors about it, but everyone just assumed it was tension and the stress of keeping up with the accelerated pace of our lives. I never really believed that, but I didn't want to be a complainer. I knew it was true that I was now doing more in a day than I had previously done in a week, so I just trudged along.

However, besides the exhaustion, something strange was happening to my body. Being an athlete, I had always had a strong, compact frame. Now I would look in the mirror and feel scared at the deterioration of my body's muscle tone. I told only Paul and my doctors of my vain concern.

"Elizabeth, you're forty-one," Paul responded. "You haven't been exercising and you've had two children. Stop worrying." That was fine for him to say, but I didn't buy it. Something was going on, but I couldn't figure out what it was.

My friends did not really notice any drastic change in me and kidded me about turning forty-two in a few weeks.

"Relax, Elizabeth," was the repeating refrain. No one wants me to get sick, and I think there is sometimes a collective denial among us all. We hold on to our best hopes until facts force us to face the worst.

I finally went to Michael Gottlieb. He ran a CPK test to check for toxicity to AZT. CPK stands for creatine phosphokinase, an enzyme that is released by muscles when they become severely damaged. My test results were off the charts. The test showed that AZT was making my muscles produce a lot of CPK and it was destroying them. My body was eating itself up.

I stopped the drug immediately. AZT is extremely toxic. I was lucky because I used it for almost two years without experiencing any side effects. Some people have ghastly reactions right away—headaches, vomiting, anemia, and diarrhea. One of the more serious complications is the suppression of bone marrow which produces white blood cells. That's why we had to stop AZT with Ari.

AZT was the only drug that had been federally approved for the treatment of AIDS. It's believed to effectively prolong the life of people with AIDS by slowing down the progression of the disease which in turn delays the onset of the opportunistic infections that kill most AIDS patients. But not everyone can take it; some people cannot tolerate the powerful and toxic antiviral drug.

When Gottlieb told me I had to stop taking AZT he was able, at least, to offer me another option—DDI (dideoxyinosine), which would be available in a few weeks. Some call DDI a "cousin" to AZT. Like AZT, it's an antiviral whose mechanism against the virus is to terminate a part of the virus's DNA chain so that the virus doesn't replicate. In early clinical trials it showed relatively little bone marrow toxicity, but ultimately how toxic—and effective—it was against the virus remained to be seen. It had not been approved by the government for widespread use but was in FDA Phase II clinical trials and was being made available to many others on a compassionate use basis. I became one of the guinea pigs the drug is being tested on. I was lucky to have an alternative. It would have been far more depressing to let go of the only proven lifeline doctors have been able to offer.

But going from AZT to DDI isn't like switching from Tylenol to Advil. It's very scary. It puts you right back in touch with how vulnerable you are. Like AZT, DDI is a powerful and potentially dangerous drug. When I read the list of reported side effects in the informed consent agreement, I almost lost my nerve:

> Seizures, inflammation of the pancreas; abnormal liver function; pain, weakness, tingling or numbness in the hands/arms or feet/legs (related to nerve damage); low neutrophil (white blood cell) count, transient skin rash; headache; light-headedness; increased uric acid (which can lead to gout, [painful joints] and kidney damage) and elevated creatine phosphokinase (a protein released by damaged heart or muscle tissue) in the blood; irritability; excitability; and difficulty in sleeping. Electrocardiographic changes may occur which might indicate heart damage.

Reading and signing the consent form was horrible. I know they don't know what may happen to me on this drug. I know this drug may not work. It may cause me more harm than AZT and I may have to stop using it as well. And then what?

But despite all the risks, if you are HIV-positive or an AIDS patient, you feel lucky to be a DDI guinea pig.

I decided I would sign. I would use the drug my doctors were recommending but I wouldn't rely on it. I would keep myself strong in any and every way I could. Whether it be good nutrition, vitamins, Chinese herbs, acupuncture, exercise, or therapy. I would fight back from the toxins of AZT and not let this virus hold me hostage.

Now that we had identified the problem, I wanted to know if the effects on my muscles were reversible. No one really knew, but Michael thought they were. I wanted to reclaim my body by immediately working out five days a week and getting myself back in shape as fast as I could. But I was forbidden to exercise by a muscle specialist who said I might permanently damage my muscles unless I waited until the toxins were completely cleansed from my body. I waited and then I went to work.

Two days a week, Gaylene, a new but dear and wonderful friend, and I would work out: sit-ups, steps, cross-country ski machine. I'd pump iron and imagine power surging back into my body. I started to feel really strong again and it was wonderful. My body was mine again.

In mid-October, we got word of the results of our year-long work in Washington. Ten million dollars had been directed to pediatric AIDS research. Tom Harkin had done what he had said he would. It was a beginning but certainly not enough. The time bomb continued to tick. Now we'd have to wait another year for more.

In October and November, Jake celebrated his fifth birthday and I celebrated my forty-second. Jake was doing well. His T-cells had dropped once but gone back up. Every six weeks we were still very anxious when his blood work was done. Waiting for those numbers never gets easy. We'd look at this son of ours and see a kid who was really becoming a person. He was funny and cute. I treasured the mornings when he'd climb into bed and say, "Mom, let's cuddle." I loved seeing him hit the baseball clear across the yard. He is strong and has a good sense of himself, which we used to balance the fear.

I think we both decided we should enjoy our birthdays this year and we did. Jake had his own piñata because he wanted to get *all* the candy, and I had a repeat of my party from the year before. It was a wonderful, raucous, dancing frenzy. Since I was on DDI, liquor was off-limits so my tequila shooters had to be waived, but the energy was mine. I vaguely remember Susan and me standing on the tables and dancing as the evening wore on. This year Paul's back was better so he could dance too. Everyone had a great time, especially me.

During these months many things were building to a crescendo. "60 Minutes" was filming the many hours they would distill down to a fifteen-minute segment on me, Paul, and the Foundation. Susie, Susan, and I were working with Chiat/Day/Mojo, an advertising firm that was helping us create the Reagan public service announcement, and Susan and I were preparing the materials we would need for the 1990 assault on Washington for pediatric AIDS funding. It was an exciting and stimulating time.

On Halloween, "60 Minutes" came to the house and filmed Susan and me working at my kitchen table. Before they got there we tried to pretend we weren't excited, but of course we were. However, once they arrived, I think it was amazing how relaxed we were. We just went on as though no one was there. Actually, we were under a great deal of pressure and couldn't waste time worrying about lights and cameras. We hadn't felt very successful in Washington that year. The ten million dollars appropriated for research was only half of what was needed, and no extra pediatric clinical trial money had been found. Once again we had to state our information clearly so that people would understand the problems and how we felt they might be addressed. We were working relentlessly. We were determined to do better in 1990.

A few days before a trip to Washington there is always electricity in the air. Our office is one fairly small room. We have seven desks in it and usually at least five people. When something exciting happens or when we are under a great deal of pressure, everyone feels it. We'd have requests in for meetings, but it always ends up that confirmations aren't made until the last minute. Susan would hang up the phone, swing around, and announce we had some congressman confirmed, an hour later two senators would be set. Senator Hatch's office called; the meeting with the drug company was on. Senator Metzenbaum's office called; the meeting with Kennedy was finally on. Each time a call came in, the energy level heightened. You could almost touch it.

Susan and I left for Washington. We had written a formal request letter to the White House in hopes of getting a meeting with President Bush. Unfortunately, we had gotten a rather standard reply saying they were sorry but he was "very busy."

We weren't really counting on much help from the White House. The Reagan administration had been unable to offer money and leadership. The Bush administration, while saying the right words, wasn't willing to make the hard choices either. Six months later, on the day of the opening of the International AIDS Conference in San Francisco, President Bush was in North Carolina raising one million dollars for Jesse Helms. I've learned to pay attention to actions, not words. Words won't save any lives if they're not backed up with the necessary commitments. As far as I'm concerned, you can't support the battle against AIDS and support Jesse Helms.

President Bush now seems to be wavering even on the battle itself. At a press conference in Washington on September 17, 1990, he said that while he was saddened by the thousands of deaths from AIDS, he wasn't convinced that any more money would help curb the tide of the epidemic. "I wish somebody could convince me that if you could only spend a quarter of a billion dollars more, we would have the answer," Bush said.

It seems at this point in life we would realize that there are no guarantees. Our S&Ls weren't guaranteed. There is no guarantee that the one billion dollars a month we spend in the Persian Gulf will ensure a free Kuwait, lower oil prices, or stability in the region. We're willing to commit huge funds in other places with no guarantees, but it seems to me the White House is looking for an excuse not to fully support this war at home. More people have died from AIDS here than in the Gulf or Vietnam, but once again no one really seems to care.

Even without any White House visit, our trip to Washington was important. Our first scheduled meeting was with a representative from Burroughs Wellcome, the drug company that manufactures AZT. "60 Minutes" was trailing us around the capital on this trip as well.

Everyone seemed to think the Pediatric AIDS Foundation was my creation. Susan and Susie, who had been co-founders, were, unfortunately, almost ignored in the crush of publicity surrounding me and Paul. I was especially glad that Susan was with me on this trip because I wanted her included in the political segment of the "60 Minutes" piece. We had made almost every trip to Washington together and she had been crucial to our success. The Foundation was my idea, but without Susan and Susie it would never have become a reality. If "60 Minutes" was going to show me in Washington, it should be the way it really was: Susan and me together.

By the end of two days, we hated it. We were grateful they were there, but it was also a great inconvenience. They followed us everywhere. It was not like our usual trips to Washington, but we knew the piece could have great impact. It would put the Foundation on the map and determine whether or not we would be taken seriously. It could educate millions of viewers to the issue of pediatric AIDS. We played ball, keeping our fingers crossed that the piece would help us achieve our goals. Once they were done we laughed about how surprising and unpredictable life can be. We had just done "60 Minutes." There was a great desire to pinch each other to make sure it was all real.

After a day and a half, Susan prepared to go back home. I was going to stay an extra day to finish the meetings we had set up.

It was a long day and turned out to be one of the hardest I'd had in Washington. We were in a meeting with Mel Levine, the congressman from our home district. Because he didn't sit on any of the committees that directly impacted pediatric AIDS issues, we hadn't yet met Mel.

Mel started to explain that his wife knew me from a "Mommy and Me" group when Ariel was just nine months old. This caught me off guard because I work hard to emotionally separate my personal life from my Washington business.

All of a sudden, Ari was in the meeting and I hadn't brought her in. Mel had. As I was trying to sound intelligent, I was also trying to stay calm. Then Susan looked at her watch, stood up, and said she'd have to leave for the airport. We hugged each other, said a professional good-bye, and I finished the meeting with Mel.

I walked out feeling that the emotional fault line inside was about to split wide open. All of a sudden I missed Ari terribly. I wanted to be that mom in the playgroup again, raising my children just like everyone else. I was trying to get to the Rayburn Building and I stopped a stranger to get directions. He could see that I was crying and asked if everything was all right. I felt all wrong. I felt out of place. I couldn't hold it together. I shouldn't have been there. I said I was having a hard day and tried to smile. I knew I needed to pull myself together, that the next meeting would be difficult. I didn't know if I could do it.

Ten minutes later I had forced the tears to stop and I was meeting Mike Stephens, who is the key person for Congressman Natcher on the House Appropriations Health Committee.

We were disappointed in our inability to bring Mike Stephens around to our point of view in 1990. I wanted to find out what happened. Were we somehow too naive? Did we misunderstand part of the process? I felt vulnerable when I walked into his office. Few people hold your hand in Washington, so I knew I had to stay sharp.

His argument was that there was enough money flowing into the existing institutions at NIH. He firmly believed that people like Sam Broder, the head of the National Cancer Institute, and Tony Fauci had the funds, but *chose* not to spend any of them on pediatric AIDS. He just didn't think that they had been talking straight to me, that if they thought it was important, they would make sure the money was there. I was very confused. I was already feeling vulnerable; now I felt raw.

Sam Broder had impressed me with his integrity and had told me specifically that he didn't have the money he needed to run his existing program, let alone set up new ones. Tony Fauci had not been as specific, but it was painful to even imagine that they had been running circles around me without my knowing it.

I looked at my watch and realized it was four-forty-five. I was late for a meeting with Senator Kennedy that I had tried to set up on each of my previous trips to Washington.

The first person I saw when I sprinted into the Russell Building was Sam Broder, the man I had been speaking about only moments before. When I looked at Sam, he knew I was upset.

He asked what was wrong. I blurted out, "I just got out of a meeting with Mike Stephens and he's saying you could be running programs you are not running. I just don't know who to believe anymore. Sometimes I think everybody is just using me and I'll never understand what is going on in this damn town. I need to help Jake and I'm afraid I can't. Now I'm even late to meet with Senator Kennedy, so good-bye!" Poor Sam, I'm sure he never knew what hit him.

I flew into Kennedy's office. "Hello, I'm Elizabeth Glaser and I'm sorry I am so late."

The staffer looked at me and in the hushed tones of Senate propriety said, "He waited for you for a while, but then he couldn't wait any longer."

"But when I called you said he was running late!"

"Yes, Mrs. Glaser, but not half an hour late."

I asked if I could wait for Senator Kennedy to return. But when he returned, the meeting lasted only ten minutes, and I left feeling I had failed to move him.

The day was over. I was running on empty and my quota of optimism had been spent. Tired and discouraged, I trudged over to Senator Metzenbaum's office, hoping that Joel Johnson would be there to help me understand what had happened with Mike Stephens.

He was. But when he said, "What's wrong?" in his calm and kindly way, I just fell apart. "Joel, I don't know what I'm doing. They're running circles around me. I can't cut through the bullshit. Maybe I shouldn't even be doing this work at all. I'm so confused. I just want to go home and be with my family and never, ever come back to Capitol Hill!"

I was crying, yelling, and blowing my nose and the aide whose desk is next to Joel's got up and said, "I'm going to the bathroom." He flew out of the office.

Joel let me go on for a few more minutes and then he said, "Elizabeth, listen to me. Be quiet long enough for me to tell you something. You may be naive about the way Washington works, but you are not stupid. The work you are doing is important. You know that. You're not making any big mistakes and you've accomplished a hell of a lot in a very short time. You're new to this game so you'll have to take my word for it: you're doing fine. Washington is the land of incremental change—one step forward, two steps back. Don't get down on yourself when you have a day like today because it's perfectly normal."

Joel's reassurances helped calm me. He gave me a ride back to my hotel, and I went upstairs to get ready for dinner. I called Sam Broder to apologize and try to explain why I had been so upset. "Sam, are you lying to me? Do you have the money to do this work?"

"No," he said. "All our money is already in programs."

"Well, what should I have said?"

And then Sam taught me a great lesson about Washington—how to stop the bullshit. He told me if I ever had a meeting like that again just to say I wasn't there to find out what Sam Broder or Tony Fauci could do, but rather to find out what Mike Stephens or whoever I was talking with could do.

Six months later, I would say just that in my next meeting with Mike Stephens. And with his help and the support of Natcher and two wonderful congressmen—one from Maryland, Steny Hoyer, and one from Massachusetts, Silvio Conte—the House would appropriate ten million more dollars for basic, fundamental pediatric AIDS research and

$23.8 million to supplement the pediatric clinical trial units. Whatever the Senate did this time at least the House had come through.

As the day ended I was exhausted but I had already made dinner plans with my old high school boyfriend, Harold Steinitz. We talked about old times and what our friends from high school were doing. We talked about our lives and how things don't always turn out the way you expect them to.

After Harold left I got into bed and thought for a long time about my life. I looked back at all the turning points and at the choices I made and knew that there was nothing I would have done differently.

That might sound strange, but my whole life has been rather consistent. One lesson I have learned from AIDS is not new. We all know it. The difference for me is that AIDS makes it impossible to ignore.

The lesson is that I have to appreciate my life. I have to appreciate what I do have rather than yearn for what I don't have. I have learned to worry about what really matters and let go of the rest. Some people get so wrapped up in minutiae that they are too tired to appreciate the beauty and goodness that is all around them.

I live with a sense of urgency because I have no choice. The challenge in my life is not to give up. The challenge for me is to find a way to keep fighting. The challenge for me is to live as fully as possible so I don't waste time, and so I enjoy the time I have. The challenge for me is to continue to care and love.

But that challenge is in every other life, too. Most people just don't realize it, but if you are not enjoying your life, then you are wasting time. If you don't find a way to solve your problems and work hard at it, you are wasting your time. If you complain without looking for a solution, then you are wasting your time. Wasting your time is the same as wasting your life. People who waste their lives make me angry.

On that last day in Washington, I felt discouraged, sad, and sorry for myself. When that happens, I find someone to talk to, because I've learned that if I don't I'll sink into an even deeper despair. I was lucky that Joel was there. At home, when I get despondent, I'll call Lucy or Lynn and say,

"I don't want my life; I want someone else's life. Everyone has a better life than I do."

And Lucy or Lynn will say, "That's true. You have every right to feel sorry for yourself, but you are doing the best you can."

When I hang up the phone I ask myself how long I want to keep feeling that way. The answer is "Not long," because it doesn't feel good. So I say that I hope by tomorrow I'll feel better.

As I was flying back to L.A. and rehashing the trip in my mind, I realized that a lot of people are unwilling to take risks in Washington because they want to protect both their egos and their jobs. Staying the same is synonymous with staying safe.

But in the nearly two years I had been traveling to Washington, I had found people who were willing to take risks to do what was right. Orrin Hatch, who's both a Republican and a Mormon from Utah, represents a tried-and-true conservative constituency, yet he's never backed away from the issue of AIDS.

Likewise, Howard Metzenbaum always helped us, regardless of whom he might anger. He's not afraid of a fight and that's the kind of person we needed, someone who didn't wait for us to ask for help but offered it immediately.

Now we knew our challenge was to keep the issue vital. We needed more people willing to take risks and fight hard. Washington has a short attention span and we knew that we had to keep the legislative pressure on or complacency might set in. That was where "60 Minutes" could make the difference.

The rest of November we were busy working on the Reagan public service announcement, completing shooting on the "60 Minutes" spot, and exploring the possibility of doing a prime-time documentary on pediatric AIDS. Medically, I was stable and I had adjusted to the DDI without any of the horrible side effects I'd read about on the consent form. Although my T-cells were still low, I was otherwise asymptomatic and felt great. Time was moving fast and before we knew it, Christmas was upon us.

Paul and I had decided to spend the holidays away from home again, and we left the week before Christmas to go skiing with Jake and our friends the Seymours in Telluride, Colorado. There wasn't very much snow, but there was enough to keep Jake happy.

At first, Jake refused to go to ski school. When I told him that he couldn't ski with me until he took a lesson, the next day he did. By the third day, I could meet Jake at the bottom of the hill at lunchtime and ski with him all afternoon. I never thought I would see a child of mine learn how to ski. Skiing thrills me, and I had dreamed about the day when I could ski with Ari and Jake.

Ari tried to ski but she was too young and then too sick to ever learn how. But Jake is so well coordinated and agile that he picked it up the instant he decided it was something he wanted to do. It was as though the days were filled with magic. It was hard to imagine, but I was beginning to feel whole. Skiing with Jake filled me with joy. Watching him master a run and fly down the mountain with his arms outstretched was the most wonderful moment I could have imagined.

I was feeling fine until Christmas Eve. We were riding back to our condominium on the bus. The night was peaceful, quiet, and calm. It was so beautiful and silent. Tears started falling, but I brushed them away so no one would know I was crying. I managed to hold myself together just long enough to get back to our condominium and then when Jake went next door to say hello to the Seymours, I collapsed on the bed and the sadness overtook me.

I cried and cried until I started to shake. Paul sat beside me and took me into his arms. "I miss Ari, I miss Ari so much," was all I could say. He said softly, "I know . . . I know."

The tears were furious and left me exhausted. But Paul hung in there with me. He stayed calm and strong and available for me to lean on.

Jake came back and I blotted my face with a washcloth and got him into his pajamas and ready for bed. I read him a story, but he was so tired that he fell asleep before I even finished. I stayed beside him for a few moments, lulled by the rhythm of his breathing and warmed by his small body beside mine.

I remembered being a little girl and overflowing with excitement on Christmas Eve. It was the most magical night of the year for me. Even in Telluride. I still felt the magic.

That was what had made me cry. I was surrounded by beauty, mystery, and joy and it reminded me of my sadness and loss.

I got into bed with Paul. I was tired but grateful for the strength of his presence and the steadfastness of his love. As I coasted slowly into sleep, I hoped to dream about Ari. It was my only chance to see her and touch her again. But that night, all I did was sleep.

As we had the year before, we spent the second half of our vacation in Hawaii. Paul and I were slightly apprehensive about going back there because the previous year had been so difficult and depressing for us. But we had a wonderful time, swimming and snorkeling. Paul played golf and I played tennis. Jake is a beach rat and made friends with every child within walking distance. We had come a long way in one year.

We all feel very close to Ari in Hawaii because it is so beautiful and we see so many rainbows. Whenever we see one filling the sky in a giant and colorful plume, we always feel as if Ari is saying hello.

It is not so surprising, perhaps, that I had the dream in Hawaii that I had yearned for in Colorado. It was the dream I had been waiting for. I was walking alone in a forest that felt mysterious, but in a magical way. The sky was lush with cumulus clouds, but they were so low they almost touched my head.

As I walked, there were three rainbows in a row, one behind the other. Warm sunlight melded the colors of the three rainbows together like a piece of beautiful stained glass. Walking through the rainbows, I felt Ari's hand come down through the cloud to touch me. "Hi, Mom," she said.

Startled, I looked up and said, "Hi." I reached up toward her through the low cloud and she took my hand.

I said, "Ari, can I come up there with you?"

"Yes, you can," she said, and she pulled me up beside her.

"Can you give me a hug?" I asked.

She wrapped her arms around me and in the dream I could feel her, I could actually feel the warmth of her body that I yearned for.

Then I awoke. I kept my eyes closed and tried to stay motionless so I could slip back through the stillness into the dream. I wanted to feel Ari's hand in mine. I wanted to feel her embrace, her warmth. I miss everything about Ariel, but I miss her hugs so desperately.

In the sixteen months since her death, it was the first time I had ever found Ari again in a dream. The dream blessed me with contentment and possibility. Now, when I go to sleep each night I know I might see Ari again.

New Year's Eve in Hawaii was as difficult for Paul as Christmas Eve had been for me in Colorado. The beginning of a new decade was nothing Paul wanted to celebrate because it filled him with such piercing fear.

Paul and I got married in 1980 and Ari was born the following year. The decade began for us abundant in hope and promise, and ended with despair. For Paul, entering another decade escalated his fear. Not being able to rely on the future is an odd feeling. I cope with that by living one day at a time. Right now I can live in the moment much better than Paul.

Paul tends to look down the road, and whenever he does that, he gets terrified. New Year's Eve made him feel scared and depressed. He became moody and withdrawn, and while I tried as best I could to talk him through it, I couldn't. The lessons of Santa Fe were useless. I couldn't make them work. We were once again alone in our struggles.

I have an immediate focus to my life now; Jake and the Foundation. Both require tremendous energy, commitment, and drive. Paul's dynamic is a different one and, I think, much harder, given our situation. If he is directing a thirty-million-dollar film and is in charge of a crew of 140 people, there is little time to think about anything else.

But when Paul writes screenplays in between films, his journey is an interior one. He has to go deeper and deeper into himself every day, which is a lonely and often claustrophobic experience.

While the New Year began with difficulty for Paul, it began optimistically for me. Jake and I were both stable and strong. In January, I took my yearly ski trip to Aspen. It was as good as always. The Foundation was gaining momentum and had a full agenda of legislative goals. President Reagan was filming our public service announcement. We were planning a pediatric think tank in Santa Barbara for early winter. Another million-dollar fund-raiser was planned for L.A. in the spring. The "60 Minutes" piece would air in February.

Paul had gone skiing in Aspen with his friend Gene Sey-

mour and so he wasn't home on February 4, the night the
segment aired. I had asked to see it early, but CBS said that
wasn't possible. I was seeing it for the first time like everyone
else. I invited some of my closest women friends over for dinner. I had to be doing something on Sunday afternoon because I could hardly sit still.

Friends on the East Coast started calling after they saw
it and everyone's reaction was great. They felt the spot was
both moving and informative. That was reassuring, but I had
to see for myself.

At seven o'clock, my friends and I crowded around the
television in the den and as soon as we heard the "tick, tick,
tick" of the stopwatch at the beginning of the program, we
grew still. Ed Bradley's deep voice filled the room as the program began:

> In 1981, the Glasers had a baby girl. The birth was a
> difficult one and the mother was given seven pints of
> blood. It never dawned on them that the blood could
> have been contaminated . . .

That was the most public I had ever been. We faced hundreds of people at the *Immediate Family* benefit, but those
were all Hollywood people, many of whom we knew. Now
my family, our story, was being seen by fifty million Americans.

Seeing Ari's face fill the screen made me proud. The piece
was filled with some of our favorite snapshots of her and she
looked so beautiful. We had spent so many, many hours with
her in the den, propped up on the sofa. Being in that same
room with her face filling the television screen was hard to
comprehend.

Paul and I talked about the pain of isolation when we were
first diagnosed. Bradley summed up Ari's illness and we told
the story of how intravenous AZT made it possible for her
to walk and talk again. I discussed the Foundation, and they
then showed me and Susan in Washington and Susie here in
L.A.

One of the moments I liked best in the spot, because it is
what I feel so deeply in my heart, came right at the end. I
said, "You don't want to lose your hope. We don't know
when an answer might be found for this disease that might

change all of our lives. Where do you go? You love your kid every day. You walk outside and you appreciate your life, even though it is horrible, because you have it. You learn to love what you have now."

As the piece ended in L.A., everyone was excited. They hadn't made us seem tragic. The Foundation came off well. We were serious players in Washington. Susie's fund-raising role wasn't covered, but we were proud of what the three of us had accomplished.

The next morning I left for Washington. I was walking through the L.A. airport when I noticed people giving me the thumbs-up sign. Occasionally someone would look toward me and say, "Way to go!" or "We're praying for you."

These were all people who had seen "60 Minutes." I was flabbergasted by the positive and enthusiastic reaction. All of a sudden it felt as if the whole world knew who I was and they were encouraging me. Strangers were responding to me and that had never happened before.

It was immensely gratifying, but also disconcerting. I felt very confused. It seemed all of these good things were happening only because Ari was dead. The Foundation had funded a research lab at UCLA, named for Ari. At the ceremony people applauded, but this was the place where my daughter died. It didn't make any sense to be praised for something that resulted from Ari's death.

"60 Minutes" aired and suddenly I was being treated like a hero, but I was talking about everything I had learned through her death. I knew amazing things were happening in my life, but I couldn't really let them in because somehow it all felt wrong when I looked at it that way.

I was doing what I felt I had to do, because I believed that my speaking out might benefit others as well as help me not feel like a victim. If people can relate to me as a woman who is HIV-positive, they may be more sympathetic to others living with this disease. If people can understand that my children are HIV-positive, perhaps they will be more compassionate toward the thousands of other HIV-infected children.

But in February, while I could feel proud of what I was doing, I couldn't get enjoyment from it. I was doing a job and there was so much that needed to be done. I will not feel satisfied until compassion starts spreading as fast as the virus.

Santa Monica is not typical of much of the rest of the country. As AIDS spreads through rural America, many people still live in deep fear and appalling secrecy.

A doctor who treats AIDS in the South tells of a patient who, on the days he goes for treatment, gets up before dawn and hides beneath a blanket on the back seat of his mother's car. She comes out a few hours later and drives him to the clinic. When they return home, he stays under the blanket until it is dark again and he can slip back into his house.

This is why there is still such a crucial need for leadership right from the top. When President Bush turns down a chance to speak at an AIDS conference in San Francisco so he can appear instead at a fund-raiser for Senator Jesse Helms, it's a signal that the moral compass of America is still far off the mark.

When I got to Washington, it was time to get down to business. Each trip to Washington had become more and more important. We needed more money in 1991.

A month earlier, Barbara Boxer, the congresswoman from San Francisco, had asked if Paul and I would participate in hearings on AIDS. We refused at first, because the hearings were going to be in Los Angeles. Paul and I had never testified. We thought it would be important, but if we were both going to speak, we felt we should try to do so before as wide an audience as possible. So we told Boxer that we might be willing to do it if it was held in Washington. That was in the works and we were talking with her often.

Barbara Boxer became one of our favorite people in Washington. She became one of the new leaders we were looking for. She is an extremely dynamic and exciting woman. She says she wants to help and then she makes things happen. That was our kind of person.

She had arranged for Susan and me to meet with Speaker of the House Tom Foley and Congressman Richard Gephardt, House Majority Leader. At the last minute, Congressman Steny Hoyer, who chaired the AIDS caucus, joined us. We didn't know it at the time, but Hoyer was the other new friend we were looking for. Steny became our strongest advocate that year, and it was largely his leadership that got pediatric AIDS research the money it so desperately needed in 1991.

Susan left that night and I stayed on for another day of

meetings that ended with an appearance on the "Larry King Live!" television show. CNN was hard news and that's where we wanted to be. I had never done live television before and this was challenging. I felt I held my own.

Shortly after I returned home to Los Angeles, the Foundation sponsored the think tank in Santa Barbara, at Ted and Susie Field's oceanfront ranch. It was our second and was very different from the one we'd had a year before in Bethesda.

Susan coordinated the entire weekend with Art Ammann, Dick Stiehm, and Phil Pizzo. A year before we had twelve doctors, but now we brought in thirty doctors and researchers from around the country for a weekend of intense, creative brainstorming about pediatric AIDS. All of the Foundation's funded researchers were included in this group. It was a way of evaluating where we stood and where we needed to go. It was relaxed and informal, which is important because there is so little coordination in the epidemic. The doctors need to see each other as friends working toward the same goal. Researchers tend to be isolated in their labs or hospitals and usually only see each other at large conferences.

There were no formal papers. Instead, Susan organized the conference around forty-five-minute presentations and discussion sessions. The Foundation had also invited our first Scholar Awards recipients. We had funded three outstanding young researchers for a year to pursue specific areas of investigation.

I felt enormously proud when I saw the best and the brightest doctors and researchers talking and learning from each other. I felt so proud of Susan and Susie and all we had managed to accomplish since the days of sitting around the kitchen table with legal pads and felt-tip pens eighteen months before.

When we started the Pediatric AIDS Foundation we hoped to be out of business in a year. We wanted to raise as much money as we could, funnel it into research, and then close the door as the government took over. No one could have imagined that in slightly over a year, the Foundation would have emerged as the driving force behind the issue of pediatric AIDS.

The reason we could never have imagined doing what we're doing is because we were sure others—professional lobbyists, government officials—were. As proud as I am about what we have accomplished, I still hate the fact that we had to do it at all.

My daughter died from AIDS. My son's life hangs in the balance, and I have been infected with the HIV virus for nine years. Don't think we are unique. There are at least one and a half *million* other Americans just like me who are either living with AIDS or who are HIV-positive. There are twenty thousand children just like my children. One of whom could be your child or grandchild.

The numbers increase every day. Someone dies of AIDS every twelve minutes. Someone is infected with the AIDS virus every fifty-four seconds. In America, 212 new cases of full-blown AIDS are diagnosed *every day*.

Where is the outrage? Where is the alarm? This is certainly no time for complacency. In its first decade, the AIDS epidemic claimed over eighty thousand lives. According to government estimates, four times that number will die within the next three years.

We are making progress on the war against AIDS, but it is far from over. It certainly isn't won.

If you wait until AIDS affects you directly, it will be too late. Today is the time to care. Today is the time to teach your children what they need to know so they don't become infected. Today is the time to change your behavior if you are in a high-risk group.

AIDS has no medical cure yet, but it can be prevented. Millions of research dollars are being spent to develop a vaccine against AIDS. But right now, what will keep most people safe is a penny's worth of latex in a condom. Education is the only vaccine we have. Parents and schools have to unite to teach children and adolescents what they need to know to stay safe. And the world has to educate itself to help people with AIDS, not ostracize them.

I am a teacher. The lesson of my life, in the end, is a very simple one. Love. My life is not a lesson about AIDS; my life is a lesson about love. Love your life. Love the life you live now. Don't wait for it to start tomorrow. Don't wait for someone or something to make it perfect. I want my life to last a long time, but if it doesn't, I know I will have lived fully right up until the end.

•   •   •

On March 13, 1990, Paul and I went to testify in Washington. Barbara Boxer had scheduled her hearings before the House Budget Subcommittee on health issues.

It was a monumental moment in our personal lives; the culmination of our struggle to move forward despite our pain to try and make a difference in the lives of others. We had worked hard on our testimonies, because we felt so much was at stake. Paul, my reluctant hero, was not overjoyed at the prospect of putting himself in the middle of a media spectacle. He hated being a celebrity when he was in a detective show. Having attention focused on him now because of his family's tragedy is a lot harder. But he joined me. He stood by me as a husband to say, "This is my problem, too, and if you don't wake up, it will be yours as well."

Paul realized that in our society's distorted value structure, people would pay attention to us because of his role in a hit TV show. We knew the hearings gave us a chance to step up to the plate on behalf of every child and every person with AIDS. Everyone with AIDS is somebody's child.

We had no idea how much news coverage there would be. We hoped it would be the hard news people. They could make a difference by calling attention to the problem on TV sets all over the country. We woke up tense and anxious.

The day of the hearing was a marathon. It began with "Good Morning America." They were happy to have just me and Susan, no celebrities needed. We were the experts. The day ended with "Nightline." In between there were newspaper, radio, and television interviews.

At nine that morning, we drove to Capitol Hill. We were all quiet in the car. No one knew what to expect. Paul and I reviewed our testimony. The car pulled up outside the Rayburn Building, and Susan, Paul, and I climbed out. We walked in silently and took the elevator to the third floor, stepped out, turned the corner, and were face-to-face with a wall of cameras and photographers.

I looked at Paul, and he looked at me. We took each other's hand, held our heads high, and walked ahead.

The hearing room was jammed with reporters and TV crews. It seemed like every news station in town, including ABC, CBS, and NBC, was there. CNN covered our testimony almost in its entirety. The lights were bright and burning hot. When it was our turn to testify, Paul began speaking in a strong, slow voice. He told the committee how I had become infected, how we had lost Ariel, how I had begun looking for solutions in Washington. Then he said:

This is not one child with a disease. This is a disease that is striking entire families. In the most generous of perceptions, I was lucky. I had the help of a strong support system of family and friends. This is unusual however—most families with AIDS have no supports at all, sometimes not even from the parent. How are they to survive if we do not provide the resources to help them?

The basic medical questions that plagued my child remain unanswered and the commitment from our government came too slowly and our daughter, Ariel, died. I am here to talk about the past only so you will understand that living with AIDS is living with a time bomb.

Paul spoke for a few more minutes and then it was my turn. I felt so many emotions careening inside of me. I had been fighting back tears during Paul's testimony. I took a drink of water. My voice cracked but I began very, very slowly.

"No mother ever really believes that her child is going to die. I did not." The tears started to fill my eyes but I wouldn't let them come. I talked about our efforts to save Jake, about all we still didn't understand about Ariel.

"Why had she stopped growing? Why had my son become infected when not all children born to infected mothers are infected?"

I talked about how additional allocations for research could answer many questions, and how at that time no one was even asking them, much less answering.

"If the federal government moves at the pace it is accustomed to, my son will probably not live." Saying those words was painful, so I took a moment's pause. "Creative approaches can save lives. We need a plan of action, but it must be implemented now, not slowly tomorrow."

I had outlined the money needed and pleaded for full one-hundred-percent funding. After several more minutes, we were done. Congresswoman Boxer asked a few questions. Then we stood up and left the hearing room. The cameras had stopped; the flashbulbs had stopped. We walked into the hall and once again looked at each other.

We had come farther than either of us ever imagined. We had testified in Washington, the Foundation had found its place, and Paul and I were still together.

We were climbing a mountain whose peak we would never reach. But with wisdom and love, each step felt firm, and so we were not too scared to keep going.

As we left the Rayburn Building, we heard the receding echoes of our own voices and only hoped that someone out there would listen.

EPILOGUE

Here is what is truly amazing about life. Things change. In May of 1990, I went back to Santa Fe to meet with a therapist named Darby Long. Darby had been working for sixteen years with cancer patients and over the last seven years saw a number of people with AIDS as well. She believes that attitudes, beliefs, and emotions significantly impact one's health. A friend intuitively knew that Darby would be able to help settle some of the questions that eluded me. I wasn't as sure, but with Paul's encouragement, I decided to give it a try.

I arrived in Santa Fe believing certain things to be true. I thought I could never find a way to escape the pain and sadness Ari's death left in me. I thought I had lost her forever. I thought I could never take Jake blueberry picking on Pleasant Mountain.

I was wrong. The first day, I let myself feel all the grief and loss I usually keep locked inside me. I told Ari, "I miss you so much. I don't know what to do," and Darby said a really strange thing. She said, "Ask Ari what to do!" I thought, *This is silly, Ari can't talk. She's dead.* I lay crying and then said to myself, "Elizabeth, just try it." In my own voice that only I could hear, I said, "Ari, I miss you so much. What should I do?"

And then something amazing happened. Inside me there was an answer. It was my voice, but it was Ari's voice too.

She said, "Mom, don't be sad. I am fine. I am always with you." She said, "We are doing this work together. Trust your instincts, move ahead. You can do it." She said, "Your life is amazing, Mom. Enjoy it. Enjoy Jake. Enjoy Dad. Enjoy it all." As I found Ari's voice, her love filled me, and some inner peace was mine.

I know Jake and I are vulnerable but no one knows what will happen. Right now I choose to believe it will all be fine.

I have been freed. So much of my pain is gone. Now when I watch Jake hit a baseball, I glow with pride. I read him a book at night, and I can love him completely. We can cuddle, roll, jump, play, and I see him, no longer his sister.

I took him to pick blueberries, and we relished the sweetness of life.

On September 12, 1990, I walked with Jake to Crossroads Elementary School. It was his first day of kindergarten. We held hands as we crossed the street. With his short hair and freckles, his backpack and lunch box, he looked like the cutest kid in the whole world. We got to the gate and without hesitation he turned to me and said, "Bye, Mom," and walked off. I stood there with the same mixture of pride and sadness I always feel when I'm loving Jake. A number of parents gave me warm hugs, and as I watched Jake walk into his classroom, tears filled my eyes. We had finally made it to Crossroads. Jake was almost six and hope was still ours. My life had certainly not turned out the way I expected; but while tomorrow would bring what it would, today was glorious.

In the beginning I felt there were no angels to help us. I felt alone in a fight to save my children's lives. But over the years, angels have come into our life. Real live angels who reached out to help. One at a time. Slowly at first, but they came and I believe they will continue to come for a long, long time.

I know I have a job to do and I am now enjoying it, because Ari is with me in her own way. I am challenged by my life. I have no vision of where it will go and that makes it exciting. Every day has become an adventure.

I know there are terrible problems in the world and I want to be a part of solving them. I want to be a part of helping the world care again. I have come to see that what I learned about love in Santa Fe with Paul goes way beyond just us.

I can meet the world with that love. I can bring it to my home. I can bring it to my office. I can bring it to Washington. It is mine, and there is a great deal of it to give.

Now that I know Ari is always with me, I need not hold on to the sadness and grief. They can float away, and in their place I find great joy.

Every day now is a miracle and knowing that makes me smile.

Acknowledgments

I wish to say a very special thank you to Laura Palmer, who walked unflinchingly into my life, who journeyed with me back into a painful past so that I might learn and grow, and who joins me in working to create a future that has more hope, more love, and more caring.

To my publisher, Phyllis Grann, I would like to say thank you for allowing me the opportunity to write this book. Thank you for helping to give me the confidence to trust my feelings and my words.

To my editor, George Coleman, it was your idea. You believed I had something to tell that was of value. Without you this book would not be. You have offered guidance, direction, and a very clear eye.

To Andrew Zeller, whose work on this manuscript was invaluable. To all of you, my team at G. P. Putnam's Sons, I say thank you.

To Esther Newberg, whose humor and support has meant so much to me, thank you for holding my hand with courage and integrity.

There are so many people who have helped us in the last four years. It may be hard to imagine that so many people could be important. But, in fact, each and every individual has made a difference in my life since our diagnosis. Some are there all the time and others just for brief moments, but all together we have been lucky that many friends and family have reached out to help.

To my family, the Meyers, there are no words that can really express the gratitude I feel for your unending love and support. To Mom and Dad, Edith and Max, who undid their lives to help me glue mine together and who raised me to be the person I am today, no thanks will ever be enough. To my brother, Peter, and his wife, Janet, and my ninety-two-year-old Nanny Belle, I say thank you for your constant love.

To Paul's family: his father and mother, Sam and Dorothy Glaser, who gave him an understanding and wisdom that has helped us all; his sister and brother-in-law, Connie and Billy Kantar, and their wonderful children Alisa, David, Deborah, Jonathan, and Ruth; to Paul's sister Penny and her children Manuel, Eva, and Rachel; to our cousins the Moskows, Donna and Michael and their children Keith, Allison, Kenny, Cliff, and Carla, you have all become like my own family. We needed you and you never let us down.

To Lynn and Lucy, my oldest friends, who loved me when I felt unlovable; who watched me grow and never held me back, but rather pushed me on; who supported me when their own families were calling. And to Lynn's wonderful husband, Frank, and Lucy's wonderful husband, Doug, who reached out with love and support as well. I love you and thank you.

To Susie and Susan, the two best friends anyone could ever imagine. Your love and commitment to me, my family, and the Pediatric AIDS Foundation can never be equaled. We have shared it all—pain and joy, loss and growth. Without you I could never be who I am today. And to Susan's family, Robert, Francesca, and Daniela De Laurentis, and to Susie's family, Peter, Erik, and Heather Zeegen: you not only loaned me your wives but let us become a part of your families as well. My thanks go beyond words.

To the Seymours: Judie, Gene, Amanda, and Josh, the thanks are unending. You embraced each of us in your own special ways and you let our family join yours in the hardest of times. I thank you with all my heart.

To our friends—the list seems endless, but the love and loyalty of every single person made a difference in our lives. Rena and Jerry Kramer, Suzanne and Jeff Buhai, Hilary and David Neumeister, Priscilla and James Stephens, Carol and

Ron Herman, Jodie and Jeff Gold, Claudia and Walter Teller, Linda and Jimmy Burrows, Jan and Mark Victor and their children Shannon, Bret, and Haydn, Ellen and Bruce Gilbert, Andrea Eastman, Preston Fisher, Bill and Denny Friedman, Marlo and Steve Erlich, Barbara and Billy Finklestein, Dawn Steel, Allyn Stewart, Cynthia Wick, Gary Adelson, Jeremy and Richard Dreyfuss, Tim Zinnemann and Meg Tilly, Janet and Steve Goldstein and their children Jarred and Maris, Havi Scheindlin, Jane Fonda, Rita Braver and Bob Barnett, Sol and Shirley Turtletaub, Arlene and Alan Alda, Cher, Marlene and Lee Canter, Jake Bloom Robert Pipes, Gaylene Ray, and Forrest Stewart—Thank you all so very much.

To Graciela, Maria, Anna, Palma, and Alfonsia, I thank you from the bottom of my heart for helping to make our house a home in spite of all odds. You have all joined our family, most especially in our hearts.

To our neighbors who welcomed us on the block regardless of our medical reality. You helped us to feel like we belonged and gave us strength to continue. Thanks to Lynda and Allen Jayne and their children, Andrew and Cathy, Madeleine and Greg Gorski and their children, Brigid, Pete, and Leo, Genie and Gene Shank, Valerie and Richard Hermann and their children, Douglas, Michael, and Jason, Joyce and Jack Zimmerman.

To the families from First Presbyterian Nursery School, I thank each and every one of you. You helped us survive what we thought we couldn't. You offered your love and support and embraced us wholly. No words will ever be sufficient. And a very special thanks to a very special few. Our director Mary Hartzell, Jake's teachers Joanne Mandakas, Gwen Rinehart, Lisa Scemama, and Scott Davis, and Jake's friends' parents and our friends, Alan and Nina Miles, Fatenah and John Barbow, Dana and John Meyer, Diana and Daniel Attias, Belita and Joel Rudnick, Christine and Gustof Soderberg, Marianne and Guy Dill, Charlotte and Charlie Morgan. And to Jake's most special and dear friends, Tommy, Louie, Neemah, Skylar, Zakary, Eric, Rachel, Ali, Harry, Cindy, you help keep each day exciting and we thank you for that.

To our Crossroads family, Joanie Green, Mimi Baer, Paul Cummins, Cathe Jacobs: in the worst of times, you were our family. You saw our tears and fears and never flinched. Your strength kept us going.

And to Ari's most special teachers—Akimi Watanabe, Bonnie Hockman, Evelyn Winkler—a special thanks for allowing her to bloom.

To our wonderful and special doctors, Dr. Richard Stiehm, Dr. Jay Gordon, Dr. Linda Nussbaum, Dr. Chris Ito, Dr. Michael Gottlieb, Dr. Jim Blechman, Dr. Peter Vink, Dr. Napolean Lee, Dr. Cassandra Mayhan, Dr. Richard Fine and Shawnee Fine, and Dr. Paul Geller. Thank you for holding our hands as we all walked through unchartered terrain.

To our talented and caring therapists and counselors who helped us sort through the rumble of our lives. A special thank you to Dr. Harry Brickman, Dr. Beatriz Foster, Susan Jay, Ph.D., Jonathan Omer-Man, Marianne Williamson, Dr. Richard Friedman, and Darby Long.

To the wonderful nurses who helped us through the hardest times of all. Our love and thanks to Lesa Grovas, Nancy Potash, Laurie Reyen, Peggy Gong, Debbie Delaney, Donna Yoshamura, and Herb.

To Lloyd Zeiderman and Peter Benzian, our friends and advisors who sit on the Foundation board of directors. I want to thank you for all the moments when I never have time to say it. You have helped me to meet my dreams.

To my second family, who make our little office a wonderful and magical place to be. I thank you all for making every day an adventure filled with challenges, love, affection, and fun. My thanks to Beth Freeman, Francesca Bill, Jan Fox, Leslie Russo, Allison Moskow, Sherri Rivera, Patricia Stitch, and Cyd Wilson.

To the Foundation advisory board members, I thank you for helping us meet goals that almost seemed impossible: President and Mrs. Ronald Reagan, Mrs. William E. Brock, Bob Burkett, Alfred and Kathryn Checchi, Kitty Dukakis, Michael Eisner, Susie Field, Senator Paula Hawkins, Elton John, Michael Ovitz, Steven Spielberg, Jonathan Tisch and Mrs. Pete Wilson.

And our health advisory board members: Mary Boland, Yvonne Bryson, Margaret Heagarty, Anna Belle Kaufman, James Oleske, Gwendolyn Scott, Coleen Conway-Welch and Lori Wiener.

To my special friends who through Foundation work have

helped so much. I say thank you to Bob Johnson, Scott Iverson, Chiat/Day/Mojo's Laurie Coots, Cami Pollack, Ruth Spitzer Rosenfield, and Rob White. To Chuck Sloan and Mark Pollack, to Diana Ho and Larry Dressler, Denise Martin, Josh Baran, and Paul Costello.

To the special people in Washington who helped me learn what I needed to know. Who took that time to meet with me and returned my calls. However things work out, I have appreciated it. To Joel Johnson, Kevin McGuiness, Nancy Taylor, Tim Westmoreland, Maureen Burns, Polly Gault, Mike Iskowitz, Terry Burn, Susan Campbell, Mike Hall, Mike Stephens, Kay Casstevens, Barbara Masters, and Johnny Hemphill, I say thank you.

A most special thanks to Senator Orrin Hatch and Senator Howard Metzenbaum. You united, and so many benefited. Your commitment has given children with HIV hope for a better future, a more understanding and compassionate America.

To Senator Tom Harkin, Senator Lowell Weicker, Senator Alan Cranston, Congressman Steny Hoyer, Congresswoman Barbara Boxer, Congressman Silvio Conte, Congressman Mel Levine, Congressman Henry Waxman—my thanks for helping in what often feels like a lonely battle.

To my heroes at NIH, who have been both professionals and friends, I have not only the highest respect but the deepest gratitude for your involvement in my life. A very special thank-you—from the bottom of my heart—to Dr. Phil Pizzo. My gratitude also goes to Dr. Sam Broder, Dr. Tony Fauci, and Lori Weiner. To Dr. Dwane Alexander and Dr. Toni Novello, my thanks as well.

A special thank-you to Jim Allen and Sam Matheny.

And a very special thank-you to Dr. Art Ammann, who heads the Foundation health advisory board, and is a dear and trusted friend.

To the Rays, the Whites, the Kushniks, the Frieds, the Rodgers, the Lykins and all the other families who are working so hard to make a difference. I am proud to be in such company.

And to Ari's dear friends, Francesca, Amy, Taylor, Sara, Nicole, Sophie, Allwyn, and Vanessa, who know more about life than they should. Ari and I will always love you.

•   •   •

And to my husband, Paul, who has walked through fire with his family and survived. You are one of the strongest and most sensitive men I could ever imagine. I love you more deeply than even I yet truly understand. Thank you for being you and for being mine.

A Note to Readers

In October 1990, the House and Senate conferenced the 1991 appropriations budget. The pediatric AIDS basic research money was increased by ten million dollars, totaling twenty million. The pediatric clinical trials were appropriated an extra 23.8 million dollars. It was *half* of what was needed. This money, while making a difference, won't reach researchers for at least twelve to twenty-four months.

That same month the Pediatric AIDS Foundation could have dispersed 2.2 million dollars to researchers around the country who are looking at critical pediatric and maternal transmission questions.

There were six important grants that went unfunded because we only had 1.7 million dollars in the bank.

Every day lost can never be regained. The crisis is here. The time is now. If you can help, please do.

The Pediatric AIDS Foundation
2407 Wilshire Boulevard, Suite 613
Santa Monica, California 90403
(213) 395-9051
(800) 488-5000

Elizabeth Glaser